3

D1351613

FOR RETURN

Athelston

EARLY ENGLISH TEXT SOCIETY

Original Series No. 224

1951 (for 1946)

PRICE 12s. 6d.

Athelston

A MIDDLE ENGLISH ROMANCE

EDITED BY

A. McI. TROUNCE

B.A., B.Litt. Oxon.
M.A. Western Australia

LONDON

PUBLISHED FOR THE EARLY ENGLISH TEXT SOCIETY
BY GEOFFREY CUMBERLEGE, OXFORD UNIVERSITY PRESS
AMEN HOUSE, E.C.4
1951

*This volume is a revised re-issue of the text which
appeared in 1933 as no. XI in the Publications
of the Philological Society, from which the Early
English Text Society has acquired all rights in
the book.*

. C.T. O

QUEEN MARY
COLLEGE
LIBRARY

37787
PR 1119. Az
224
C

A 94
224

English L
10.5.57

TO
MY MOTHER

Please note that this book is o.s. 224, the first volume to be issued for 1946. The Secretaries regret that o.s. 223, which completes the issue for 1945 has been slightly delayed. It will be ready shortly and will be sent to all who have subscribed for that year

CONTENTS

INTRODUCTION

1. The Manuscript

The poem of *Athelston* is contained in one manuscript only, No. 175 of Gonville and Caius College, Cambridge. The most authoritative account of the manuscript is in the *Catalogue of the Manuscripts of Gonville and Caius College*, by M. R. James, 1907–8, pp. 199–201. The manuscript is one of a fine collection given to Caius College by William Moore, a seventeenth-century alumnus of Caius, and University Librarian, of whom it is recorded ' that through his whole life (he was) a diligent collector and transcriber of the choicest manuscripts which he could possibly purchase by love or money : all of which he gave to Caius College '.[1] Our manuscript (which is of vellum, size $9 \times 6\frac{5}{8}$ in.) is certainly a choice one, neat and pleasant in appearance. It consists of seventy-nine leaves, each divided into two columns. The number of lines in a column varies, in *Athelston* from thirty-four to thirty-eight. The manuscript belongs to the early fifteenth century, and, according to M. R. James, is in at least two hands. The contents, all English verse except for one fragment at the end, and chiefly romances, are as follows : (1) *Richard Coer de Lyon* ; (2) *Sir Ysumbras* (in a rather smaller hand) ; (3) a Life of St. Catherine ; (4) a piece entitled *Matutinas de cruce* ; (5) the poem of *Athelston* ; (6) *Beues of Hamptoun* ; (7) a fragment of religious prose, *De spiritu Gwydonis*. *Athelston* alone of these pieces lacks a title, and this accounts, doubtless, for its not being listed in the mention of this manuscript in the *Catalogi MSS. Angliae et Hiberniae*, Oxford, 1697.

The poem of *Athelston* begins a little below the concluding

---

[1] John Venn, *Bibliographical History of Gonville and Caius College*, 1349–1897 (Cambridge, 1897), I. 192. It is a curious circumstance that the virtual founder of Gonville and Caius Coll., William Bateman, bishop of Norwich 1344–53, should be the ecclesiastic, who, as I suggest (Intro. 6 *d*, and note to 465–6), may have been a model for *Alryke* in the poem. It would be a singular, if not a unique, coincidence, that would enable us to connect a known personality in such a way with both the composition and the preservation of a romance. *Athelston* might, in that case, bear a sub-title, ' William Bateman's poem '.

prayer and *Amen* of the previous piece, and its beginning is marked by a large illuminated *L* in the word *Lord*. It extends from page 120 *a* to page 131 *a*, and contains 812 lines, which are written as verse, but without any divisions between stanzas. The lines begin with small capitals. Although, as James's examination shows, many leaves are missing from the manuscript, the part containing *Athelston* is intact. It seems on the whole to have been a careful and intelligent piece of copying. The script is not inelegant, though occasionally a little cramped. Words for erasure are marked with a line through and dots beneath. Some of these corrections, at 303, 423, 615, 787, 792, 803, suggest that the scribe was taking some liberties with his original, but of what nature I cannot determine. The versions of at least three of the poems in the manuscript, *Sir Ysumbras*, *Athelston*, and *Beues of Hamptoun*, seem to be connected with the south of the East Midlands, and the puzzling introduction of St. Edmund into the poem of *Athelston* connects it with Bury St. Edmunds. It is not unusual for Middle English manuscripts to be found in later times near the place in which they were written.[1]

2. THE STORY

The outline of the story is as follows:

'Four messengers (who may perhaps be understood as men of high birth) meet by chance on the highway near a forest, and celebrate their meeting by entering into a formal bond of sworn-brotherhood. Shortly afterwards the eldest of the four, named Athelston, becomes king of England, and proceeds, as he was bound to do, to fulfil his compact by sharing his good fortune with his brothers. The eldest of the three, Wymound, is made Earl of Dover; the second, Egeland, is made Earl of Stane (or Stone), and given the sister of Athelston, called Edyff, as his wife; the third (and last) brother, Alryke, is made Archbishop of Canterbury. Egeland and Edyff have two sons who have reached the ages of fifteen and thirteen before the story resumes its course. Wymound becomes jealous because of the favour shown by Athelston to Egeland and his family, and, under an oath of secrecy, falsely accuses Egeland and Edyff of plotting

[1] Dr. M. R. James kindly informs me that MS. Gonv. and Caius 175 has, as far as he can see, no trace of provenance. He doubts if it is monastic.

against Athelston's life and kingdom, and after making the accusation retires to Dover. Outraged by this news Athelston summons Egeland and his family to London on a pretence of wishing to knight the two sons, and as soon as they arrive hurls them all into prison. The queen intercedes unsuccessfully for the prisoners, and the king in his rage kicks her, and kills her unborn child. The story now takes a new turn, when the queen by a messenger summons Alryke, the Archbishop of Canterbury, on the ground that Alryke would have more influence over the king than she had. The ride of the messenger is described in some detail, several places on the route from Westminster to Canterbury, along the famous pilgrims' road, being mentioned in the account. The archbishop, in answer to the summons, rides post-haste to London, and at Westminster pleads with his sworn-brother for a fair trial for the prisoners. The king angrily refuses, deprives Alryke of his office, and banishes him. Alryke's spirited rejoinder is to excommunicate the king, and place the realm under an interdict. He rides back to London, and is met by the barons, who, when they discover the state of affairs, promise him and the Church support against the tyranny of the king. Conflict is, however, avoided by the submission of the king, who yields up his intended victims to Alryke, and asks for absolution, which is granted. The end is not yet, because Alryke insists that all the accused persons must undergo ordeal by fire. This they do successfully, first Egeland, then the two children, then the Countess, who is taken with the pains of labour as she passes through the fire, and shortly afterwards gives birth to a boy, who later becomes St. Edmund. The king, having lost his heir by his own violence, adopts the newly born child and promises him the succession. All that remains now is to have the traitor punished. The archbishop demands that Athelston shall reveal his name; but the king is unwilling to break the promise he has given to his sworn-brother. He consents to do so in confession, after Alryke has threatened to cause him to go through the fire himself. The traitor, Wymound, is then summoned from Dover, taxed with his crime, and, by order of the king, put to the ordeal, at which he fails. He is pulled from the fire by the children, to whom he confesses that he committed the treachery out of pure envy. After this avowal he is dragged at the horses' feet through the streets of London, and then to the

Elms, the place of execution in London, where he is hanged.'
The poem has an opening and a concluding prayer.

The story falls quite clearly into five divisions : stanzas 1–5,
the oath of sworn-brotherhood ; stanzas 6–27, the treachery of
Wymound ; stanzas 28–60, the archbishop's protest, and his
triumph over the king ; stanzas 61–2, the birth of St. Edmund ;
stanzas 63–75, the punishment of the traitor. The three strands
of the plot are connected in various ways—Alryke is the chief
binding link, as he is active and prominent in each of the three
developments ; next to him in constructive importance is
Athelston. The queen is used at the critical joining-place
(stanza 28) to summon the archbishop to the help of the
prisoners. The birth of St. Edmund is connected with the
other strands by the fact that the king's killing his heir allows
him to give the kingdom to St. Edmund, and by the fact that the
saint is born of the countess while she is undergoing the ordeal.
The poem shows considerable narrative skill, but the prominent
part played by Alryke in the second half of the poem, whether
it indicates interpolation or not, does reveal a lack of unity in
the poem. We get an immediate impression that an old story
of sworn-brotherhood has been rehandled to give it a religious
turn, and that the signs of the remodelling remain.

3. The Analogues

Analogues for the chief elements in the story are not hard to
find, either in English itself, or in Old French poems. The
attempt to assemble the parallels has not been made before,
because other investigators, induced by the preponderance of
Old English names (*Egeland* has been ignored or side-tracked),
have been anxious to credit *Athelston* to native English effort,
and have proceeded to look for its origins in Old English history
or legend. But, as I shall show, *Athelston* has many conventional
features, most of which had their origin in Old French literature,
and until one has allowed for this borrowed element, one cannot
begin to compute what may be more original in the poem.

3 *a*. In English, *Amis and Amiloun*[1] has remarkable resemblances to *Athelston*. Each treats of the fortunes of men
who are sworn-brothers and who suffer through treachery.
Stanza 5 of *Amis* shows a similar quick growing-up of the two

---

[1] Ed. E. Kölbing (Heilbronn, 1884).

sons in the preliminary part of the story, as in Stanzas 6 and 7 of *Athelston*. The children are very beautiful ; the king wants to knight them ; the mothers express themselves as very pleased with their sons' success. The origin of the treachery is almost exactly similar—Amis and Amiloun are betrayed by a 'chef steward of alle his (the duke's) lond ' :

> For þai were so gode & hende,
> & for þe douke was so wele her frende,
> He hadde þerof gret envie.   (ll. 211–13.)

The traitor goes to the duke with 'wordes grame'. Moreover, the traitor wishes to become the sworn-brother of Amis, and begins his treachery after the latter's refusal. The imperative demand of the bond of brotherhood is shown :

> Whiles þat I may gon & speke,
> Y no schal neuer mi treuþe breke,
> Noiþer for wele no wo.   (ll. 370–2.)

The traitor is cursed by the author at the same place in each poem. The duke's reaction to the traitor's story is similar :

> þe riche douke gan sore agrame :
> ' Who haþ,' he seyd, 'don me þat schame ?
> Tel me, y þe pray ! '   (ll. 794–6.)

Then follows the violent anger of the king, trial by ordeal—in *Amis*, a duel—and the death of the traitor. The wife of the duke, like the queen in *Athelston*, is willing to become *borwe* (Fr. *sun plegge*) for Amis when he is accused through information laid by the steward. Amis rides furiously for Amiloun to get his help, as Alryke rides to give it ; and the similarity in situation and in phrase cannot be accidental. Compare stanzas 35 and 36 of *Athelston* with the following passage from *Amis* 973 ff. :

> Amorwe Sir Amis made him ȝare
> & toke his leue for to fare
> & went in his jurnay.
> For no þing nold he spare,
> He priked þe stede, þat him bare,
> Boþe niȝt & day.
> So long he priked wiþ outen abod,
> Þe stede, þat he on rode,
> In a fer cuntray

Was ouercomen & fel down ded ;
Þo couþe he no better red,
    His song was : ' Waileway ! '
& when it was bifallen so,
Nedes a fot he most go. . . .

We may note that Amis's hurried ride is similar in the Anglo-
Norman version,[1] and this fact casts some doubt on the suggestion of Miss Hibbard [2] that Alryke's ride was the subject of an
English ballad.   The appeal for help from one brother to the
other has the same accent in each poem :

' Broþer,' seyd Sir Amis þo,
' Ywis, me nas neuer so wo,
    Seþþen þat y was born ; '
                    (*Amis* 1069 ; cf. *Athelston* 439).

Amiloun rescues Åmis (and the lady), as Alryke does Egeland
(and his wife), and brings about the death of the traitor ; but
whereas *Athelston* ends at that point *Amis* has many further
developments.   Since *Amis* is earlier than *Athelston*, borrowing
or close affiliation is, I think, certain.

3 *b*. The *Erl of Tolous* [3] has similarities to *Athelston* both in
situation and expression, but is of later date.   Having regard
to *Athelston* as a whole, we find the best parallels in French
chansons de geste.   *Parise la Duchesse* [4] is a French *chanson*
bordering on a *roman* of about A.D. 1200.   Its substance, in so
far as it resembles *Athelston*, is as follows.   Traitors, disappointed
of power, plan to destroy the queen who is opposed to them.
They send a gift of poisoned apples, one of which is eaten by
the king's brother in the presence of the queen.   She is there-
upon falsely accused of a murder, and Charles, easily deceived
and egged on by the traitors, angrily threatens her with violence,
though she is with child.   The queen protests her innocence,
but nevertheless is doomed to be burnt, unless she is cleared in
the ordeal by battle.   The queen appeals for help to the old
count Clarembaut, who has been in retirement from the court.
Suspecting foul dealing, Clarembaut approaches the king, who
scornfully rejects his advice and bids him flee.   The queen

[1] *Amis e Amilun*, ed. E. Kölbing, 446 ff.
[2] *P.M.L.A.* XXXVI. 224 ff.
[3] Ed. G. Lüdtke in *Sammlung engl. Denkmäler*, III.
[4] Ed. F. Guessard et L. Larchey, Paris, 1860.

shows herself with her unborn child to the king, but he is adamant and orders her to be dragged to the fire. Finally, he allows exile instead of death, and from this point the poem is more diffuse in the manner of the *roman d'aventure*. There follows a journey to Cologne, during which the queen is suddenly delivered of a son, for whom a glorious future is predicted. Ultimately, the king begs forgiveness of the queen, and the archbishop of Cologne blesses the reunion. The duchess gets an acknowledgement of the crime from the traitor, Beranger, before he is drawn and hanged.

The general resemblance of this story to *Athelston* is obvious; there are also closer similarities in detail. When the traitor is to announce his news, he has exactly the method of Wymound for drawing out the king. The journey to Cologne is along a pilgrim route, and places and incidents along the route are named. Particularly to be noticed are the religious accompaniments of the birth; the lady addresses a long and very devout prayer to the Virgin Mary and recalls the birth of Christ.

The *chanson* of *Gaydon*,[1] related to *Parise la Duchesse*, is in some respects more like *Athelston*. Thibaut, the traitor, proposes to alienate Charlemagne's affection from Gaydon, and also, if possible, to poison Charlemagne in order to get the throne. The deadly nature of the apples sent as a gift is accidentally revealed as in *Parise*, and the traitor falsely accuses Gaydon. Charles, in anger, swears not to eat or drink till he has punished the culprit. Riol, duc de Mans, intercedes for Gaydon, but is silenced and dismissed by Charlemagne. After his defeat in the ordeal the traitor confesses his falsehood and agrees that his place is in Hell with Ganelon, the famous traitor of the *Chanson de Roland*. A prominent role in the latter part of the poem is played by the two young nephews of the hero, Gaydon.

An examination of *Athelston* shows that it reproduces fully and accurately the type of the traitor; and this fact is to be emphasized in view of the attempts to see in *Athelston* a purely English poem. The main outlines of the type—envy, covetousness, ordeal, and punishment—had been fixed in Ganelon[2] of the *Chanson de Roland*, and later developments as in *Gaydon* made the type self-conscious. *Sir Wymound* in our poem is a complete sketch of the traitor. He *hadde gret envye* (79–88) of the favour

---

[1] Ed. F. Guessard and S. Luce (Paris, 1862).

[2] *P.M.L.A.* XXXVI. 119 ff.

shown to Egeland by Athelston : ' He þouȝte ... False lesyngys
on hem to make, To don hem brenne and sloo ' ... 'þorwȝ wurd
oure werk may sprynge.' He excites Athelston's curiosity
about his bad news (124–6); he protests his affection for
Athelston in a phrase almost exactly equivalent to that of
Gaydon (*Athelston* 137–8). The king reacts to the news as
Charles does in the *chansons*, where the traitor insinuates that
Charles is to be both deposed[1] and poisoned. The traitor in
Athelston exhibits covetousness (724–5). He undergoes an ordeal
by the order of the king, and not, like the others, by the order of
the archbishop; and he fails at the ordeal. At the instance
of the two young sons of Egeland, he confesses his treachery :

> He louyd him to mekyl and me to lyte ;
> þerfore enuye I hadde.

He is then drawn with five horses through London and hanged
at Tyburn, which penalties seem to be a confusion of the
traditional punishment of the traitor in the *chansons* with the
legal penalty of drawing and hanging. There are, of course,
traitors, especially stewards[2] (Fr. *seneschal*), in other English
romances, but in none of them is the traitor of such central
importance, or so completely furnished with the traditional
traits as is Wymound in *Athelston*. I imagine also that the
author knew he was drawing the typical traitor, since I think
the name *Wymound* can be shown to have signified rascality to
Englishmen of the fourteenth century.[3] It is to me inconceiv-
able that any English poet could have drawn such a figure
without going to the source for it—the French *chansons de geste*.

3 c. In order to gather the parallels together I propose to
give now a brief account of two poems, or compositions in verse,
in Middle German texts,[4] which are themselves closely connected
with French *chansons*, but which resemble *Athelston* in some
respects more closely than do the *chansons* from which they
both derive. The first is the legendary account of the ordeal
undergone by Richardis (or Richgard), the wife of the Frankish
king, Charles the Third, called the Fat. Charles the Third as
well as being emperor was king of the West Franks, and the

---

[1] See note to 142.
[2] *Journal of Eng. and Germ. Phil.*, 10, p. 429.
[3] See Intro. 6 *a*.
[4] Both originally Frankish.

tale of Richardis was a Frankish tale which spread to Germany, and, as I think, to England. It is contained in lines 15406–515 of the rhymed *Kaiserchronik*.[1] This chronicle was composed about the year 1150, probably at Regensburg, which was a centre of the saga-cult of Charles the Great. The parts of the chronicle dealing with the German kaisers is mainly sober history, and the account of Richardis's ordeal stands out by reason of its plainly legendary matter and artificial form.[2] The course of the narrative is as follows : The king took a wife who was true and upright, *aller boshaite was si fri* (cf. *Athelston* 61–3). Envy of her good qualities raised up enemies against her, *Si begriffen si mit lugene* (cf. *Athelston* 82–3). A counsellor of the king, Sigerat (or Sighart), hints at a discovery so serious that its like had never been before ; he dare never tell of it (cf. *Athelston* 121–6). The king demands the truth for the sake of the realm's honour (cf. *Athelston* 145–7). The queen is accused of loving another man, and the informant bids the king hang him on a tree if he is speaking falsely. The king rushes to his chamber, strikes the queen *ainen michelen vusteslac* and upbraids her violently. Greatly moved she scornfully denies the charge. Charles, shaking with rage, taxes her with adultery and with disloyalty to the realm. She agrees that she were worthy of death, if guilty. She says she will appeal to God (i.e. undergo the ordeal, *iudicium Dei*) to prove her innocence. She sends forthwith for four bishops, who give her absolution. She makes the proper legal and religious preparations for the ordeal. On the day of the ordeal bishops and barons and a great quantity of other folk gather. The queen appeals to God to deprive her of the crown if she is guilty. She advances then with uplifted eyes amid many blessings from the bystanders. She puts on the waxen shift, which was set alight and burnt up without harming the woman. All rejoice, and *sprachen deo gracias* (cf. *Athelston* 590, 614). The bishops take their leave, and the king has the traitors hanged. The general resemblance of this to the form of the traitor-story we have been discussing is plain ; certain particular resemblances to *Athelston* may be brought forward. First and most important, the whole story is contained within the framework of the treachery and its punishment.

[1] *Die Kaiserchronik eines Regensburger Geistlichen*, ed. E. Schröder.
[2] *Ibid.*, Intro., p. 67.

Unlike the *chansons* it contains no matter irrelevant to this one theme. To note are the assurance that the wrongly accused person was actually not capable of falsehood ; the king's violent treatment of the queen ; the ordeal, differing from that in the French *chansons* ; and the bishops' departure before the king punishes the traitor.

I add now a second poem (Middle High German), *Morant und Galie,* written originally about 1200 and included in the compilation known as the *Karlmeinet,*[1] of the beginning of the fourteenth century. The poem is accepted by Ehrismann as being a German version of an episode in the saga-history of Charles the Great, and based upon a lost Old French poem. Its resemblance to the tale of Richardis is very marked, but it adds some features which bring it closer to *Athelston.* It opens with a prayer for Paradise, and an announcement of a tale of treachery, just as *Athelston* does. Then Rohart, the leading villain, adjures his companions to stand by him in his project. He has an envious hatred of Morant, and wishes to oust him from Charles's favour. Morant, having been at the court, gets leave to depart. The traitors then make a charge of adultery against Morant and the queen. Charles, greatly perturbed, takes the traitors into his confidence, and they counsel him to send messengers for Morant *mit vrme segele ind breve* (cf. *Athelston* 193–6). Morant is commanded to the court, along with his two nephews. He suspects no trouble. When he arrives at the court, the accusation is made to him and the queen. She utters loud complaints, and high words ensue between Morant and Charles. The two accused persons are fettered and imprisoned. A friend of the queen pleads for the prisoners, and the ordeal—of battle—is appointed. The villain, Rohart, disguises himself as a pilgrim in the attempt to avoid the ordeal. He is of course defeated. Charles makes an elaborate humiliation and shows his repentance by the promise of rich gifts. Then follows the punishment :

> Da man sy dreckede durch de stat . .
> Bis an de stette gibet . .
> An eynen galgen, was nuwe
>   Wael vaste ind ho.   (Cf. *Athelston* 801–9.)

---

[1] *Karlmeinet,* ed. Adelbert von Keller, pp. 325 ff. ; Gustav Ehrismann, *Geschichte der deutschen Literatur,* III. 123 ff.

Then the conclusion :

> Got mit syner mechte
> Ind syner groesser gode
> Beneme uns sulche gemode,
> Want untruwe ind overmōt
> Nemet selden ende gōt. (Cf. *Athelston* 810–12.)

I think it will be agreed that, if a *chanson* like *Morant und Galie* did exist, it would make an excellent starting-point for the story we have in *Athelston*. Add the sworn-brotherhood and the birth of the saint, substitute the ploughshare ordeal—all readily available to a writer of a *chanson*—and the substance and method of *Athelston* are complete.

4. These parallels I have cited indicate that the judgement of Miss Hibbard that *Athelston* shows no signs of having passed through the hands of French story-tellers[1] needs some revision. Practically the whole of the outline of the poem is derived, but good use has been made of the framework, and I wish now to examine in some detail the two most prominent features of the substance of *Athelston*, the sworn-brotherhood and the judicial ordeal. A full and accurate understanding of these two institutions, as well as of their use in stories, is necessary if we are to appreciate the achievement of our poem, or its weak points. They are comparatively rare in English poems, are both very interesting, and they have not been anywhere discussed in a fashion suited to my present purpose.

Sworn-brotherhood[2] was a widespread social custom of great antiquity. By it men bound themselves with an oath to be faithful to each other till death. It descends almost certainly (in western Europe) from the old Germanic custom which survives as the blood-brotherhood[3] of Old Norse laws and sagas. *Gísla Saga Súrssonar* is an excellent example of a blood-brotherhood story, not only because it gives the only full description of the ceremony, but also because it shows the weight attached by the Norsemen to this kind of brotherhood, both as a social institution, and as a story motive, a means of launching a tragic narrative. With the coming of Christianity,

---

[1] *P.M.L.A.* XXXVI. 226.

[2] J. Flach, *Le Compagnonnage dans les Chansons de Geste* ; G. H. Gerould, *Social and Historical Reminiscences in the Middle English 'Athelston'*, *E. St.* XXXVI. 193.

[3] M. Pappenheim, *Die altdänischen Schutzgilden*, p. 21.

brotherhood by mingling of blood gave place to brotherhood by
taking an oath. Sworn-brotherhood carried the obligation of
fighting alongside the ' brother ', of sharing goods with him, of
claiming his wer-gild (in heathen times of avenging him). Outside Scandinavia there is very little mention of the relationship
in legal documents ; one law, however, of Edward the Confessor
does show that the status was recognized in England.[1] There
is no English word to describe the relationship until the later
manuscripts of the *Anglo-Saxon Chronicle* (twelfth century),
where in two places (ann. 656, 1016) the word *wedbroþer* is used,
probably borrowed from Old Norse, which has a rather rare
veðbróþir. Sworn-brotherhood may be looked upon as a special
development of the Germanic ' comitatus ', and as having some
of the poetical possibilities contained in the intense loyalty of
that bond.

French *chansons de geste* have a number of examples of
sworn-brotherhood, and it seems to me one of the strongest
arguments for a French original behind *Athelston* that the
treatment of this motive in our poem agrees, as against the
Old Norse use of it, with some conventions of treatment established by the *chansons*. There is no doubt that the poets of
the *chansons* felt the beauty of the relationship, as we may see
from a passage in *Girart de Vienne*,[2] describing the bond between
Roland and Oliver—the original sworn-brotherhood of the
chansons. Its recurring note is *Je vos aim plus que home qui
soit né*. I mention some leading points of a *chanson*, *Daurel et
Beton*,[3] which, like *Athelston*, begins with a bond of sworn-
brotherhood and continues with treachery and an ordeal by
fire. Beuve D'Antone, a knight at Charlemagne's court, for an
unexplained reason chooses *comte Gui* for companion, i.e. sworn-
brother. The oath is taken on the Bible in the presence of
witnesses. Beuve leaves to Gui all his possessions, including
his wife, if he dies without issue. Beuve is singled out for
favour by Charlemagne, and is given Ermenjart to wife, along
with a dowry of Poitiers. Gui is immediately envious of Beuve
and resolves on his death. Then events follow as in the
other traitor stories, with this difference that the lady herself
claims the ordeal by fire to save herself from the traitor Gui.

[1] F. Liebermann, *Die Gesetze der Angelsachsen*, I, p. 641.
[2] *Girart de Vienne*, ed. Tarbé, p. 155.
[3] Ed. Paul Meyer (Société des Anciens Textes Français).

Ultimately the son, Beton, avenges the wrong-doing of the traitor.

The *chanson* of *Aye d'Avignon* is closer to *Athelston* in the respect that it connects the act of faithlessness with disappointment at the distribution of estates. Charles, to reward Garnier, son of Doon, would have given him a fief if one had fallen vacant; as it is, he gives him his niece, La Belle Aye, and some treasure. These had been previously promised to Berenger, who now demands that Garnier give them up. He refuses; then Berenger exclaims: 'Car hui departiront les nostres amistiez'. This breaking of the friendship is in strict accordance with the code of the *chansons*, where any breach on the part of one brother entitled the other to abrogate the bond.

One feature of the treatment of sworn-brotherhood in the *chansons* merits special attention in relation to *Athelston*, namely, that it was definitely considered as being superior to the marriage-tie. In the French *Ami et Amiles* the bride of Amiles has to swear an oath in these terms: 'Que vos panrez Amile le baron au loement d'Ami son conpaignon!'[1] The position as regards the wife is stated even more pointedly in *Athelston*. When the queen, after her pleadings with the king have failed, is dispatching the messenger to Alryke, she says to him:

> He wole doo more for hym, I wene,
> þanne for me, þouȝ I be qwene. (ll. 306-7.)

This is to be taken as a statement not so much of the queen's own weakness as of the bishop's influence, in that he is the sworn-brother of Athelston. For it must be carefully noted that his first plea to Athelston when they meet (441-6) is based solely on his position as a sworn-brother; his use of his ecclesiastical authority follows only after the failure of the other instrument. This discussion of differing moral claims is exactly in the manner of the *chansons*.

The vitality of sworn-brotherhood as a story-motive in the *fourteenth* century as evidenced in *Athelston* must surely be attributed to the fact that Scandinavian influence was strong

---

[1] *Ami et Amiles* represents, as Flach says, 'le compagnonnage idéal dans toute son énergie et toute sa pureté'. One may contrast the way in which in Chaucer's *Knight's Tale* 1129-69 sworn-brotherhood is held inferior to 'love'.

in the East Midlands, and that the descendants of the Norsemen must have cherished memories of sworn-brotherhood.[1] It
is to be noted as significant that both in *Athelston* and in *Amis
and Amiloun* sworn-brotherhood never gives way to the attempt
made to use it for religious purposes. In *Athelston* Alryke
pleads as a sworn-brother before he acts as an archbishop;
Athelston himself is very unwilling to break his word to his
sworn-brother, Wymound; and even Wymound shows some
compunction (176–7). In *Amis and Amiloun* the clash is plainer,
since Amiloun helps his brother in what he knows to be an im-
moral cause, and in the face of a warning from heaven that he
would be afflicted with leprosy. The situation in which Amiloun
is involved is, in the technical sense, a tragic one, and he makes
his choice as the heroes of the old sagas, who with their 'aesthe-
tic view of conduct'[2] preferred that their conduct should be
dramatic rather than righteous. But a romance must have
a happy ending, and this is duly arranged when the Church has
been obeyed. So in a lesser degree, but quite unmistakably, the
king in *Athelston* prefers the old barbaric virtue to the new
morality of the Church, and the happy ending is for a moment
endangered. I think that the poem of *Athelston*, along with
Amis, earns an added spiritual dignity in reflecting though
faintly the old heroic virtues,[3] and, as a literary form, has a
particular interest because it combines with a romance these
hints of sterner tragedy.

5. The other institution, besides sworn-brotherhood, which
figures prominently in *Athelston*, is the judicial ordeal, the medieval *iudicium Dei*, and like sworn-brotherhood it is an institution
which is very ancient and whose history is obscure. By it
a person was subjected to a test with fire or water to determine
whether he was guilty or innocent, and in Christian times the
result was accepted as the judgement of God, a supernatural
verdict. The poem quite clearly introduces this practice, when
Alryke says:

> Sere, off gylt and (= if) þay be clene,
> Þis doom hem thar nouȝt drede.   (ll. 574–5.)

---

[1] Cf. also the beautiful and vigorous ballad of *Bewick and Graham*,
Child, No. 211, Vol. IV, pp. 144–50. See also Gerould, *op. cit.*

[2] E. V. Gordon, *Introduction to Old Norse*, p. xxxii.

[3] It is interesting to observe that the *Battle of Maldon* was probably
written in the East Midlands.

Again, in ll. 775–6, Athelston says:

> Let hym to þe fyr gon,
> To preue þe treweþe in dede.

When the result of the ordeal is seen it is characterized as a *myracle*, l. 617. What ordeal is used in *Athelston*? It is the ordeal of walking through fire, which was, of course, not a legal ordeal, but a legendary one. The poem, however, apparently confuses this ordeal with the one of walking over nine red-hot ploughshares, although the word *plowȝ-lengþe* or *-lenge* cannot actually mean ploughshares:

> It [the fire] was set, þat men myȝt knawe,
> Nyne plow-lengþe on rawe. (ll. 570–1.)

The institution of the ordeal was well known in Anglo-Saxon times;[1] but the ploughshare ordeal is not mentioned at all in Anglo-Saxon documents, and the few instances in post-Conquest laws are, according to Liebermann, due to interpolation from Frankish laws.[2] He remarks on the *Tale of Emma and the Ploughshares* and on *Athelston* that the Emma incident is 'eine Tradition seit Ende 12. Jhs., aber unhistorisch. In der Dichtung *Athelston* schreitet der Graf durch Flammen neun Pluglängen weit; der Bischof segnet den Weg neunmal; offenbar unwirklich und aus fremden literarischen Erinnerungen'.[3] The ordeals which we know to have been used in England were gradually superseded by the Norman trial by combat, and were abolished early in the thirteenth century.[4] It was therefore likely, as has been remarked,[5] that a popular poem, composed more than a century after ordeals were abolished, should be confused about their nature, especially since the ploughshare ordeal was foreign to England. In the poem of *Athelston* the ordeal is given not only to Egeland and Wymound, who are accused of crimes, but also to Egeland's two sons and his wife, who are apparently innocent, and, most curious of all, Alryke threatens Athelston with it as a merely punitive measure. We are thus directed away from England to find parallels for the ordeal story, and German

---

[1] See Liebermann, *op. cit.*, *Iudicium Dei*' passim.

[2] *Ibid.*, I. 406–7, 416, 484, 604–5, and footnote; II. 386.

[3] *Ibid.*, II. 386.

[4] *Encyclopaedia Brit.*, S.V. ORDEAL.

[5] Beug, 'Die Sage von Athelstan' (*Archiv für das Studium der neueren Sprachen und Literaturen* 148, p. 191).

and Scandinavian sources have good store of such material; but, before I examine these sources, I think it helpful to assemble the passages of *Athelston* which refer to the general procedure in ordeals, because they are best explained by passages in the English laws describing English custom. The actual procedure did not differ much from one country to the other, because it was regulated by the Church.

There was a prescribed ritual of service before the ordeal, examples of which may be seen in Liebermann, I. 401–3, and some of the examples are quite old; he quotes a Northumbrian service of the ninth century. Lines 585–7 of *Athelston* refer to this ritual:

> Nyne syþe þe bysschop halewid þe way,
> Þat his weddyd broþer scholde goo þat day,
> To praye God for þe ryȝt.

This blessing of the element by which the test was to be made was a necessary part of the service. I quote one such blessing from Liebermann, I. 419: '*Benedictio ferri ferventis* :—Deus omnipotens . . . dignare exaudire nos . . . orantes ad te pro benedictione huius ferri . . . mitte in hoc ferrum vim virtutis tuę ac veritatis, ut in eo semper per misericordiam et virtutem tuam verissima iustitia, quę tibi soli cognita est, fidelibus tuis . . . declaretur.' This was followed by the *Oratio*: 'Deus iudex iustus . . . te suppliciter rogamus ut . . . si innocens de prenominata causa . . . hoc ferrum ignitum in manus acceperit . . . illesus appareat.' Lines 627–8, if they are spoken by the bishop, are to be regarded as corresponding to the *Oratio*; if they belong to the queen, as is possible, they constitute a protestation of innocence, which the heroines of these ordeal stories usually make.[1] According to the laws, the ordeal of hot iron was held inside the church, and in the legend of Emma the ploughshares which she trod were placed inside Winchester Cathedral. Of course, the ordeal of fire as described in *Athelston* cannot take place inside a church. I think, nevertheless, that the ordinary procedure as described in the laws may supply a meaning to two unexplained lines of the poem connected with the ordeal. I quote from Liebermann, I. 387, a Latin version of Old English laws (936–1000) dealing with the ordeal of carrying hot iron: 'Novem pedes mensurati distinguantur in ter ternos, in primo

---

[1] See note to 625 ff.

signo iuxta stacam teneat pedem dextrum; in secundo sinistrum; inde transferat dextrum pedem in tertium signum cum ferrum proicitur, et ad sanctum altare festinet.' The lady is described in 633 of *Athelston* (and Wymound in 786) as going *Fro þe lengþe into þe prydde*, which may mean going through the fire 'length- wise, *either* the first third of the way, *or* till the "tertium sig- num".' An illustration of Kunigund's ordeal (in Alwyn Schultz, *Das höfische Leben zur Zeit der Minnesinger*, I. 268) shows her standing still on the last ploughshare; and we shall see, when investigating other foreign legendary ordeals, that the subjects sometimes linger over the ordeal to show their confidence in their cause. I suggest also, but not with much assurance, that 591-2 (repeated in 615-16)

> Þey offeryd hym with mylde chere
> Vnto seynt Powlys heyȝe awtere

might find their explanation in the hastening to the altar (*ad sanctum altare festinet*) as soon as the ordeal had been undergone. The ordeal had to be conducted by the bishop or his representa- tive (Liebermann, I. 485); and in our poem the archbishop, Alryke, directs proceedings for the ordeal in London. The laws enjoined that the ordeal should take place 'in conspectu adstan- tium', and the crowd is clearly evidenced in *Athelston* (570 and 589-613). The clothes had to be taken off: 'Ita missa expleta, homo predictus in ecclesia exuatur non sólum laneis vestibus, verum etiam femoralibus' (Liebermann, I. 417). In *Athelston*

> From hym þey token þe rede scarlet,
> Boþe hosyn and schoon, þat weren hym met.
>
> (ll. 582-3.)

After the ordeal the burned limb was inspected, 'et si sanies crudescens in vestigio ferri repperiatur, culpabilis et inmundus ducatur; sin autem mundus extiterit, laus et gloria Deo refera- tur' (Liebermann, I. 429). The inspection to see whether the limb was healed took place usually after three days, and it will be observed that in *Athelston*, as in the other legendary accounts, the inspection takes place *immediately*, and no harm at all is done to the limbs.

> He was vnblemeschyd foot and hand;
> Þat sawȝ þe lordes off þe land,
> And þankyd God off his myȝt. (ll. 588-90.)

C

The mention of *foot and hand* seems to result from confusion of the ordeals of carrying iron and treading iron, unless it is used as a metonymy for ' over the whole body '. Line 590 shows the customary thanksgiving. It will be seen that, though the references are fragmentary, they do recall in a more or less authentic fashion the greater part of the procedure associated with the ordeal.

So much for the ordeal in general, and as an institution. When we turn to its use in stories, we find that the material is almost entirely outside England—and is indeed chiefly the ' Richardis ' tale referred to previously, or stories closely allied to it. I have cited the parallels of the *chanson de geste, Parise la Duchesse*, and of the allied German poem, *Morant und Galie*, where a tale of treachery is combined with an accusation (of adultery) against a woman, and she is threatened with fire not as an ordeal, but as a punishment. But the ' Richardis ' tale has this feature which brings us nearer to *Athelston*, namely, that the lady herself is subjected to an ordeal and survives it. The existence of this tale of Richardis and the wide vogue it had[1] provide the best explanation, if not the only one, for a remarkable feature of *Athelston*—that, though Egeland is the chief offender, Edyff, the woman, has a more prominent part in the ordeal.[2] In addition, it will be noticed that from the beginning it is specially insisted that the wife must accompany Egeland (191, 214); and that, when Egeland and his family are arrested, it is the countess who makes the protest (245-9); indeed, Egeland speaks only once in the whole poem, and then what he says relates to the fitness of the wife for the journey to London. It would seem that the ' Richardis ' tale has been combined with a story of the treachery-cum-ordeal type of the *chansons*, and has been made predominant, probably because the ecclesiastical revisers chose to have it so. I leave aside for later discussion the question whether *Athelston* derives directly from the tale of ' Queen Emma and the Plough-shares ', *which is itself of foreign origin*; briefly, I do not believe that any direct connexion between the two can be established. It is interesting to observe, as bearing on the possibility of a tale like that of ' Richardis ' having entered into the composition of *Athelston*, that different versions of the German tale use

[1] F. J. Child, *English and Scottish Popular Ballads*, Pt. III, pp. 36 ff.
[2] Miss Hibbard, *op. cit.*, p. 226.

different ordeals, and one of them, in the *Annales Reginonis
Monachi*,[1] the ploughshare ordeal.   In this account the queen
offers to be tried ' aut singulari certamine aut ignitorum vom-
erum examine.   Erat enim religiosa foemina '.   The religious
aspects of this ordeal of a queen are much farther developed in
the most famous of the stories akin to the ' Richardis ' tale,
that of Kunigund (St. Cunegundis), the wife of the emperor
Henry the Second.   Kunigund was a very pious lady who
preserved her chastity though married, and was historically, as
well as in legend, a notable supporter of the Church,[2] and was
allied with the bishops who presided at her ordeal.   One detail
of her passage over the ploughshares, which in most accounts
are twelve in number, is a good parallel to a feature of Edyff's
ordeal.   It is said of her : [3]

> Stans super extremum vomerem reveranda, supremum
> Regem laudavit, per quem satanam superavit.

This I take to be an action corresponding to that described
in *Athelston* 634-5 :

> Stylle sche stood þe fyr amydde,
> And callyd it merye and bryȝt.

As to the cheerfulness under the ordeal, one may compare
what was said of Bishop Poppo, when converting the Danes :
' hilari et jocundo vultu nec fumum incendii se sensisse testatus
sit.'   The tale of Cunegund appropriated to Gunhild, daughter
of Emma, who took the name of Cunegund, survives in English
literature in the fine ballad *Sir Aldingar*.[4]   Having supplied
these parallels to the tale of Richardis and of *Edyff*, I imitate
the caution of Child, who draws back from any attempt to show
their interrelations.   But the parallels do indicate that the
ordeal of Edyff in *Athelston* is similar to those just cited, and that
such an ordeal had strong religious associations, which would
give a chance to an English reviser to increase the prominence
of the bishop as the champion of the Church.

The use of the number nine in the *Athelston* ordeal—*nyne
plowȝ-lengþe, nyne syþe þe bysschop halewid þe way*—causes

---

[1] Pistorius, *Scriptores*, I. 87.
[2] Anna Gebser, *Die Bedeutung der Kaiserin Kunigunde* (Berlin, 1897).
[3] *Vita St. Cunegundis*, Pertz IV (not VI, as Grimm has it), 820 b.
[4] Child, *Ballads*, Pt. III, pp. 36 ff.

us to look to Scandinavian sources. None of the German
accounts I have seen mentions the number nine, while it is
frequent in Old Norse incidents. In *Heimskringla*, III. 301, it
is told of Harald, when claiming to be the son of Magnús, that
' hann fastaði til járns, ok var sú skírsla gǫr, er mest hefir
verit gǫr í Nóregi, at IX plógjárn glóandi váru niðr lǫgð, ok
gekk Haraldr þar eptir berum fótum, ok leiddu hann byskupar
ii.' And of Bishop Poppo in *Heimskringla* :[1] ' en síðan mon ek
ganga yfir glóanda járn í trauste heilagrar þrenningar 9 fet ...'
It is true that the tale of Emma mentions nine ploughshares,
and that an Old English law of 936–1000 (Liebermann, I. 387)
enacts that the hot iron must be carried *novem pedes*. But
these are both of late date, and since the nine feet are unknown
in the earliest English laws on ordeal, and in the ' Kunigund '
legend the number of ploughshares is twelve, it is probable
that the number nine in England represents the adoption of
the Scandinavian habit. The extension of the nine from the
number of *plowȝ-lengþe* to the number of times the bishop
blesses the way looks like a popular confusion among people
who knew some stories having that number in connexion with
ordeals. So also, in the legend of Emma, the queen and the
bishop give each nine manors to St. Swithin's. Thus the
account of the ordeal in *Athelston* as well as of sworn-brotherhood seems to show Scandinavian influence in important
particulars.

5 *a*. This is a convenient point at which to examine Miss
Hibbard's contention [2] that the poem of *Athelston* needs nothing
to explain its material except a knowledge of the tale of *Queen
Emma and the Ploughshares*.[3] The substance of the legend is
as follows : Emma, mother of Edward the Confessor, is accused
of adultery with Alwyn, bishop of Winchester, by Robert,
archbishop of Canterbury and favourite of Edward, and she
is put in confinement at Wherewell. She manages to communi-
cate with the bishops who were her friends, and suggests an
ordeal to prove her innocence. At the instigation of Robert,
who also adds a charge of attempting to poison the king (when
he was young), Emma is awarded an ordeal of nine red-hot
ploughshares. Robert decamps to Dover, ready to flee if things

---

[1] Jacob Grimm, *Deutsche Rechtsalterthümer* (1899), II. 577.
[2] *P.M.L.A.* XXXVI. 223–44.
[3] *Annales de Wintonia* (Rolls), pp. 20 ff., for the year 1043.

go badly. On the appointed day Emma undergoes the ordeal
in the presence of the king and the assembled barons of England,
and proves her innocence. Edward humbles himself before his
mother, and receives correction from her and the bishop.
Robert flees to France, and Godwin, whose exile he had pro-
cured, returns, as also does Edith, wife of Edward the Confessor.
Emma and the bishop both give nine manors to St. Swithin's
to commemorate the occasion.

Miss Hibbard seeks to sustain two propositions : (a) that the
poem of *Athelston* is based on the legend of Emma and the
Ploughshares as told first by Richard of Devizes,[1] a monk of
St. Swithin's, Winchester, fl. 1191 ; and (b) that the poem was
based immediately on the version of the legend which appears in
the Chronicle of Richard of Cirencester,[2] a monk at Westminster
about 1350. I think, however, that it can be shown quite
simply and briefly that Richard of Cirencester could not have
been the source for the material of *Athelston*. The extant
versions of the Emma legend, nine in number, divide themselves, as Miss Hibbard recognizes, into two groups : those
which derive from the original Winchester legend as printed in
the *Annales de Wintonia*, and those which depend on the
shortened version of Ranulph Higden in the *Polychronicon*
(Rolls) VII. 161. The Winchester version includes certain particulars which the Higden abridgement leaves out, among others,
these : (1) mention of Dover as the place where the traitor
stayed while the ordeal was in progress ; (2) mention of Emma's
praying immediately before she underwent the ordeal ; (3) the
blessing of the ploughshares ; (4) the taking off of the shoes
and hose, and the doffing of the clothes. But all these four
particulars occur in the poem.[3] Moreover, one of these items,
the stay at Dover, is the chief argument Miss Hibbard advances
for identifying the stories at all ; yet it is present in the poem,
and *not* in Richard of Cirencester. Therefore, even if *Athelston*
is in any way connected with the legend, it is much more
closely related to the Winchester version than to the version of
Richard of Cirencester, on which Miss Hibbard's case is based.
She does make one—as I shall show—unfortunate attempt to
connect Richard of Cirencester with the Winchester source, as

[1] See *Dictionary of National Biography*.
[2] Ricardi de Cirencestria, *Speculum Historiale* (Rolls).
[3] Miss Hibbard identifies Robert with *Wymound* and Emma with *Edyff*

against Higden's version. She says that the original Winchester
account mentions that Robert fled 'extra Anglia', that Higden
in the corresponding place has 'in Normanniam', and that,
since Richard of Cirencester has 'extra Anglia', he must have
known the Winchester source. Unfortunately for this argument,
a foot-note to the very page of the *Polychronicon* cited by
Miss Hibbard gives the readings of other manuscripts of Higden
as 'extra Anglia(m)'. Therefore we may dismiss entirely the
idea that Richard of Cirencester was the compiler of the
material for the poem, at least so far as Miss Hibbard's
evidence is concerned; and with Richard of Cirencester dis-
appears the whole of the elaborate construction of guesses
erected by Miss Hibbard upon him as a foundation.[1] I might
mention here in passing that I shall show in discussing the
topography of the poem that it is indeed closely identified with
London, but with London as opposed to Westminster.

Is the poem connected with the legend of Emma in any way?
Or did it make any use of the ballad on Emma which we know
to have existed from a reference in Warton's *History of English
Poetry*?[2] Miss Hibbard maintains (*op. cit.*, p. 226) that unless
we accept the connexion we have no explanation of: (1) the
importance of the Church in *Athelston*, and the prominent part
played by a woman; (2) Dover as the place of stay of Wymound;
(3) the name of the archbishop, Alryke. With regard to the
first I have shown that the 'Richardis' type of tales of ordeals
always gives prominence to the Church and the bishops.
'Dover' has to be interpreted along with the other places on
the London–Dover road, and is in any case not infrequently
mentioned in romances, as in *Havelok the Dane*. As for the
name Alryke, there are dozens of examples in the Domesday
Book for Kent. I conclude, therefore, that although it is
tempting to find a connexion between the only two stories in
England which refer to the ordeal of the nine ploughshares, I
can find no evidence for the connexion. Of course, I cannot
positively assert that the two were entirely independent; but
of this I am sure, that to assume the connexion creates more
problems than it solves, and hence that the balance of probability is very much against it.

[1] With Richard of Cirencester disappear also the arguments connected
with the name of *Alryke*.

[2] Ed. W. Carew Hazlitt (London 1871), II. 96–7.

5 *b*. I have now assembled the borrowed material in *Athelston*, so far as I have been able to find it during an extensive, though by no means exhaustive, search in likely places. I may at this point summarize this material in order to clear the way for a consideration of the more particularly English sources. I have suggested that the framework of the story comes from the *chansons de geste*, along with conventions of treatment so accurately reproduced as almost in themselves to warrant the assumption of a French original. We have a story beginning with an act of treachery and falsehood, ending with the punishment for that act, and taking a course between that beginning and end according to the examples in the *chansons*. There also the men concerned are sometimes sworn-brothers. The accusation is made against the king's favourite and the king's wife, and a judicial ordeal is appointed, involving both man and woman, because the first has to fight to prove the second's innocence. The 'Richardis' tale (connected with the *chansons*) adds Germanic ordeals for the woman, ordeal by fire, which is legendary, and other legal ordeals, such as treading hot plough-shares. We have also a trusted adviser of the king being summoned by the queen to help in the difficulty, and the 'Richardis' tale has the constant feature of bishops as sup-porters of the accused lady. The actions both of the queen and of Edyff in *Athelston* are closely paralleled in the analogues cited. We have also a birth corresponding to that of St. Edmund, and frequently two young sons or nephews of the hero involved in his misfortunes. We have every action of Wymound's, including, be it noted, his desire to avoid the ordeal, that is to say, the motive for his going away to Dover, which Miss Hibbard thinks to be supplied by the Emma legend. No adequate investigation of *Athelston* can possibly ignore this material and these parallels, and they account quite plainly for most that is in the poem.

Naturally, the *Athelston* poet combines these well-known motives and situations in his own way. He takes the treachery-cum-ordeal story and develops it on the ordeal side, as one may suppose, to serve his religious purposes. He sends to the ordeal not only Egeland but also his two sons, his wife, and Wymound. It appears at first sight that he has allowed his religious zeal greatly to outrun his artistic discretion, not to mention mere probability. But I do not think he is quite so stupid as he has been represented. With regard to Edyff, it is true that the poet has nothing to correspond to the 'adultery' charge, which goes with the story of the woman under the ordeal. But he does take pains to associate Edyff with Egeland's supposed treachery (163, 245 ff.), and to prepare for Edyff's arrival at the court to share her husband's fate (214 ff., 229). With regard to the ordeal undergone by the sons, we have shown that the *chansons* give examples of two young sons (or nephews) being involved in the disaster to the hero. Moreover, it often happened in England that the family of an alleged or convicted traitor was made to suffer with him (Liebermann, I. 644). We may recall the action of Henry the Second in sending every relative of Becket's after him to Pontigny. Lines 172–4 of *Athelston* seem to refer to this custom :

> Boþe he and hys wyff, hys soones twoo,
> Schole þey neuere be no moo,
> In Yngelond on þat stede.

But the ordeal for Wymound does seem to be dragged in, since the king knows he is guilty. An attempt, however, is made by the poet to provide an issue for decision by the ordeal, since he causes Wymound, ineptly enough, to deny that he ever made the falsehood (765). Two circumstances of the procedure in English trials of the thirteenth century may be recalled : firstly, that the king could not punish a baron without fair trial, and this fact is very likely referred to in 767; and secondly, that traitors were subjected to the most complicated and terrible series of tortures, when they were executed.[1] The author evidently intended to make as much use as he could of the ordeal, but he did so with at least a modicum of discretion. With regard to the particular ordeal the poet uses, there seems to be a confusion between the legendary ordeal by fire, and the ordeal of the ploughshares, which was not actually used in England. This confusion may have been due to misunderstanding of a foreign original, or to the poet's taking up into a French original some material from popular—originally Scandinavian—tradition where confusion had already occurred. Another difference to note between *Athelston* and its (likely) sources is that the material conventionally attached to the accused woman,

---

[1] See, for example, the account of the execution of William Wallace in *Flores Historiarum* (Rolls), III. 124.

violent treatment from the king, outcries, protestation of innocence, ordeal, has been divided between the queen and the king's
sister. Lastly, we may observe that the situation in which
king, favourite, villain, and helping bishop are all sworn-brothers
makes a splendid opening, although it raises problems in conduct
beyond the scope of our poet.

6. THE ENGLISH MATERIAL

The way is now clear for a consideration of the English
material in *Athelston*. The principal matters may, I think, be
dealt with in the answers to these four questions : (1) How does
it come about that Old English names are so prominent ? What
do these names represent ? (2) Is *Athelston* of the poem to be
identified with the historical Athelstan, successor of Edward the
Elder on the throne of Wessex and England, and *seynt Edemound*
with St. Edmund of East Anglia, King and Martyr ? (3) How
does the figure of *Alryke* (the bishop as helper of the woman)
come to assume such outstanding importance with his
paraphernalia of ecclesiastical rite, especially the interdict ?
(4) Whence come the particular and accurate references to places
in London, and on the road through Canterbury to Dover ?

6 a. *The Names*

ATHELSTON (r. w. *ylkon*) 26, *Athelstane* (r. w. *name*) 185 = OE.
Æpelstān. The form *Athelstane* is the only one secured by
rhyme, but it may not have been in the original. Since this
form is not actually used for the king himself, and in view of 26,
I keep the usual *Athelston* in the title.

EDEMOUND (r. w. *ground*) 649 = OE. *Ēadmund*. The second
element of the compound proper name (from the *-ou*-spelling)
seems to have preserved a strong secondary stress ; or the
spelling may be a sign of a French (Anglo-Norman) original.
The inserted *e*, which the metre indicates to have been pronounced, may perhaps be compared to the three syllables in
Engeland (England), as in *Havelok the Dane*, 59, 61, 63, &c. It
is worth noting, however, that in the romance of *Bevis* the
English versions of the section with the ' London ' incident,
ll. 4294 ff., write *Edgar*, while the Anglo-Norman versions have
Edegar ; and also the Anglo-Norman *Vie seint Edmund le Rey*
(Rolls, 1892) has at least a dozen instances of a trisyllabic
' Edmund '.

EDYFF (r. w. *wyff*) 47, *Edyue* 192 is the OE. woman's name
Ēadgifu, which was borne by the historical Athelstan's step-
mother, and by two of his sisters.

ALRYKE (named only once) 51, r.w. *wyke* (OE. *wĭce*), *lyche*,
ryche. The number of phonological possibilities in deriving this
name is embarrassingly large. From Zupitza to Miss Hibbard
it has been assumed that Alryke represents the OE. *Ælfric*, and
that the *f* has disappeared : this is likely enough. We know
also that an Ælfric, a candidate for the archbishopric of
Canterbury, appears as *Ælricus* in a Latin life of Edward the
Confessor [1] ; that there are several instances of the name *Alric*
in OE. records [2] ; and, further, that the *Anglo-Saxon Chronicle*
mentions a number of Ælfrics who were prominent ecclesiastics.
But suppose a French poem anywhere behind Athelston, and
other possibilities arise. *Alryke* could easily have been cor-
rupted from *Ailryke*, and any *Ail-* in a French form may
represent OE. or ME. *Egel-* or OE. *Æpel-* [3]. I mention this
merely to show the futility of basing an argument, as Miss
Hibbard does, on the assumption that *Alryke* necessarily represents the OE. *Ælfric*. A suggestion which may be worthy of
consideration in view of the likely Scandinavian influence in
Athelston is that the name is identical with the recorded Old
Norse name [4] *Alrekr* < * *Alríkr* = Gothic * *Alareiks* [5]. That such
a name would be borrowed into English with the *-i-* is proved
by the *Eʒricus* (OWSc. *Eiríkr*) quoted by Björkman on p. 38 of
his *Scandinavian Loan-words in Middle English*.

EGELAND 62, 116; *Egelond* 44; *Egelan* r. w. *nan* (OE. *nān*)
579; *Egelane* 161, 705, 717 : this name is a problem. There is
nothing in Old English resembling it, and, moreover, very few
names at all in *-an*, or *-and*. The rhyme at 579–80 seems to show,
as Zupitza supposes,[6] that *Egelan* (without the *d*) is the proper
form ; and if we accept this we may find parallels for the adding

---

[1] *Vita Eadwardi* (Rolls), pp. 399 ff.

[2] *Anglo-Saxon Chronicle* (Laud MS.), ann. 789 (see Z's note to 51). See
also W. G. Searle's *Onomasticon Anglo-Saxonicum* : several examples of
Ælric (p. 30), *Alric* (p. 67), *Elric* (p. 226).

[3] R. E. Zachrisson, *Influence of Anglo-Norman on English Place-Names*.

[4] See, for instance, the Index to *Origines Islandicae*, I. 644 ; also Noreen,
Altisländische Grammatik, p. 48; (possibly) *Victoria County History of
Yorkshire*, II. 163.

[5] Schönfeld, *Altgerm. Personen- und Völkernamen*, p. 10.

[6] See Z's note to 441, *E. St.* XIII. 351.

of an homorganic *d* to words ending with *n*.   Jespersen, in his
Modern English Grammar, I (pp. 218–19), has a collection of such
words, mostly from mod.E. ; in *Piers Plowman*, C-Text, Passus
VI, l. 79 (ed. Skeat, 1886), we have *Symondes* as the genitive of
Simon ; Fabyan's *Chronicle*, p. 349, has *syr Symonde Mounforde*.[1]
This addition of a *d* is more likely than the loss of a final *d*
after *n* as in *laune* (lawn) from *launde*, which is rare and post-
Middle-English.   But if *Egelan* is the proper form of the name,
where does it come from ?   The only similar names I have been
able to find are in Old and Middle High German.   Förstemann [2]
has *Agilan*, *Agilanis* (recorded before the period of *i*-mutation),
and *Egilano* (ablative).   But despite the rhyme with *nan*, I am
not convinced that *Egelan* does represent the original form of
the name.   Of course, if *Egelan* were an English name in use at
the time (as were *Wymound* and *Athelston*), then the rhyme
might be decisive.   But if the name comes from a literary
source, the matter is not so certain.   Förstemann has a number
of examples of a name which would give a ME. *Egeland*.   We
find a *Hekilant* several times.[3]   There is also a feminine *Egilanda*.[4]
Names in *-land* are very common.   Curiously enough the name
Egeland is borne by the present High Commissioner for S. Africa.
If we suppose *Egèland* to have been the original name, I think it
possible that the form without the *d* may be accounted for by the
assumption of an Anglo-Norman original.   The *Vie seint Edmund*
(Rolls) rhymes the name *Edmund* either with *-und* (438, 531) or
with *-un* (*mesprisun* 3291, *felun* 3698).   The Anglo-Norman
practice (and possibly the English use, independently) may be
connected with the frequent French assonances in *-n* and *-nd*.
But whether we adopt the form in *-an* or in *-and*, I think that
what evidence is available points to a German source for the name,
and this is interesting in view of the fact that German stories seem
to have been used in *Athelston*.

WYMOUND (79, 691) is either OE. *Wīgmund*, *Wīmund* (which
is rare), or ON. *Vīgmundr*.   The spelling *-ound* may indicate an
Anglo-Norman original ; see also *Edemound*, p. 25.   Wymound in
Athelston is, as I have shown above, a fully typical traitor, and

---

[1] Cf. also the rhyme *Symond* : *pownde* (*Le Bone Florence* 1372–3), and the
spelling *Aþelstond* (*Reinbrun*, stanza 6) ; *Symownde* = Simon (*Prompt. Parv.*)

[2] Förstemann, *Altdeutsches Namenbuch*, p. 28.

[3] *Ibid.*, pp. 717, 1003.

[4] *Ibid.*, p. 23.

there is some evidence that the name itself connoted rascality. In the Miracle play of the York-cycle dealing with the Crucifixion,[1] the third executioner is called (*sir*) *Wymond*, and the name is only applied to him when the other two executioners are protesting that he is late with the cross which was to bear Christ. The *sir* addressed to a common soldier must have implied derision, and it seemed that the title might be taken to label him as a villain, because an enemy of Christ. The idea that the name befitted a low fellow may be evidenced again by its being chosen for the comic Charlemagne in *Rauf Coilӡear*, where the king is the butt of the collier.[2] A further reference, for which I am indebted to Dr. C. T. Onions, adds strong confirmation to the supposition. In a poem[3] printed in *Reliquiæ Antiquæ*, I. 133, there is a series of terms of abuse for the hare : it is called 'the stele-awai, the swikebert, the sculkere, the brekeforwart, the *wimount*', besides some other names. The general tenor of the abuse is : 'The hare is the one-not-to-be-trusted.' It looks as if we are entitled to say that Wymound was regarded as a generic term for the traitor, the villain, the rascal. This view of the name renders irrelevant any attempt to find an original for it, such as that of Beug,[4] who mentions a Wymound accused of treason in 1102. Our East-Midland author seems to have had enough originality to fit his traitor with an English name ; and if Wymound was the popular equivalent of Ganelon, may not Athelston have been thought of as the equivalent of Charlemagne ? I certainly agree with those who think that the English names of *Athelston* are interesting, but, bearing in mind the nature of the name Wymound, and the possibilities for Egeland, one must refuse countenance to any suggestion, such as Miss Hibbard's, that English history or legend will supply us with all the originals needed.

6 b. Who is 'Athelston'?

I think a caution should be expressed about the status of any conclusions one can reach on this question. I hold that any identification based on the common possession of general traits by the *Athelston* of the poem and the real Athelstan, when these traits are conventions in medieval poetry, is illegitimate and

---

[1] *York Mystery Plays*, XXXIV. 338, ed. E. Toulmin Smith.
[2] E.E.T.S., E.S. 39, ll. 241, 315, 450, &c.
[3] *Les noms de un levre en Engleis.*　　　　　　[4] *Archiv* 148, p. 192.

futile. Much the same poem could have been written if another name had been given to the king ; so far as I can see, the figure of Athelston has no individuality of character, and he is, apart from the dignity he gets from the sworn-brotherhood, merely the typical king of the *chansons*. We may, however, inquire why the name of *Athelston* was used by the poet, and the answer to that inquiry is only to be found in the fact of legends about him being current at the time when the poem in its original form was made. We know that legends about Athelstan were widespread in medieval England and that he was the only Anglo-Saxon king to be so celebrated. We have the well-known reference in William of Malmesbury to the ' cantilenis per successiones temporum detritis ', on which he based his account of Athelstan. All these references are gathered together by Beug in an accurate and useful, but rather forbidding article,[1] where it is shown that, in the Chronicles, there is an unbroken sequence of traditions about Athelstan. The most constant feature of these references is the splendour of his reign ; and his fame was not purely English, since a number of the accounts dwell on the rich embassies which came from foreign courts to sue for the hand of his sisters. It is perfectly feasible that a poet of the thirteenth or fourteenth century should regard Athelstan as the English equivalent of Charlemagne, the glorious ruler of tradition, to be celebrated in story and song.

It is also possible that the author found a tale of falsehood and treachery attached to the name of Athelstan : at any rate such a tale, corresponding rather remarkably in outline with the type as developed in the *chansons*, does appear in the important records of William of Malmesbury and Pierre de Langtoft. William of Malmesbury tells how Edwin, brother of Athelstan, was alleged by a cupbearer of Athelstan's to have taken part in a conspiracy against Athelstan. For punishment, Edwin was set in a rudderless boat, and drowned himself at sea. The cupbearer subsequently betrayed himself when he slipped and recovered himself, exclaiming, ' Sic frater fratrem adiuvat '. Athelstan, reminded of his duty to his brother, accused the cupbearer, who was tried and beheaded. Athelstan did penance for his wrong-doing. Pierre de Langtoft keeps the outline of the story, though simplified, and combines it with the famous

[1] *Archiv für das Studium der neueren Sprachen und Literaturen*, 148, pp. 181–95.

tale of Edric, whose story is fully told by Robert of Gloucester.[1]
In Pierre de Langtoft's story Edwin receives a traitor's death
in London.   That the author of our poem knew some such story
of Athelstan is possible; but the very fact that he used so little
of this excellent material indicates that he was modelling himself
on the pattern of the French *chansons de geste*.

I bring together some other points from this legendary
material which might possibly have a connexion with incidents
of *Athelston*, but which, if they do appear in the poem, bear no
recognizable relation to the accounts in the Chronicles. William
of Malmesbury has a tale of irregular birth and hence succession connected with Athelstan.   The same author also refers to
an 'Elfredus' (an actual historical Alfred), who questioned
Athelstan's title, was sent to Rome, and was there punished by
the Pope and died.   Athelstan's brother, Edmund, who suc-
ceeded him, is sometimes referred to as his son; and there was
a chance of confusion between the Eadgifu who was Athelstan's
sister and the Eadgifu who was Edmund's mother.   Throughout
the Chronicles Athelstan is a good friend of the Church, and
there is nothing in legend or history to suggest his quarrel with
the Church as related in our poem.   In the thirteenth century,
that is, quite late in the development of the stories about him,
the Chronicles connect him with the tale of the fight between
Guy of Warwick and Colbrond, the Danish giant.[2]   If this
material has been used at all, it has been greatly transformed
by being fused with something else.   Beug calls his article *Die
Sage von König Athelstan*, and maintains from the occurrence of
the treachery-motive that our poem is in the tradition; but it
is unfortunate that the only poem in English on Athelstan
should use so little of the excellent legends about him.   My
conclusion is that our *Athelston* of the poem is the historical
Athelstan in name; but I do not believe that our poet was
interested in Athelstan so much as in giving an English colouring to a well-known and popular type of story.

6 c.   Who is ' seynt Edemound ' ?

If St. Edmund of East Anglia is meant, it seems strange that
a story is preserved here without being mentioned anywhere

---

[1] *Chronicle* (Rolls), ll. 6330 ff. and 6373 ff.
[2] Beug, *op. cit.*; Gerard of Cornwall (1216); Pierre de Langtoft (1307).

else in the voluminous records of the saint. Is *seynt Edemound*
to be connected with the rest of the religious matter in the
poem? Was the saint introduced by an English and ecclesiastical
reviser or adapter of an incident similar to the birth in *Parise
la Duchesse* referred to above? Did our poet have any justification, other than a possible desire to use great English names,
for connecting St. Edmund of East Anglia with Athelstan of
Wessex or with any other Athelstan? In this connexion one
must mention the theory of Lord Francis Hervey.[1] Hervey's
case is that the *Romance of King Athelstone* solves the mystery
of the birth of St. Edmund (*Corolla*, Intro., p. xli), and this
case is based chiefly on a conjectural reconstruction of the dim
history of East Anglia at the end of the eighth and the beginning of the ninth century (Intro., pp. vii–xxv). He attempts to
prove that an Athelstan who was king of Kent from 839 to 852
was also king of East Anglia, and that this Athelstan was the
predecessor of St. Edmund on the throne. I have not come
across any authoritative verdict on Hervey's conjecture; but
the historical reconstruction seems to be reasonable; and it will
be agreed that it is interesting to find even a possibility that
St. Edmund was preceded on the throne of East Anglia by an
Athelstan, himself the subject of legends (*Corolla*, p. xvi).
Hervey's attempt at a closer identification of poem and history
is worthless, as are also the speculations of Haigh in his *Numis-
matic History of East Anglia*, pp. 6–11. With regard to Hervey's
chief theory, we may say at least that it affords a possibility that
Athelstan of East Anglia and Athelstan of Wessex were confused,
and the way opened for bringing St. Edmund into a poem on
Athelstan.[2]

6 d. Alryke and the Ecclesiastical Matter

I think, undoubtedly, that Gerould's suggestion[3] is essentially
right, that the action of Alryke in the poem reflects the conflict
in England between Church and State; although I think, also,
that his case needs modification in some respects and additions
in others. We shall not appreciate the significance of Alryke's
actions in the poem or of the evident relish with which they are

---

[1] *Corolla Sancti Eadmundi*, by Lord Francis Hervey.
[2] I omit any consideration of the St. Edmund of the thirteenth century,
since he could never have been looked upon as a king.
[3] *E.St.* XXXVI. 193.

told, unless we consider the opposition, as determined as it was creditable, which the Church in the twelfth, thirteenth, and fourteenth centuries made to the injustice and tyranny of English kings. We are on safer ground in looking to England for the explanation of Alryke's part in the poem than we are for Athelston's, because the French *chansons* afford us no model[1] of an ecclesiastic asserting the rights of the Church against the king, and threatening excommunication against him. It is notable that in the *Sege of Melayne*[2] the figure of Turpin, the archbishop, is vigorously developed in this direction without any warrant or parallel for it in the whole range of the *chansons*, where he has frequent mention. Since we have then in English these two poems with dominant archbishops, and since this difference between French and English poems corresponds to a difference between French and English history, we may assert with safety that the struggle of Church and State in England inspired the portrayal of Alryke in the poem of *Athelston*.

The connexion between *Athelston* and the *Sege of Melayne* is very close. The outline of the story of the bishop defeating the king is the same in each poem, and so many situations and expressions correspond and in such a peculiar way that we are safe in making what is usually a very dangerous conjecture, that the one poem borrowed from the other consciously and extensively. There is the same use of contrast when the bishop turns on the king (stanza 56 of *Melayne* and 44 of *Athelston*). The same phrase, *Allas þat þou was born*, is used by the bishop to the king, and the rhyme-word is *þorn*. Other similarities of situation and action occur at ll. 676–86 of *Athelston* (cf. 616–19 of *Melayne*) in threatening action against the king; at stanza 29 of *Athelston* (cf. 119 of *Melayne*) in commissioning a messenger; l. 215 of *Athelston* (cf. 1503 of *Melayne*) in using a rare tag; ll. 531–2 of *Athelston* (cf. 1357–8 of *Melayne*) in starting a new incident. I think perhaps, too, that the obscure action in *offeryd hem* (591 and 615 of *Athelston*) may be explained by a bad adaptation of the ceremony of dedication occurring several times in the *Sege of Melayne* (l. 811) and in *Rowland and Otuell* (l. 724). Three very striking verbal parallels are:

---

[1] Heinrich Massing. *Die Geistlichkeit im altfranzösischen Volksepos*, passim and p. 139 in particular; R. Kahle, *Der Klerus im mittelenglischen Versroman* (1906), pp. 145 ff.

[2] E.E.T.S., E.S. 35.

Athelston 367 :
    For dool, hym þouȝte, hys
        herte bledde ;
Athelston 368 :
    Þe teeres fyl ouyr his chyn ;

Athelston 771–2 :
    Myȝte he neuere with *crafft ne
        gynne*
    Gare hym schryuen off hys
        synne ;

Melayne 86 :
    For sorowe hym thoghte his
        hert bledde.
Melayne 1583 :
    The teris rane ouer Charles
        chynn.
Melayne 443–4 :
    That for him selfe no gyn ne
        kan,
    Noþer *crafte ne gyn.*

The mere identity of *crafft ne gynne* is notable, and, moreover,
the phrase seems to be dragged into *Athelston*. It is to be
remembered that these parallel phrases occur nowhere else in
the tail-rhyme romances : they are not part of the common
stock of expressions. There are of course differences in story
and style ; but no one reading extensively in the tail-rhyme
poems could fail to be struck by the similarities between these
two. My view is that such an accumulation of parallels could
only result from deliberate borrowing, and that *Athelston* owes
the debt because the phrases suit *Melayne* better, and because
Melayne is possibly to be dated before *Athelston*.[1]

If then many features and expressions in the quarrel between
Athelston and Alryke are similar to those in the *Sege of Melayne*,
I think it is unwise to attempt, as Gerould does, to identify
Athelston and Alryke with Henry the Second and Becket,
especially since Athelston is plainly the conventional king of
the *chansons de geste*. Nor is there anything in the actions of
Alryke which characterized Becket more than other independent
ecclesiastics, except perhaps the haughty defiance of the king
to his face, and even this may be due to the style of popular
narrative art, where sudden violent contrasts were not unusual.
Furthermore, I think that the use of the interdict in the poem
must be connected with the one great interdict in England in
the reign of King John. This event, with its spiritual and
physical sufferings, made a deep impression on all Englishmen,
and produced numerous references in chronicle, in story, and
in verse. Stephen Langton, the leader of the opposition to

---

[1] It is by no means certain ; but it would not matter much if *Athelston*
were placed before *Melayne*. The important point is the close connexion.

John, is more like Alryke in that he was associated with the
promulgation of the great interdict, and did have the support
of the barons, whereas they were opposed to Becket. Moreover,
the course of events in John's reign—defiance of the Church,
Archbishop, and clergy, interdict, excommunication, abject sur-
render of John—correspond exactly with what is told in the
poem.[1] I think the best view of the matter is that we have in
Alryke a popular picture,[2] a compound of many memories,
recalling Becket certainly, but not him alone ; and this view is
confirmed by the fact that Alryke is made to use an assortment
of penalties that was never employed by any archbishop in
England.

The chief penalty, the interdict, entails theoretically the
cessation of all the divine offices of the Church (cf. *Athelston*
473–5),[3] but actually baptism appears never to have been with-
held, and in John's reign the chroniclers [4] especially mention
its continuance. Stanza 45 seems to indicate that personal
excommunication of the king is being thought of, though
it may be that, in accordance with the demands of the dramatic
situation, the king himself is singled out by Alryke as an ex-

[1] Kate Norgate, *John Lackland*, pp. 128, 161–2, 175, 180.

[2] It is possible, in view of the likely East-Anglian composition of
Athelston, and of the general realistic tendencies of tail-rhyme poems, that
there may have been local reasons for writing a poem with a vigorous
ecclesiastic as the chief character. William Turbe, bishop of Norwich
from 1146–74, was famous as ' the most stubborn and consistent supporter '
of Becket against Henry the Second, and in 1166 vindicated the supremacy
of Church over State by excommunicating the powerful earl of Norfolk,
Hugh Bigot. This proper display of Norfolk vigour and independence
was emulated over a century later by Bishop William Bateman, who, like
William Turbe, was a native of Norfolk. The fourteenth-century bishop
defied the king and his council in maintaining his ecclesiastical dignity
against the Abbey of St. Edmund, and he forced Robert, Lord Morley,
in spite of the threats and entreaties of the King and nobles, to do penance
through the streets of Norwich ; in fact, I believe that it is not a fantastic
claim to assert that Bishop William Bateman may have been the *immediate*
model for *Alryke*; on which see the note to 465–6. At the very least,
this conclusion is justified, that, if the fashion had been set, as it certainly
was set by poems like *Amis and Amiloun* and *Octavian*, of writing romances
with a religious colouring, circumstances were favourable in Norfolk for
choosing a composition which allowed the presentation of a figure like
Alryke. (For the historical material see the *Victoria County History of
Norfolk*, II. 224 ff.)

[3] *Catholic Encyclopedia*, s.v. *Interdict*.

[4] e.g. *Annales de Dunstaplia* (Rolls), p. 30.

ample of the evil effects of the interdict. If excommunication
is meant, Alryke's action is uncanonical, since such excommunication is reserved to the Pope,[1] and in the *Sege of Melayne* 616
the authority of the Pope is invoked. Excommunication and
the interdict require absolution to remove them, as is carried
out in *Athelston* 553–4. The measures directed against the
church buildings themselves are a puzzle. To break the
churches down (478), when they are the property of the Church,
is clearly something that no archbishop would order ; and what
stoken agayn wiþ þorn means it is difficult to say. I have
discovered a case[2] when a church under interdict, St. Mary-Le-
Bow in London, had its doors and windows barred with
branches of thorn ; but if the reference is not to this, it may
be, as Zupitza suggests,[3] that some lines have dropped out
which mentioned the churchyards, which are to be *stoken*
(perhaps 'choked ', as Miss Rickert translates) *agayn wiþ þorn*.
The refusal of burial to those dying under an interdict is good
Church law, and the chroniclers note particularly the burying
in unhallowed places.[4] Lines 483–5 contain another difficulty,
because Church law does not recognize any absolution after
death for a man who dies under the ban of the Church.[5] There
are some cases on record, however, of a special commission
being granted by the Archbishop of Canterbury for the absolution after death of an excommunicated man ; and, curiously
enough, one of these (and they are rare) was granted to the
church of St. Mary-le-Bow in 1326.[6] If one could be sure that
the lines have to be taken as they stand, one would have, along
with the possible reference of the phrase *stoken agayn wiþ þorn*,
some ground for believing that the material behind our poem
was connected with St. Mary-le-Bow, especially since, as I
shall show, it is certainly connected with St. Paul's. Against
this, however, it must be said, that if the phrase *ȝiff þou be ded*
be taken loosely to mean ' if you are dying ', then 483–5 are
merely another way of stating 480–2, a recapitulation—a device
of composition used both in this poem and in others in the

---

[1] *Catholic Encyclopedia*, s.v. *Excommunication*.

[2] See note to 478–9.

[3] In his note to 479, *E.St.*, XIII. 393.

[4] See note to 480.

[5] *Dictionnaire d'Archéologie Chrétienne et de Liturgie*, s.v. *Absoute III*, *absoute des morts*.

[6] See note to 483–4.

same narrative measure.[1] Lines 486–7 seem to refer to a foreign
invasion ; but neither this nor the ordinary operation of the
interdict would explain *Hungyr, þyrst, cold, drouȝþe and sorwe.*
It seems here that the writer is piling on all the troubles and
horrors he can think of, perhaps with memories of some old
imprecations,[2] and the final threat of leaving the land bare of
everything lends support to the idea of an accumulation of
terrors without regard either to canon law or to ordinary probability. It is a minstrel's way—with hyperbole—of expressing
the awful power of the Church.

The thirteenth century witnessed under Pope Innocent the
Third and his immediate successors the culmination of the
conflict between Church and State, and the material for our
poem must have been shaped then. The reign of Henry the
Third shows numerous incidents—including some famous ones
connected with Hubert de Burgh,[3] and with Simon de Montfort[4]
—that would suggest a story (such as we have in *Athelston*), where
prelates of the Church defied the king in London. The bad
rule of Edward the Second (1307–27), who was addicted to
foreign favourites just as Henry the Third was, provoked
similar opposition from the Church.[5] It is possible, moreover,
to find actual accounts of these incidents in the Chronicles
which suggest that origin for the corresponding material in our
poem. In particular, I cite an account of the rescue of Hubert
de Burgh,[6] and another incident[7] from the year 1239 relating
to an ecclesiastic of St. Paul's, which is quite remarkably like
the corresponding part in *Athelston*. But whatever the actual
origin of our poem, it is certain that the movements of Archbishop Alryke when he defies Athelston must have been
paralleled a hundred times in actual life. He is clearly
championed by London against Westminster. He defies and
excommunicates Athelston in the chapel of the palace of Westminster. Exiled, he rides up Whitehall, where he meets his

---

[1] Cf. stanzas 47–8.　　　　　　　　　　　　[2] See note to 490–1.

[3] Matthew Paris, *Chronica Majora* (Rolls), III. 222.

[4] T. F. Tout, *History of England*, p. 128.

[5] Higden's *Polychronicon* (Rolls), pp. 303 ff. ; T. F. Tout, *op. cit.*, p. 292.

[6] H. Wharton, *Historia de Episcopis & Decanis Londinensibus* (Londini
MDCXCV).

[7] Matthew Paris, *Chron. Maj.* (Rolls), III. 543–5 ; *Flores Historiarum*
(Rolls), II. 231.

belated followers, and thence along the Strand to Fleet-Street,
past the point marking the boundary of the City of London,
where even to-day the king still waits for formal admission into
the City.   Once within the City he would be sure of protection
against the royal anger, and he meets an evidently sympa-
thetic company of barons.   He rides on up Ludgate Hill, past
St. Paul's, and down Cheapside, intending to turn south on to
London Bridge, and so along the road to Dover and France.
That he took this route is proved by the fact that he turned
and rode back to *þe brokene cros off ston*, which may be identified as a cross standing near the north gate of St. Paul's churchyard.   Here took place the submission of the king, and the
ordeal.[1]

This *brokene cros off ston* is mentioned in old records as having
witnessed important events in this struggle of the Church (and
in particular of St. Paul's Cathedral) against the King.   The
following quotation from the *Victoria County History of London*,
pp. 411–13, will show the position which St. Paul's occupied in
this matter.   'In Anglo-Saxon times it [St. Paul's] was the
meeting-place of the folk-moot.   Such tradition affected later
custom ; in 1252 the citizens swore fealty to Edward [son of
Henry the Third] in St. Paul's churchyard. . . . Their attitude
in the struggle between king and barons is definite.   In the
reign of Henry the Third the clergy of St. Paul's took part
in that movement of the church towards independence which
identified itself with the struggle for political liberty.'   Seeing
thus that St. Paul's was the recognized centre of opposition to
the king, one can appreciate the fitness of having the scene of
the king's humiliation and the triumph of the Church just outside St. Paul's.   The Broken Cross (the Old Cross was its
usual name) is indicated as the scene of some famous events in
the crisis at the end of the reign of Edward the Second.[2]   The
king's representative, the Bishop of Exeter, was brutally beheaded by the London mob just near the Cross; and when
Queen Isabella was enlisting the aid of London, her letter was
affixed to this cross.[3]   Moreover, the area at the west end of
Cheapside near this cross was associated with large assemblies,

[1] For a difficulty in this interpretation, see the note to 546.
[2] Maitland's *History of London*, pp. 469–70.
[3] Maitland, *op. cit.* pp. 76–7; Thomas Walsingham, *Historia Anglicana*
(Rolls), I. 180.

great jousts being held there at the beginning of the reign of
Edward the Third.[1] It is certain that the man responsible for
the *matter* in the second half of *Athelston* was of strong ecclesiastical sympathies and knew his London well. This association with London City renders quite untenable Miss Hibbard's
theory that *Athelston* is a Westminster poem. *Athelston* is anti-
monarchical and so anti-Westminster. The references to Westminster in the poem are the general ones which are likely to
occur whenever a Middle English poet mentions the king,
while the London references are, as I have shown, quite
peculiar.

6 e. *Places in London*

Illustrative quotations about these places will be found in
the notes to the lines concerned ; here will be set down only
general remarks or points which require special discussion. All
the places of London which are mentioned are to be found in
other records. *Westemynstyr* (palace and church), *Seynt Poulys*,
Loundone-brygge, *Flete-Strete* and *Charynge-Cros* are still situated
where they were at the time of our poem. The *brokene cros* and
þe Elmes have disappeared, and their identification is not a
matter of such certainty, but I think they can be located satis-
factorily,[2] and their location is of importance in determining
the object of parts of the poem. The *brokene cros* is the more
important of the two. If the identification given in the note is
accepted, it throws a light on the purpose of the poem, and on
some of its obscure circumstances, such as why Egeland and his
sons should be *offeryd unto seynt Powlys heyӡe awtere*. If the
ordeal took place just outside, in West Cheapside, and if St.
Paul's Cathedral was supporting the cause of the archbishop
against the king, what more natural than that a thanksgiving
should take place in St. Paul's? *Þe Elmes* was placed by
Zupitza,[3] following Stow, at Smithfield; but the reference in
our poem is almost certainly to Tyburn. Stow apparently did
not know the name of ' The Elmes' in connexion with Tyburn,
but actually Tyburn has an earlier and surer claim to the
designation than Smithfield has. It would not be a matter of
much moment except for the fact that Smithfield was within
the City, and Tyburn without, and the latter from an early

[1] Maitland, *op. cit.*, p. 470.   [2] See notes to 546, 805.
[3] See Z's note to 805.

date was the place where traitors to the *king* were executed.
Since we have seen that *Athelston* has reflections of the social
and political life of the thirteenth and fourteenth centuries, and
since we find the title of 'The Elms' given to Tyburn in a few
records of this period, it is just to claim that our writer must
have been referring to Tyburn. Wymound was punished as a
traitor by the *king*, and would be hanged at Tyburn, the royal
place of execution.

There is not much to observe about the places mentioned on
the route to Canterbury, except the remarkable fact of having
them at all. All are plainly identifiable except *Steppyngebourne* (342), and that is, apparently, Sittingbourne. The
distances are with one exception (that of the length of the road
from Dover to Gravesend) moderately accurate, and the time
allowances not impossible. Stone (342) is 17 miles from London,
and about 2 beyond Dartford ; just north of the road after
leaving Stone was Stone Castle. Sittingbourne (*Steppyngebourne*)
is 40–1 miles from London ; Osprynge 46–7 miles, and the Blee,
from where Canterbury can be seen, at the 50-mile stone.
Canterbury is 56 miles from London, and Dover 71. Rochester
alone of the important stopping places on the route is missed
out. Line 356 gives the journey from London to Canterbury as
50 miles, and Alryke's ride (381) agrees with this distance.[1] The
times allowed for the journeys are feasible, though the *noble
hors* of the messenger has a stiffer task than the *palfrays* of the
archbishop. The one messenger is, apparently, considered as
doing all the journeys (733, 356, 321) ; but 228 seems to render
this interpretation impossible, since we are told there that Edyff
is to arrive in London *Tomorwen*, that is, on the following day,
so that, if the same messenger is meant for both journeys, he
could not have ridden to Stone on the same day as the queen
wishes to dispatch him to Canterbury (299 ff.). The nearest we
can get to a time-scheme for the poem is to allow six (dramatic)
days : (1) the swearing of brotherhood ; (2) the falsehood and
the sending for Egeland ; (3) the imprisonment of Egeland and
the pleading of the queen ; (4) the queen sends to Canterbury
and Alryke sets out ; (5) the quarrel of Alryke with the king,
and the ordeals ; (6) the punishment of Wymound.

[1] See, however, the note to 324.

6 f. The Development of the Story

Little can be said with certainty about the development of the story or stories we have in the poem, but I may set down some of the probabilities foreshadowed in the discussion of the analogues. Whether these are *sources* is to me, though interesting, not a vital question; my purpose in assembling them is to exhibit as fully and as accurately as possible the *kind* of poem we have in *Athelston*, which is in the deepest sense part of the *meaning* of the poem. I suppose a French original with treachery plus ordeal, having the form of a *chanson* like that represented by the German poem *Morant und Galie*, but having other elements, as in *Parise la Duchesse*. Probably also the treachery theme concerned sworn-brothers. I do not think any English popular minstrel could have preserved the conventions of the *chansons* without a French original. This must have come to England quite early, and in England adopted, perhaps straight from Germany,[1] the elements of the ploughshare ordeal and the bishop as helper of the accused woman, that is, the 'Richardis' story. Deutschbein[2] claims that west Germany, north-east France, and England had a common stock of stories, and it is not without interest to note that the most important analogue, *Parise la Duchesse*, belongs to the area of France required, for Parise makes the pilgrim journey to Cologne. I think the poem was probably given currency in England in an Anglo-Norman version in the thirteenth century, where perhaps the English Athelstan was introduced, and the importance of the sworn-brotherhood increased by taking in some traditional tale of a compact among sworn-brothers. I think the present state of *Athelston* entitles us to suppose an English poem before the one we have, and better than it. This poem (which ought to have been preserved in the Auchinleck manuscript, but is not), belonging to the end of the thirteenth century, was an attempt by the Church to use the treachery-plus-ordeal story for its own purposes (just as it used *Amis and Amiloun*), developing the part of the archbishop, and giving the localization of

[1] Is it possible that the influx of Flemings in the thirteenth and fourteenth centuries brought German stories with it into Norfolk? The *King of Tars* (*E.St.* XI), which I place also in Norfolk, uses German material, to be found in Chronicles.

[2] *Studien zur Sagengeschichte Englands*, p. 255.

London and the Canterbury road. The remodelling of the religious part seems to have caused the confusion about the ordeals. One cannot quite rule out the possibility that whatever source the poet used for this part may have been in some way connected with a version of the 'Emma' legend known in the south of England.[1] After the middle of the fourteenth century, this poem was rewritten in the North Midlands, and then copied (and perhaps revised) in the South-East Midlands,[2] the London and Canterbury references being amplified. I put this hypothesis forward not as a solution of the problem of the development of the story and the poem, but as a brief conspectus of my discussion of the material.

7. LITERARY APPRECIATION

What is the value of the poem? I quote the verdicts that have been passed on it. Zupitza (*Englische Studien*, XIV. 324 ff.), speaks of *der lebhafte stil*, dubs its material *echt menschlichen stoff*, and avers that a *wahre herzensquickung* results when one comes to *Athelston* after *die endlosen kämpfe* of a romance like *Guy of Warwick*. Miss Rickert (*Romances of Friendship*, p. xviii) is impressed by its Teutonic ideas and Old English atmosphere, and then goes on: 'The merit of the romance is not perhaps very great, but it is full of curious ideas, and the presentation of fourteenth-century London is interesting. The two women are the most vivid characters.' J. E. Wells (*Manual*, p. 24) is enthusiastic: he calls it 'an excellent piece of narrative'. He describes various incidents as 'striking' and 'spirited'. 'The verse', he says, 'is smooth and yet vigorous, . . . the emotion intense and genuine.' Miss Hibbard (*op. cit.*) regards the poem as a unique product of native English genius, and remarks on the 'closely-knit story', 'the concrete realism', 'the great episode of the religious ordeal'. Albert C. Baugh (*P.M.L.A.* XLIV. 377) speaks of its 'constructive skill', and its 'independent creative gift'.

It would seem therefore that American scholarship had

---

[1] Miss Hibbard deserves great credit for discovering and developing the parallel between the *Emma* legend and *Athelston*, which may yet throw some light on our poem. For that which has driven her into what appear to be indiscreet speculations is nevertheless a very striking circumstance, that so many of the names of *Athelston* are Old English.

[2] See further Intro. 8 *a*.

discovered to the world a neglected masterpiece ; but my opinion
is that a good deal of the praise has been bestowed rather in-
cautiously. Baugh's eulogy is a piece of light-hearted boost,
and as such negligible. I have already indicated that I disagree
with Miss Hibbard's view of the poem. The judgements of the
three remaining commentators do give us, along with some
things I do not accept, its leading features—compactness, vigour,
use of Germanic ideas, topical references, and success in handling
the verse.

The poem is certainly well constructed in the sense that its
parts are cunningly connected and one's interest is maintained.
But it lacks underlying unity of temper, since the moral claims
of sworn-brotherhood and of the Church are not artistically
adjusted ; [1] and by this failure the poem drops far out of the
front rank. I think, too, that it is not quite sound to belaud
Athelston for avoiding the ' longueurs ' of a romance like *Guy
of Warwick*, for the two poems belong to different genres : [2]
Athelston does not attempt the elaborateness of a romance. The
leading situations are rendered with a certain effectiveness—the
initial taking of the oath, the pleading of the queen, the ride of
the archbishop and his defiant conduct (both especially spirited),
and the final discomfiture of Wymound. Others are feebler,
the ordeal and the ride of the messenger to Canterbury. The
characters are, with the exception of the vigorous portrait of the
archbishop, little more than conventional figures, but the conventions, especially in the villain, are well carried out, and there
are a few fresh touches. The struggle of loyalty and self-
interest in Wymound (176–7), the anxiety of Edyff to see her
sons honoured (229–30), the queen flinging off the garland in her
haste to help the prisoners (256–7), the archbishop comforting
the children in the ordeal (606 ff.) help to contribute an air of
reality which shows *Athelston* to be of the true East-Anglian
tail-rhyme tradition.[3] The subject-matter of the tale is extra-
ordinarily varied and interesting—the institution of sworn-
brotherhood, the trial by ordeal, the clash of Athelston and
Alryke and its background of the conflict of Church and State,

[1] Nor are they, for that matter, in *Amis and Amiloun*, but its greater
length prevents the contradiction from being so noticeable.

[2] See Miss Everett in *Essays and Studies of the English Association*,
XV, p. 116.

[3] See *Medium Ævum*, I. 2, pp. 105–6.

the reference to the Canterbury road and to London. The
verse is competent and even skilful,[1] and serves moderately
well the purpose of the straightforward narrative : and that is
saying a good deal, because these twelve-line stanzas become
·difficult if many of them have to be written. They are, in fact,
only possible with a liberal use of conventional phrases, which,
when they are mere padding, weaken the whole verbal texture ;
but *Athelston*, although in this respect it suffers in common with
other tail-line poems, is more discreet and successful than many
of its fellows. The diction of *Athelston* is conventional to a
remarkable degree ; the poet always prefers the ready-made
phrase, even when the meaning of it has to be forced ; often the
poem reads like an exercise in the fourteenth-century East-
Midland poetic diction. And yet the author manages to carry
his story along steadily. Alliteration is frequent, and though
not primarily structural contributes some of the energy of the
verse. Poetically considered, the most valuable thing in the
tale is the presentation of the theme of sworn-brotherhood, and
next to that, the portrait of the archbishop. I find it on the
whole a highly interesting poem, but an uneven one, which pro-
vokes interest rather than satisfies it—certainly no masterpiece,
but certainly no failure.

A special aspect of its appeal is that it has undoubtedly a
strong English and Germanic element. The material, along
with the names, is probably more English than in any other of
the romances, and the fact that the ballads of *Adam Bell*,
Bewick and Graham, and *Sir Aldingar* provide good parallels to
Athelston suggests the use of traditional stories. There is no
question of direct influence ; I disagree with Wells's suggestion
that ' much of the ballad quality is evident ' in the poem, and
even more with Miss Hibbard's attempt to substantiate Wells's
judgement. The method of *Athelston* is the method of narrative.
Nevertheless, I consider it likely that some of the same traditional stories may have been worked upon by both the minstrel
and the village poet who made the ballad. To this extent
Athelston has a popular and therefore an English impress. And
I would suggest also that the use of the tail-rhyme stanza for
narrative was in itself a declaration of independence against
the French couplet, which dominated narrative poetry in the
thirteenth century. There is therefore good reason for regarding

[1] See Intro. 9 *b*, and the notes on 19–21, 94–6, 149–50.

Athelston as being especially English; and, though the probability of a non-English original be accepted, the fluency and
vigour of the style (supported by the parallel of *Amis and
Amiloun*) suggest that the translation was of the free sort that
allowed for originality, in the making of alterations and additions. Such independence is a very definite mark of the tail-
rhyme 'school' of poems, which can lay claim to a larger
English element than any other part of Middle-English
romance.[1]

I might in conclusion attempt to indicate the position of
Athelston in the series of tail-rhyme romances which are the
chief contribution of the East Midlands to English literature of
the Middle Ages. They extend, as far as one can at present
judge, from the most northerly to the most southerly point of
the East Midlands, and in addition push a little beyond the
bounds north, west, and south in some examples. These poems
have been in general either neglected or despised; but there is
a good deal yet to be understood about them; and I imagine
that in the process of understanding them people will allow
them a greater worth than at present. They have certain
characteristics in common. Their material is chosen from many
quarters, but they have not much to do with the great cycles
of romances. It is in keeping with this independence that it is
often difficult to trace any originals, and for at least two of
them, *Athelston* and the *Sege of Melayne*, nothing even approach-
ing an original has been found. There is an extensive imitation
of incident, as also of verse-habit and phrase among them, and
this community of practice points to some sort of an East-
Midland school. They are nearly all popular in tone (*Ipomadon*
is a partial exception), and have a considerable element of folk-
lore and popular story. They show a very strong ecclesiastical
influence both in the type of story told, and in the method of
treatment. Sometimes, as in *Roland and Vernagu*, this religious
matter extinguishes the story. Lastly, these romances adopt
and develop the twelve-line tail-rhyme stanza, and this is a very
remarkable development, to be compared, I think, with the
more famous alliterative revival in the West Midlands. For,
despite the usually held opinion, I think that the tail-rhyme
stanza had some advantages over the couplet in the direction
of liveliness and vigour.

[1] See *Medium Ævum*, I. 2, pp. 102 ff.

If I were asked to select the best of these, I should name *Amis and Amiloun, Sir Launfal, Ipomadon, Sege of Melayne, Octavian, Athelston, Emaré, Sir Gowther,* and *Sir Cleges. Athelston* is not the least interesting of these. For neatness in narrative it vies with *Sir Cleges,* but has more dignity. In language it is inferior to more decorative poems, such as *Emaré* and *Octavian,* but its simple vocabulary is perhaps an advantage with a straightforward story. In vigour and verve it is excelled greatly by the *Sege of Melayne,* but it displays more narrative skill. It disputes with *Amis and Amiloun* the interest of sworn-brotherhood, and while it shows less emotion has more actuality. I would place *Athelston* fourth or fifth in the group, and the group itself will I believe eventually take a higher place than it is at present allotted.[1]

8. THE DIALECT

The following are the significant features of the language of the poem as evidenced in the rhymes or the metre.

(1) OE. short *ă* before a single nasal or a nasal combination remains *ă*:

MANNE 670 r. w. ANNE (Lat. Fr. *ă*); HAND 53 r. w. VACANT; LANDE 125 r. w. TYDANDE n.; STANDE 431 r. w. LEUANDE pres. part.

STRONGE 264 r. w. SOONE (OE. *sōna*) probably has *ǭ* from *ā* (by lengthening), and for the rhyming of *ǭ* and *ọ̄* cf. ll. 193, 417.

(2) OE. *ā* (ON. *á*) gives ME. *ā*:

HALE (OE. *hāl*) 674 r. w. SALE (OE. oblique case of *sœl*), and TALE (OE. *tălu*) and BALE (OE. *bealu*). ÞARE (OE. *păra*) 187 r. w. FARE (OE. *faran* with ME. lengthening). WATE (OE. *wāt*) 108 r. w. GATE (ON. *gata*) and LATE and STATE (OFr. *(e)stat*). TAN r. w. YLKAN 496, WAN 512, NON 515, SLON 518, GAN 768, is definitely Northern; but see Intro. 8 *a*. For BADDE r. w. RADDE 711, see the note to the line. JHON 761 r. w. ATHELSTONE (OE. *ā*) may be a Southern writing for an original JOHAN; cf. *Havélok the Dane,* ll. 176–7, and *Cursor Mundi,* l. 20346.

---

[1] For a reconsideration and revaluation of these tail-rhyme poems, see my articles in *Medium Ævum,* I. 2, 3, where the claims advanced tentatively in this edition of *Athelston* are clarified and substantiated.

(3) ME. $\bar{e}$ and $\bar{\varrho}$:

   (a) Gmc. $\bar{æ}$ (WS. $\bar{æ}$, non-WS. $\bar{e}$) appears as $\bar{e}$:

   STRETE 336 r. w. HETE vb. (Gmc. $\bar{e}$ with the vowel of the re-
duplicated preterite levelled into the present); and with
METE (OE. $m\bar{e}tan$). REED 364 (Angl. $r\bar{e}dan$) r. w. SPEED ($\bar{e}$,
the i-mutation of $\bar{o}$). WERE 443 (vb. subjunctive) r. w.
ENQUERE (Fr. $\bar{e}$). WEDE n. 602 r. w. ȝEDE. DREDE n. r. w.
ȝEDE 605 and BLEDE 626. DREDE inf. 565 r. w. GLEDE
(OE. $\bar{e}$) 572, and SPEDE inf. 578. LETE 760 r. w. SWETE.

This evidence shows that the language of the poem was
descended from Anglian.

   (b) Before certain front consonants (d, n, r) we have $\bar{e}$ instead
of $\bar{\varrho}$:

   LEDE inf. (OE. $l\bar{æ}dan$) 392 r. w. STEDE (OE. $st\bar{e}da$), SPEDE 785,
REDE 383, 779, GLEDE 782, NEDE 389. DED 796 (OE. $d\bar{e}ad$)
r. w. RED n. (Angl. $\bar{e}$). CLENE 426 r. w. SENE pp. and WENE
680. LERE 707 r. w. MESSANGERE, PERE, BERE n. The word
STEDE (OE. $stede$ = 'a place') creates a difficulty in the
rhymes with DED (OE. $d\bar{e}ad$) 171, REDE n. 177, REDE vb. 56,
LEDE inf. 251, because $stede$ if lengthened should have $\bar{\varrho}$.
The same apparent lack of agreement is found in WERE
(Angl. $w\bar{e}ron$) 14 r. w. BERE inf. (OE. $beran$).

(4) OE. $\breve{\bar{y}}$ appears as $\breve{i}$:

   SYNNE (OE. $synn$) 3 r. w. ÞEREIN (OE. inn). KYNNE 219 r. w.
WYN vb. and INNE 359. HYDE 536 r. w. ABYDE and RYDE.
LYTE (OE. adv. $l\bar{y}t$) 799 r. w. WYTE (OE. $w\bar{i}te$).

This clear indication of the East Midlands or the North is
rather disturbed by the occurrence of $\bar{y}$ > $\bar{e}$ in FEER 631 r.w.
PRAYER (OFr. $preiere$), though this particular rhyme seems to
have penetrated farther north than other SE. borrowings (see
Jordan § 39 anm.). CAUNTYRBERY r.w. MERY 97 is chiefly
South-Eastern, but the e before r is found in the Midlands.

(5) The non-WS. $\breve{e}$ (WS. $\breve{ie}$), the result of mutation or of pala-
talization, appears as $\breve{e}$.

   HERE vb. 63 (Angl. $h\bar{e}ran$, WS. $h\bar{i}eran$) r. w. DERE (OE. $d\bar{e}ore$)
and PERE (OFr. $\bar{e}$). ȝELLE vb. 425 r. w. DWELLE vb. SENE
adj. or pp. 427 r. w. CLENE (OE. $\bar{æ}$ raised before n).

(6) ME. *ēȝ* (OE. *ēah, ēag*, Angl. and LWS. *ē-*) has been raised to *īȝ* :

YȝE 803 (OE. *ēge*) r. w. LYE (OE. *lyge*) and DYE vb., the *ī* in *dye* being supported by the rhyme DY inf. : SLYLY 143. This sound-change is chiefly characteristic of the Midlands.

(7) Lengthening in open syllables :

This is clearly evidenced for *ă* and *ĕ*, and less certainly for *ŭ* and *ĭ*.

ă : TALE (OE. *talu*) 671 r. w. HALE (OE. *hāl*).

ĕ : STEDE (OE. *stede*) 55 r. w. REDE inf.

ŭ : COME (OE. *cuman*) inf. 709 r. w. DONE (OE. *dōn*). Spellings like SOONES (OE. *sunu* sg.) also occur.

ĭ : the only evidence is in spellings, some of which, in the variation of *ĭ* and *ĕ*, admit of other explanations :

WETE inf. (OE. *witan*, mod. E. *weet*) 667 ; WETYNG 505 ; and less certainly PRESOUN 251, SERE 62, &c., HEDYR 728, MEKYL 50, &c.

(8) Other points :

LYNG (ON. *lengja* = OE. *lengan*) r. w. RYNG shows *e* raised before the nasal combination. The word and the rhyme are rare and Northern. SEÞÞEN points to the OE. *seoþþan*.

Consonants : it is noteworthy that at 480 the *k* in DYKE is fixed as the unvoiced back-stop by the rhyme with HERETYKE, and the rhyme of LYNG vb. 535 with RYNG proves the (Northern) *g* ; but both forms occur in SE. Mid. texts (see Glossary).

(9) Treatment of final and unaccented *e* :

The following rhymes show that the final unaccented *e* was silent : DWELLE 231 inf. r. w. WELLE (OE. *wel*) ; BRYNGE 476 r. w. RYNG ; LATE 99 (OE. *late*) r. w. STATE (OFr. *(e)stat*). Cf. also ll. 58, 138, 237, 248, 384.

Several other lines, e.g. 78, 223, 527, with every appearance of being correctly transmitted, will scarcely scan if the *e* is given syllabic value.

No final *e* is secured by rhyme ; but there are lines which seem to demand the *e* for the scansion :

263 Týl þe néxte dáy at mórwe
378 Blýþe schál I néuere bé
505 Hádde þéy non kýns wetýng.

In addition, there are a considerable number of lines which

scan more easily on the assumption of a syllable on the un-accented *e* : 22, 41, 49, 86, 90, 92, 147, 177, 214, 217, 241, 242, 417, 451, 487, 492, 494, 516, 641, 740, 748, 770, 793.

For example, 177 But dó þy béste réde
or, 494 To bégge né to bórwe.

The syllables which would be affected in the above lines come from : -*e* of inf. 8, weak adjective 4, weak noun 3, feminine noun 2, possessive adj. 3 pl. 1, pres. subj. 1, weak pret. sg. 1. The metrical habit of using or disregarding the final unaccented *e* seems to have been general in the fourteenth century, even with Chaucer, where mere carelessness or roughness is unlikely. A comparison with regard to this final -*e* between *Cursor Mundi*, Robert Mannyng's *Handlynge Synne*, *Orfeo*, and *Athelston* shows that the last named is most like Robert Mannyng. But an alternative method of scansion (see Intro. 9 *b*) might affect some of this evidence for the retention of the final -*e*.

(10) Inflexions :

The following inflexions may have a bearing on the dialect or the date :

Pres. ind. 3 sg. : GOS 412 r. w. AROS.

Pres. ind. pl. without -(*e*)*n* : FYNDE 21 r. w. LYNDE (OE. *lind*); REDE 383 r. w. STEDE ; LIȜT 756 r. w. RIȜT (OE. *rihte* adv.)

Pret.-Pres. vbs. levelled in pl. and 2 sg. : SCHALLE (2 sg.) 281 r. w. ALLE ; MAY (2 sg.) 748 r. w. DAY ; WAT(E) (2 sg.) 108 r. w. STATE ; MAY (3 pl.) 370 r. w. PALFRAY.

Pres. subj. pl. without -(*e*)*n* : ȜE SPARE 374 r. w. ȜARE.

Pret. ind. pl. without -(*e*)*n* : ROD (3 pl.) 754 r. w. ABOOD vb.

Wk. pret. with -*e* : see scansion of l. 505 above.

Pres. part. in -*ande* : LEUANDE 437 r. w. HANDE ; cf. TYDANDE n. 124 r. w. LANDE.

Past part. with -*n* : IGON 95 r. w. ANON ; SLAYNE 162 r. w. PAYNE ; DONE pp. 247 r. w. SOONE ; BORN 482 r. w. ÞORN.

The inf. without -*n* occurs in numerous instances : WYRKE 4 r. w. KYRKE ; GOO 78 r. w. TWOO ; FARE 236 r. w. ȜARE ; BEE 560 r. w. FREE adj. ; FOUNDE pres. inf. 702 r. w. WYMOUND. Two examples occur with -*n*, both in contracted verbs : SLON 518 r. w. NON ; GON 775 r. w. ATHELSTON.

Nouns : nearly all nouns conform to the strong masc. type and have syllabic -*e* in gen. sg. and pl. There are no weak

plurals in rhyme. LUUE 86, NOSE 641, QWENE 254 and 286
seem to require two syllables. Similarly, NAME 147 and
KYRKE 417.

Adjectives : the weak declension of adjectives seems on the
evidence of the metre to be fully preserved, e.g. at ll. 41, 47,
49, 155, 177, 214, 241, 263, 266, 770, of which 263, 266 seem
decisive. Line 576 (repeated 774) is against this -e. BLYÞE 378
(OE. ja-stem), HARDE pl. 636 seem to show two syllables. ÞAT
ON 67, ÞAT OÞER 68 are relics of the old neut. def. art.

Pronouns : ÞEY 78 &c., nom. pl. ; HER(E) 22 &c., poss. ; HEM
39, 195 &c., dat. and acc. ; SCHE 298 &c., fem. sg. On HE, 3 pl.
or fem. sg., see notes to 611, 625.

We may, merely for convenience, summarize this dialect
material, roughly, thus :

North : the absence of $\bar{\varrho}$ < OE. $\bar{a}$; 3 sg. ind. in s ; pres. ind.
without -n ; inf. without -n ; past part. with -n ; words
lyng, dyke.

Midland : $\bar{\breve{e}}$ for $\bar{\varrho}$ before dentals and nasals ; $\bar{\varrho}$ < Gmc. $\bar{æ}$; $\breve{e}$
for WS. $\breve{\imath}e$; state of unaccented -e.

East : $\breve{a}$ before nasals.

South : the rhymes at 14, 250, 630.

8 a. Locality of Dialect

To localize the dialect of *Athelston*, I consider (following the
method of Tolkien and Gordon's *Gawayne and þe Grene Knyȝt*)
(1) local knowledge, (2) evidence of vocabulary, (3) alliteration,
(4) the rhymes.

1. Local knowledge.   The mention of an otherwise unknown
tradition about St. Edmund of East Anglia, together with the
knowledge shown of London and the Canterbury pilgrim-route,
points to the South-East Midlands as the home of the poet.
But if the original was in Anglo-Norman, which seems not
unlikely, this display of local knowledge is much less conclusive
evidence of the locality of the English poem, though it may
still point to East Anglia, if this area is indicated from other
circumstances.

2. Vocabulary.   Both from a general impression and on
analysis the vocabulary of *Athelston* is quite non-northern.
Out of some eight hundred and thirty separate words, there
are over a hundred French words to twenty Scandinavian ; and

of the latter only one (*ar* conj.) is not in use to-day, and all but
three (*layne, garte, brenne*) belong to *Standard English*. In a text
which scans well, vocabulary must be regarded as legitimate
evidence of locality.

3. Alliteration.   As regards alliteration, tail-rhyme poems
divide themselves into two groups : those that show signs of full
alliterative style, as it was known in the West or the North, and
those that use a more unobtrusive method, like what Chaucer
and modern English adopted.   *Ipomadon* (certainly North-Midland) is the typical representative of the first group, and the
poems of the Auchinleck manuscript (as I think, East-Anglian)
are consistently of the second group.   *Athelston* (see Intro. 9 c)
belongs in alliteration wholly to the second group.   The evidence
of the alliteration agrees, thus, with the evidence of the vocabulary as being quite against a northerly area for the poem.

Rhymes.   The rhymes show that the language of *Athelston*
is descended from Anglian ($\bar{e}$ < Gmc. $\bar{æ}$; $\check{e}$ for WS. $\check{ie}$) ; that it
is definitely Midland ($\bar{e}$ instead of $\bar{ę}$ before dentals and nasals) ;
and that it is East-Midland rather than West ($\check{a}$ before nasals).
For the rest, the certain evidence of $\bar{a}$ < OE. $\bar{a}$, and the absence
of $\bar{ǫ}$, together with the 3 sg. pr. ind. in *s*, seem to point to the
northernmost border of the Midlands ; but a closer scrutiny of
the evidence shows that the conclusion is not so firmly founded
as at first sight it appears to be.   Many of the northerly rhymes
occur in suspicious circumstances (see the notes): *gos, aros*
411–12 involves an awkward construction ; *wille, tylle* 121–2, an
awkward construction, bad metre, and a corrupt passage ; *leuande, hande* 437, a very bad break in the rhythm ; *tan, ylkan*
495–6, *gan, tan* 768–9, *hade, made* 699–700, bad metre ;[1] *Egelan,
nan* 580 is invalidated by the uncertainty about the name (see
Intro. 6 a) ; *dyke, heretyke* 480 occurs in a corrupt passage.   The
chief unimpeachable northerly evidence is in *wate* 108, *pare* 187,
hale 674 ; but one may put forward some considerations to show
that *these particular $\bar{a}$-rhymes* are not in any strict sense to be
connected with the North.   It is not possible here to give a
complete proof of the truth of this assumption ; I shall state
summarily the principle I believe to be true for tail-rhyme
poems : that *pare* (or *ware* or *sare*), if in rhyme-sequences with

---

[1] Unexceptionable $\bar{a}$-rhymes with *tan* (*Horn* 553), or with *made* (*Athelston*
791 ; cf. *Amis* 283) are found in East-Anglian poems ; see *Medium Ævum*
for 1933.

care or *fare*, points not to the North (as usually understood) but to Norfolk. The chief bases for this conclusion are : (1) that *Amis and Amiloun*, whose vocabulary places it in Norfolk, has a preponderance of rhymes proving *ā* over rhymes proving *ǭ* ; these *ā*-rhymes are nearly all in *-are* sequences, involving the forms *pare, mare, sare* ; (2) that the tail-rhyme *Guy of Warwick* (intimately related to *Amis*), which has unmistakable evidence of the South-East Midlands, still shows an appreciable number of these *-are* sequences, with the same words as *Amis* ; (3) negatively, that, in the plainly northerly versions of tail-rhyme poems (of the Thornton MS.), characteristic features (which are also excellences) of the early (Auchinleck) tail-rhyme poems are clearly and demonstrably missing. An explanation for this state of affairs might be found in the extremely conventional nature of the rhymes used in the East-Midland tail-rhyme stanza, which retained the sequences in *-are*, on account of their usefulness, after the spoken language had developed *ǭ* ; and, secondly, in the possibility that the northern part of East Anglia, being a strong Scandinavian centre, and in some degree isolated from the south of England, might have remained an *ā*-area longer than the Midlands in general. Therefore, in tail-rhyme poems, sequences in *-are* can point to the north, but of East Anglia. The other *ā*-rhymes of *Athelston*—*wate, state* 108, *hale, sale* 674—are conventional in the North-Midland group of tail-rhyme romances, headed by *Ipomadon* (perhaps about 1350); so that they do not compel us to put *Athelston* itself anywhere near the North. With the above considerations in mind, and in view of the testimony of local knowledge, vocabulary, and alliteration all pointing away from the North, I consider that Norfolk affords the best hypothesis as a place of composition for *Athelston*. There may be one or two dialectal features— such as *lyng, ryng* 535—which would be out of place in Norfolk ; but the idea of a rehandling of the story in the North Midlands would agree with what I have already suggested about the development of the story in the poem, and also with the general tendency for tail-rhyme composition to extend from where the Auchinleck group was written out to the North Midlands and Lincolnshire. A difficulty, or at least a surprising circumstance, if one accepts Norfolk for the place of composition, is that there is no certain evidence of *ǭ* in rhyme. All we have is *Jhon*, *Athelston* 761 as a possible example, and another if we emend

801–2 so as to have *so, to* for the rhymes (see note).[1] In this
connexion one must mention what seems to be a similar case of
the operation of conventional rhyme-habits—*Octavian* (Camb.
MS.), which has an overwhelming preponderance of *ā*-rhymes
(in -*are* sequences) over rhymes in *ǭ*, an almost completely non-
northern vocabulary, and some specifically East-Anglian words
and usages. I think, therefore, that the slender evidence for *ǭ*
need not rule Norfolk out. East Anglia is a more likely place
than the North Midlands or Lincolnshire to find a number of
Southern or South-Easterly rhymes which *Athelston* has : *were,
bere* 13; *stede, lede* 251; *prayer, feer* 631; *ende, fynde* 375. We
may say, therefore, that the strictly linguistic evidence is not
inconsistent with a localization in Norfolk, which is on other
grounds not only a satisfactory choice, but almost an inevitable
one. For these tail-rhyme poems are so remarkably and so
intimately related in style (see *Medium Ævum*, I. 2, 3) that,
given one poem fairly localized, the others can be ranged round
it with practical certainty. *Amis and Amiloun* provides the
fixed point, and since *Athelston* is not only obviously of the
Auchinleck (East-Anglian) tradition in style, but also closely
related to *Amis* in some features, especially in the treatment of
sworn-brotherhood, the propriety of attributing *Athelston* to the
same area as *Amis*—Norfolk—will be clear. The numerous
southern forms within the line point to a copyist of somewhere
farther south than the original, working, probably, near the
place (Cambridge) where the manuscript is now located. I think,
therefore, that with all the evidence in view one may hazard
some such statement as the following about the places concerned
in the composition of the poem. I suppose an original poem
in Anglo-Norman[2] written at Bury St. Edmunds; next, the first
English version composed in Norfolk; then (though less certainly) a rehandling towards the North Midlands; lastly, a copying in the South-East Midlands.

9. The Verse

The stanza used in *Athelston* is one of twelve lines, having
four rhyming couplets of four-stressed lines, these couplets

---

[1] Perhaps another example in *com : anon* 417.

[2] This hypothesis is favoured by (1) the three syllables in *Edemound*,
the spelling in *Wymound*; (2) the confusion of names (*Steppyngebourne*);
(3) the parallel of *Amis and Amiloun*; (4) the treatment of the name
Egeland (Intro. 6 *a*).

being divided one from the other by a shorter so-called tail-line of three stresses. Within this framework the rhyme-arrangement differs in various poems. The four tail-lines rhyme with one another, but the relation of the rhymes used in the couplets is of three kinds. The commonest scheme is aab ccb ddb eeb, that is, with different rhymes in each of the couplets. A second arrangement is aab aab ccb ddb, that is, with the same rhyme in the first and second couplets. A third arrangement represented by a single poem, *Duke Rowlande and Sir Ottuell*, is aab aab ccb ccb, where only three rhymes are used. *Athelston* belongs to the first and most numerous class.

Of the seventy-five stanzas of *Athelston* fifty-three show no variation from the scheme aab ccb ddb eeb. Of the remainder, ten stanzas (17, 20, 21, 22, 32, 33, 55, 57, 58, 69) have only six lines, three stanzas (59, 60, 72) have nine lines, while stanza seventy-three has 15 lines. Stanzas 35, 50, 51 have only four rhymes, 46 only three, and stanzas 25, 41, 42, and 45 are plainly corrupt. What is the cause of these variations in rhyme-arrangement and in length of stanza? The fact that there are practically no such variations in long and good specimens like *Ipomadon* and *Amis and Amiloun* would seem to show that the best practice did not allow any mixture. Nearly all the poems, however, have divergences from the normal, some to a lesser and some to a greater extent.[1] Mere accident and the difficulty of managing a large number of twelve-line stanzas might well account for some instances of variation from the norm. Any one of the couplets would on occasion be liable to repeat any one of the others, though, in practice, we do not find the third couplet repeating the rhyme of the first. Some poems like *Emaré* seem to mix the four-rhyme stanza or the five-rhyme arbitrarily, and in others, like *Athelston*, we may suppose that the presence of four-rhyme stanzas (i.e. aab aab ccb ddb) is due to the accidental, or even careless, use of the same rhyme twice, or to bad transmission.

The second variation from our norm of twelve lines consists of sections containing six, nine, or fifteen lines, each of which is illustrated in *Athelston* as well as in most of the other poems. Apart from the question of something lost, I think the nine- and fifteen-line sections might be due to mere inadvertence, especially on the part of a reciting minstrel, who could very

---

[1] See E. Rickert's edition of *Emaré* (E.E.T.S., E.S. 99), p. xix.

easily miss out one of the triplet-sections or add an extra one,
just as he did with the couplets. When a loss or tampering
has taken place, I do not think it worth while to emend, as
Zupitza does at l. 776,[1] unless one has a complete parallel as
a model. The ten stanzas which have only six lines each seem
to require a different explanation, since a six-line tail-rhyme
stanza did exist previously and was very popular as a lyrical
measure in the thirteenth century, besides being used in ll. 1–
475 of *Bevis of Hampton*, in *Sir Ferumbras* after l. 3411, and in
Chaucer's *Sir Thopas*. Six-line stanzas occur here and there in
the twelve-line poems, and one certain instance of a six-line
stanza deliberately employed is the concluding prayer of *Octavian*. With a poem like *Athelston*, that appears to have been
worked over, I think it quite conceivable that the revisers
should occasionally content themselves with a six-line stanza.
Zupitza makes an attempt to prove lacunae wherever these six-
line stanzas occur,[2] but his arguments are always inconclusive
and sometimes very weak. His assumption that the original
must have had only twelve-line stanzas is justified; but our
present text is too far removed from its pristine integrity to be
restored. I consider that to attempt additions where the six-
line stanzas occur is to risk supplying what never was at any
time in the story.

9 a. The Rhymes

The rhymes of *Athelston* are with inconsiderable exceptions
accurate,[3] and as compared with some of the tail-rhyme poems
more widely eclectic and varied. The following peculiarities
may be observed, and these are shared with other poems of the
same species. *The French accentuation is generally retained in
words borrowed from French*, as at 20, 245. *English words of
two syllables sometimes rhyme on the lighter syllable*, as at 93,
96, 353, 356. This is quite common in these East-Midland
poems with the syllable *-yng* of the present participle. Another
characteristic practice is that of *assonance*: *n, m* 43, 561 (the
commonest); *nt, nd* 52; *mb, nd* 282; *ng, mb* 636; (*o*)*p*, (*o*)*d* 393;
nd, ng 489; *rw, lw* 524. The assonances with nasals and dentals
are a feature of nearly all the tail-rhyme poems, and they may
be an inheritance from popular tradition; Laȝamon's *Brut* often

---

[1] See Z's note to the line.   [2] Z's notes to ll. 225, 350, 620.
[3] Peculiar rhymes are mentioned in the notes.

shows the same correspondences, especially of *n*, *m* and *ve*, *þe*, which are the commonest in the tail-rhyme poems. Their use in tail-rhyme poems was due, without doubt, to the extensive need for rhymes, but it never degenerated into a licence. There are some instances of *the use, for the purposes of rhyme, of the same word twice, or of two words from the same stem, or of two words having the same sound*—a practice observable in all the tail-rhyme poems, and in Chaucer. It occurs in *Athelston* at 135 with 141, 147 with 153, 171 with 180, 201 with 210, 213 with 222, 278 with 284, 434 with 440, 455 with 464, 599 with 605, 728 with 734, 767 with 776, 791 with 800—all these in the tail-line, where they are less noticeable than in the couplet.

The tail-rhyme stanza consists essentially of four sections terminating in the four tail-rhymes, and in the early, perhaps the most typical, examples of the style, enjambement over the section is not used to any great extent. The stiffness of movement which would theoretically result from this arrangement is avoided by various devices, rhetorical and rhythmical. As the style progresses, enjambement, along with other signs of freedom, increases, and we can distinguish several stages, the difference between which is a question partly of time, partly of locality, and partly of the habits of individual poets. In *Horn Childe* and *Amis and Amiloun* the tail-line generally concludes the sentence, and frequently the second line of the couplet does so, with the tail-line as accessory. *Octavian*, which may be about 1340, is still fairly faithful to the four-section arrangement. The next, or middle stage, is to have a fairly frequent use of run-on lines at the third or ninth line, with a few at the sixth line, or half-section, and the tail-line used more frequently as part of the narrative. This stage is represented by *Le Bone Florence*, which is of fairly late composition and not purely East-Midland, and by the *Sege of Melayne*, where the freedom is due in part to an individual element in the style. An increased tendency to freedom within the stanza, as in *Sir Gowther*, leads us to the third stage in *Ipomadon*, which is certainly not the latest of the poems, but which, besides using metrical freedom within the stanza, often has a run-on line from the end of one stanza to the beginning of the next. *Athelston* is about at the second stage, in that the tail-line is often part of the narrative, and enjambement is used over the three-line section, as at stanzas 3, 51, 52, 64. Its metrical practice is rather like that of *Le Bone Florence,* which is, however, somewhat farther from the original practice of the stanza.

9 *b. Metre and Rhythm*

Athelston on the whole scans well if some allowance is made for extra unstressed syllables. I call such syllables ' extra ' merely for convenience in describing them in relation to a regular line with two syllables in each foot : I do not think it legitimate to compare these rhythms with the regular line of French extraction. *About one-eighth of the lines have not the first un-stressed syllable,* and this proportion holds, roughly, for all the tail-rhyme poems. Some lines, 61, 73, 325, 577, 759, scan best if *words with ' r ' followed by a consonant* (e.g. *eerl) are allowed two syllables.* Line 628 (and perhaps 568) seems to show a disyllabic *fyr,* a possibility suggested by several lines in *Lybeaus Desconus,* 605, 628, 1868. *Many lines, about one-eighth, have extra syllables consisting of unaccented words and syllables.* Other tail-rhyme poems have a similar usage, and the northerly poems, which are more heavily alliterated, have also more extra syllables—a coincidence to be expected. Lines with initial stress and with extra unaccented syllables constitute the characteristic verse of the tail-rhyme measure, and give it, even without the tail-line, a movement different from the couplet-verse.

Every one has recognized that the rhythms of these tail-rhyme poems are more closely related to Old English rhythms than are those of the ordinary couplet. Lines beginning with a stress (like the OE. *A*-type), the uneven number of syllables, and the frequent alliteration are clear signs of the ancestry of the verse. But I believe one may go farther and extract certain rhythms, with unaccented syllables missing, which are definitely established as correct in these tail-rhyme poems. Bülbring, in what is, I think, a very important article in *Studien zur englischen Philologie,* 50, has systematized the rhythms of alliterative poems like the *Avowynge of Arthur,* which have a tail-line following a group of *three* rhyming lines. He has shown beyond any question the existence of two rhythms as follows :

> Tho sóth(e) fór to sáy
>
> and   ne hím to déth(e) díȝte.

Each of these lines lacks an unstressed syllable, but there is this difference, that when the two stresses are thrown together

at the *beginning* of the line, one of them may fall on a comparatively weakly accented syllable, whereas, when they occur at the
end of the line, the two words must be words of strong accent.
Lines similar to these (sometimes actually identical lines) occur
here and there in the ordinary tail-rhyme poems, with alliteration and even without it :

Amis and Amiloun 994   So stróng slép(e) ȝéde him ón
　　　　　　　　1269　Schal bé þi móst fón

Horn Childe 474 and 828　Mán móst olíue

Roland and Vernagu 397　þat wél stróng wére

Libeaus Desconus 2085　þat ís my móst(e) cáre

Ipomadon 171　Bóth(e) fár(e) and nére
　　　　　8098　My ówne wítte I wýte

Octavian (Camb. MS., where such lines are frequent) :
　　　　12　Wéll(e) óftyn sýthe
　　　183　As láw(e) wás in léde,
　　　210　Wyth fúll(e) gládd(e) chére
　　　702　And bét(e) hým no móre

Isumbras 262　Réd(e) góld schal bé þy méde.

To be added to these as evidence of the alliterative ancestry of
the verse are many lines with an unstressed syllable missing at
the caesura.

　Lines of *Athelston* which either certainly or probably belong
here are 134, 292, 345, 378, 491, 494, 505, 565, 748. If the
scansion is accepted, we have a direct glimpse into a metrical
tradition for these poems anterior to the French couplet, and
this is interesting in poems whose matter and attitude are often
of a decidedly Old English and Germanic cast. In addition,
this scansion reduces the evidence within the line for the
preservation of final unaccented *-e*, as given in the Intro. 8 (9).
This metrical material was used with excellent effect in narrative, although those who accept the orthodox opinion about
tail-rhyme poems—that they are ' crude and dull ' or ' decadent '
—will think the dictum a strange one.   I have attempted elsewhere (in *Medium Ævum*, I. 2, 3) to show that the detractors
are mistaken, and I cannot, even if I would, repeat here what is
said there.   But, in order to draw attention to the rhythmical
effectiveness of *Athelston*, it is necessary for me to mention—
very briefly—one or two general critical considerations, which

must affect one's judgement of tail-rhyme verse as a medium for narrative. The chief objection brought against these poems is that they are full of stock expressions and other conventional material; but this is really no criticism at all until the purpose and use of the conventions have been examined; and indeed the very establishment of conventions recognized as such must be reckoned an achievement. Within the conventional limits these poems create what is virtually a new genre, because, by means of the stanza and of the tail-line, dramatic and lyrical elements are built into the *framework* of the narrative. I may mention (without any attempt to prove it here) that the chief among the dramatic elements so introduced were numerous signs of the relation between the reciter and his audience. With the tail-line enters the minstrel in person : hence the *Lystnes, lordyngys,* the *wiþouten lesyng,* and the hundred other more subtle devices; hence also the use of alliterative phrases, which sanctified by time would create an intimate bond of sympathy between reciter and hearer. A lively air was imparted to the verse, which, as I believe, gave Chaucer his first and decisive lessons in intimate narrative. The success of the poems—their vigour, humour, and emotional appeal—arises directly from the stanza, which enabled poets to organize the narrative material, and from its rhythmical possibilities, which favoured lively narrative. Specific instances in *Athelston* will illustrate the truth of these claims.

Athelston is a fairly late example, and attains to a kind of smooth conventionality; its mastery of the rhythm of the late period, that is, without many stock expressions in the tail-line, is remarkable; stanza after stanza speeds on its way with an easy flow superimposed on the groundwork of the native vigour of the measure. For particular effects one may note stanza 4, ll. 6 and 12, for 'a simple instance of the 'epic formula', and the 'emotional comment', with another example of the latter at the end of stanza 15, of the sort caricatured in *Sir Thopas.* St. 6 at the end gives a good example of the 'lyrical ornaments', which appear frequently in *Amis and Amiloun.* Line 12 of stanza 8 is mainly a 'filling-up' phrase, such as one must and can make allowance for, as one must also for the redundancy of ll. 1–3 of stanza 9. St. 10 at the end is an example of the quiet emotional appeal which results from apt phrase and rhythm in this measure, and which explains why Wordsworth could use it in his exquisite, ' Three years she grew in sun and shower'.[1] St. 13, in the first three lines, shows excellent rhythmical and rhetorical use of the tail-line, while l. 12 gives us an example of the ordinary confidence between reciter and audience. St. 18 shows the convenience of the two halves of the stanza for question and reply. St. 19, especially in the second half, has an astonishing mastery of rhythm. St. 38, l. 9 gives us one of the commonest of the so-called ' tags ', which is no more mere ' filling ' than any other conventional epic title. St. 52 is perhaps the best example in the whole poem of the particular quality of the stanza in the late style, where the difficulties of the tail-line are turned to excellent account. St. 35 shows a completely convincing rhythmical dexterity. St. 56 is a fine example of the tail-rhyme method of presenting, as Ten Brink says, a picture in each stanza, and how could the effect of the last line have been attained in any other medium ?

If approached in accordance with the method outlined here, *Athelston* and the other tail-rhyme poems exhibit an interesting and effective instrument of expression—the result of an art which, rather than rough and popular, as is commonly supposed, is, in fact, complex and sophisticated. Of course, the stanza had its dangers ; the management of the difficult stanza-form was liable to become more important than what was said ; the tail-line might degenerate into a mechanical use of stock devices. But in the whole of the tail-rhyme romances there are few passages where these defects weigh to any degree against the general success of what is in effect a highly individual art-form. As I have indicated, however, the one way *not* to read them is to begin with a conviction that the tail-line would be better away.

9 c. The Alliteration

To complete the account of the metrical structure of the poem I add a few remarks on the alliteration. The alliterating phrases are frequent; a full list is given in Zupitza's edition (the *Epilegomena* in *E. St.* XIV). *Athelston* does not exhibit anything like full alliterative style, and this lack marks off the East Midland poems, like *Athelston* and *Amis and Amiloun*, from tail-rhyme poems whose general appearance and vocabulary indicate that they belong to the south-eastern area of Northern

---

[1] See W. P. Ker, *English Literature : Medieval*, p. 131.

English.[1] But at the same time I do not think it correct to say
that alliteration had become merely ornamental. Most of the
alliterative phrases were traditional, and I imagine that in
writing or declaiming the lines the minstrel would get added
emphasis when the syllables were stressed with alliteration;
indeed we have some lines (referred to in the Intro. 9 *b*),
especially 292, 345, 565, which, as I think, show the alliteration
as still possessing metrical value.

A comparison of the alliterative phrases of *Athelston* with
those of other areas may not be without interest. A few occur
in *Laȝamon*, the most interesting being *biscop, boc-ilæred*. A considerable group is known to West-Midland alliterative poetry,
including *neyȝed . . nere, trewþe trewely, deþ is diȝt, nykkyd wiþ nay,
semely to se, kevere out of care*. About an equal number (25–30
each) occur in other tail-rhyme poems, but not (or not commonly) in the West Midlands, including *worthy lord in wane,
myre ne mos, hende in halle*. Finally, there seem to be phrases
used in *Athelston* but not in the other romances, some taken
from popular speech, *lygge low, to begge ne to borwe*, and others,
it would appear, showing that the feeling for alliteration was
active in supplying new phrases, e.g. *dome . . dye*.

10. The Date

With all the material set out, it is possible now to attempt to
date the poem. The dating is necessarily risky, since we do not
know the locality of the poem, and the state of the final *-e*,
which ought to help the dating, varies with the locality. The
latest date is that of the manuscript, early fifteenth century,
perhaps about 1420.[2] I feel we should allow a certain amount
of time for a manuscript history to explain the apparent corruption of places of the text, and that might bring us to about
1400. No final *-e* is preserved in rhyme; but there are at least
hints that some final *-e*'s, particularly in the weak adjective,
were permitted within the line. *Athelston* is at any rate later
than *Amis and Amiloun* (which is in the Auchinleck MS.) as
regards final *-e*. That gives us a period, roughly, from 1320 to

[1] This same fact marks off East-Midland tail-rhyme poems absolutely
from poems (also called tail-rhyme) like *Sir Percyvelle of Galles*.

[2] The handwriting cannot, I think, belong to any time near the latter
half of the fifteenth century.

1400. But *Athelston's* extensive use of conventional phrase from many of the tail-rhyme romances, and in particular the apparent connexion with the *Sege of Melayne* bring us to the latter half of the fourteenth century. That was the dating of Zupitza, who, however, considered that the manuscript belonged to some time before 1400. If my identification of the *Broken Cross* is right, we can be rather more accurate. It was not called the *Broken Cross* till about 1370, and was destroyed in 1390 ; see the note to l. 546. We may therefore designate the last quarter of the fourteenth century as the time of composition. This dating would get some confirmation from the reference to St. Anne, whose special popularity in England dates from the last quarter of the fourteenth century. I cannot discover any connexion between *Athelston,* with its Canterbury references, and Chaucer's *Canterbury Tales.*

SELECT BIBLIOGRAPHY

1. EDITIONS.

Ancient Metrical Tales, ed. C. H. Hartshorne, London, 1829. Inaccurate.

Reliquiæ Antiquæ, ed. T. Wright and J. O. Halliwell, 2 vols., London, 1841–3.

'Die Romanze von Athelston', ed. J. Zupitza, 1889, in *Englische Studien*, XIII. 331 ff., and XIV. 324 ff. Excellent text; prolific notes; literary investigation of the poem inadequate.

Corolla Sancti Eadmundi, ed. Lord Francis Hervey, London, 1907. Text valueless, but interesting historical introduction, relating to St. Edmund.

Middle English Metrical Romances, ed. W. H. French and C. B. Hale, New York, 1930. Careful text, with footnotes, a few of which are useful.

   Two other editions have been promised at different times, but do not seem to have materialized: One, as announced in E.E.T.S. volumes for 1913–14, to be 're-edited by a pupil of the late Prof. Zupitza'; and another, by a pupil of Miss Hibbard at Wellesley College (see *P.M.L.A.*, XXXVI. 240).

TRANSLATION.

Early English Romances in Verse, Edith Rickert (The New Medieval Library, Vol. 8), London and New York, 1908. Though a free translation, not negligible.

2. HISTORIES OF LITERATURE.

A Manual of the Writings in Middle English, by J. E. Wells, Yale Univ. Press, 1916; with supplements.

Geschichte der deutschen Literatur bis zum Ausgang des Mittelalters, by Gustav Ehrismann, 3 vols., München, 1918–22–27.

Esquisse historique de la littérature française au moyen âge, by Gaston Paris, 1907.

Les Légendes épiques: Recherches sur la formation des chansons de geste, by Joseph Bédier, Paris, 1908–13.

Mediaeval Romance in England, by Laura A. Hibbard, Ph.D., New York, O.U.P., 1924.

3. ANALOGUES AND LITERARY SOURCES.

Studien zur Sagengeschichte Englands, by M. Deutschbein, Halle, 1906.

'Die Sage von König Athelstan', by Kurt Beug, *Archiv für das Studium der neueren Sprachen und Literaturen*, 148, pp. 181 ff. A full collection of references, including mention of *Athelston*.

'Athelston. A Westminster Legend', by Laura Hibbard, *Publications of the Modern Language Association of America*, XXXVI. 223 ff. Ingenious, but poorly based.

'Le Compagnonnage dans les chansons de geste', by J. Flach (*Études romanes dédiées à Gaston Paris*, pp. 141 ff.), 1891.

The Introductions to the *chansons de geste, Aye D'Avignon, Gaydon, Gui de Bourgogne, Parise la Duchesse*, edited in 'Les anciens poètes de la France'.

Gisla saga Súrssonar, ed. Finnur Jónsson. For Sworn-brotherhood.

4. HISTORICAL AND SOCIAL BACKGROUND.

Domestic Manners and Sentiments in England during the Middle Ages, by Thomas Wright, London, 1862.

Die Gesetze der Angelsachsen, herausg. F. Liebermann, 3 vols., Halle, 1898. For the ordeal.

Dictionnaire de la Théologie chrétienne et de Liturgie, publiée par Le R. P. dom Fernand Cabrol, Paris, 1907.

Der Klerus im mittelenglischen Versroman, by Richard Kahle, Strassburg, 1906. An excellent dissertation, accurate, full, and interesting. The pages for reference to *Athelston* are 14, 22, 124, 145 ff., 153.

Heimskringla, Nóregs konunga sǫgur, udgivne ved F. Jónsson, Copenhagen, 1893–1901. For references to the ordeal.

Hasted's History of Kent, enlarged by H. H. Drake, London, 1886.

Stow's Survey of London, &c., new ed. by William J. Thoms, London, 1876.

Memorials of London and London Life in the XIII, XIV, and XV centuries, by Henry Thomas Riley, London, 1868.

The History of London from its Foundation by the Romans to the Present Time, by William Maitland, London, MDCCXXXIX.

The Victoria History of the County of Norfolk, London, 1906.

Topographical History of the County of Norfolk, by Francis Blomefield, London, 1806.

For volumes in the Rolls Series used for illustrative matter, see citations in the footnotes.

5. LANGUAGE.

Über die örtliche Verbreitung der zwölfzeiligen Schweifreimstrophe in England, by Oskar Wilda, Breslau, 1887. Valuable as showing that the tail-rhyme romances are grouped in the NE. Midlands, but a little out of date.

Zupitza's *Epilegomena* to his edition of *Athelston, Englische Studien,* XIV. 330 ff. A splendid array of the linguistic material; concludes for NE. Midland.

Fourteenth Century Verse and Prose, edited by Kenneth Sisam. Referred to as 'Sisam'. Invaluable for text, comment, and glossary (by J. R. R. Tolkien).

Jordan = R. Jordan *Handbuch der mittelenglischen Grammatik.*

N.E.D. = New English Dictionary.

6. METRE.

Englische Metrik, by Dr. J. Schipper, Bonn 1882, esp. Vol. I, pp. 342 ff.

Studien zur englischen Philologie, 50, pp. 509 ff., by K. Bülbring. An attempt—painstaking, acute, at times rather forced, but on the whole successful—to find a system in the verse of the rhymed and alliterative poems of the N. and NE. Midlands in the fourteenth century.

Die alliterierenden Sprachformeln in Morris' Early English poems, by Johannes Fuhrmann, Inaug. Diss., Kiel (Hamburg, 1886).

'The Tail-rhyme Strophe,' by Caroline Strong, *Publications of the Modern Language Association of America,* XXII, p. 371. A comparison of the English strophe with a similar one in Latin and French. Has one important conclusion, that the English stanza is not based on the French.

THE TEXT

THE manuscript is quite legible, except for a very few places where the margin or a blur has destroyed part of a word. As far as the actual reading of the text is concerned, there is practically nothing to alter in Zupitza's transcription. In a few lines, 51, 222, 270, 483, he misspells a word; he is possibly wrong in 423; and he omits to mark a few abbreviations. The spelling of the manuscript has been kept, except in the use of the double *f*'s, which needs some explanation. They occur frequently throughout the poem where we should expect a single *f*, both initially, and finally in words with a long root-syllable, like *wyff* 73. The scribe certainly knew that *ff* was equivalent to capital *F* since he uses it at the beginnings of lines, e.g. l. 2. On that account probably, Zupitza rejects the initial *ff*'s while retaining those in other positions; and this compromise, which I too adopt, has this to recommend it, that the initial *ff*'s look uncouth, and can scarcely have any phonetic significance. I have not been able to discover any principle in the scribe's use of them. Any particulars in which the text as presented differs from the manuscript—words completed, emendations, &c. —are indicated in footnotes to the text. I have followed Zupitza in expanding the sign for the plural and gen. sing. of nouns as *-ys*, since where it is written in full it is most usually *-ys*, e.g. l. 1 plural, l. 64 gen. sg. A problem was presented by a long *r* in the final position with what looks like an abbreviation for *e* attached to it. Some *r*'s with long tails occur fairly often in *Emaré* (ed. E. Rickert, Intro. xiii), in which the final *-e* is almost uniformly silent; but I believe these are different from the letter in *Athelston*, which has a decided loop back and a thick stroke on it, as in *swer* (with this *r*) in the facsimile. The problem was solved for *Athelston* by the occurrence of the word *Douere* in l. 80 with this contraction, whereas in other places, e.g. l. 40, it is spelt with a final *-e*, and also by the form *lettr*, l. 206, with this *r*. I have, accordingly, expanded the *r* always to *re*. Expansions and contractions are not indicated in the text, italics being excluded, because it was desired above all else to make the text look like reputable English poetry. With this same end in view, I have, wherever possible (and without notice), rejected Zupitza's hyphens for words divided in the manuscript, e.g. *nopyng* 797, *apase* 611, *tomorn* 445. The capitals of the manuscript agree with the usual method of writing verse; the punctuation has, of course, to be added. About the latter a word of explanation may be given. The punctuation is rhythmical rather than logical, intended to indicate the movement of the stanza, especially in its freedom, according to my view of it given in the note to 19–21. I have used many dashes, as the sort of stop which allowed a free interpretation of enclosed phrases. These dashes correspond sometimes to Zupitza's brackets, 40, 545, but elsewhere to his and other editors' full-stops, 69, 251, 569, 689, 797, 803. Similarly, I have preferred colons to full-stops, 37, 68, 455, 680, 716, and commas to stronger stops, 20, 212, 453, 603, 688, and I have omitted stops, 163. The text has been prepared from rotographs of the manuscript, checked where necessary by inspection of the manuscript at Cambridge. For courtesy in connexion with these matters I have to thank the authorities of Gonville and Caius College, and of the University Library at Cambridge.

ATHELSTON

1

Lord, þat is off myȝtys most,   [120 a]
Fadyr and sone and holy gost,
    Bryng vs out off synne,
And lene vs grace so for to wyrke,
To loue boþe God and holy kyrke,   5
    Þat we may heuene wynne.
Lystnes, lordyngys þat ben hende,
Off falsnesse, hou it wil ende
    A man þat ledes hym þerin.
Off foure weddyd breþeryn I wole ȝow tel,   10
Þat wolden yn Yngelond go dwel,
    Þat sybbe were nouȝt off kyn.

2

And alle foure messangeres þey were,
Þat wolden yn Yngelond lettrys bere,
    As it wes here kynde.   15 [120 b]
By a forest gan þey mete
Wiþ a cros, stood in a strete,
    Be leff vndyr a lynde.
And, as þe story telles me,
Ylke man was of dyuers cuntre,   20
    In book iwreten we fynde –
For loue of here metyng þare,
Þey swoor hem weddyd breþeryn for euermare,
    In trewþe trewely dede hem bynde.

3

Þe eldeste off hem ylkon,   25
He was hyȝt Athelston,
    Þe kyngys cosyn dere;

Z = Zupitza   5 *small* g *in* God *throughout*   6 we *supplied* Z
11 woldē wilen Z; *so* 14   go] gon *for* gun Z   12 kynde MS. kynne Z
23 *only* eu ma *visible*   24 trewþe *first* e *smudged; possibly* o

F 2

He was off þe kyngys blood,
Hys eemes sone, I vndyrstood ;
   Þerfore he ney3yd hym nere.   30
And at þe laste, weel and fayr,
Þe kyng hym dyyd withouten ayr ;
   Þenne was þer non hys pere
But Athelston, hys eemes sone ;
To make hym kyng wolde þey nou3t schone,   35
   To corowne hym with gold so clere.

4

Now was he kyng semely to se :
He sendes afftyr hys breþeryn þre,
   And gaff hem here warysoun.   *neward*
Þe eldest broþir he made eerl of Douere—   40
And þus þe pore man gan couere—
   Lord off tour and toun.
Þat oþer broþer he made eerl of Stane—
Egelond was hys name,
   A man off gret renoun—   45
And gaff hym tyl hys weddyd wyff
Hys owne sustyr, dame Edyff,
   Wiþ gret deuocyoun.

5

Þe ferþe broþir was a clerk,
Mekyl he cowde off Goddys werk :   50
   Hys name it was Alryke.
Cauntyrbury was vacant
And fel into þat kyngys hand ;
   He gaff it hym, þat wyke,
And made hym bysschop of þat stede,   55
Þat noble clerk, on book cowde rede—
   In þe world was non hym lyche.
Þus avaunsyd he hys broþer þorw3 Goddys gras,
And Athelston hymseluen was
   A good kyng and a ryche.   60

35 schon *hard to make out*; *Z adds* e   38 þree *Z*   46 weddyd
wyff *right side of* y *and all the final* d *gone*; w *and* ff *indistinct*   51 his *Z*;
the only instance where Hartshorn and Wright are correct against Zupitza
57 þe *above the line*

6

And he þat was eerl off Stane –
Sere Egeland was hys name –
   Was trewe, as ȝe schal here.
Þorwȝ þe myȝt off Goddys gras,
He gat vpon þe countas   65
   Twoo knaue-chyldren dere.
Þat on was fyfftene wyntyr old,
Þat oþer þryttene, as men me told :
   In þe world was non here pere –
Also whyt so lylye-flour,   70
Red as rose off here colour,
   As bryȝt as blosme on brere.

7

Boþe þe eerl and hys wyff,
Þe kyng hem louede as hys lyff,
   And here sones twoo ;   75
And offtensyþe he gan hem calle
Boþe to boure and to halle,
   To counsayl whenne þey scholde goo.
Þerat sere Wymound hadde gret envye,
Þat eerl off Douere, wyttyrlye,   80
   In herte he was ful woo ;
He þouȝte al for here sake
False lesyngys on hem to make,   *lies*
   To don hem brenne and sloo.

8

And þanne sere Wymound hym beþouȝte :   85
' Here loue þus endure may nouȝte ;   [121 b]
   Þorwȝ wurd oure werk may sprynge.'
He bad hys men maken hem ȝare ;
Vnto Londone wolde he fare,
   To speke wiþ þe kynge.   90

61 eerl *written above deleted* kyng   80 þat eerl *Only* þ *of* þat *actually*
visible; faint indication of letter more likely to be a; *spacing indicates* þat
rather than þe   82 for *originally before* al, *but erased there and placed in*
proper position after al *above line*

Whenne þat he to Londone come,
He mette with þe kyng ful sone.
   He sayde : ' Welcome, my derelyng.'
Þe kyng hym fraynyd soone anon
Be what way he hadde igon,   95
   Wiþouten ony dwellyng.

9

' Come þou ouȝt be Cauntyrbery,
Þere þe clerkys syngen mery
   Boþe erly and late ?   *a favourite tag .*
Hou faryth þat noble clerk,   100
Þat mekyl can on Goddys werk ?
   Knowest þou ouȝt hys state ?
And come þou ouȝt be þe eerl off Stane,
Þat wurþy lord in hys wane ?
   Wente þou ouȝt þat gate ?   105
Hou fares þat noble knyȝt,
And hys sones fayr and bryȝt,
   My sustyr, ȝiff þat þou wate ? '

10

' Sere,' þanne he sayde, ' wiþouten les,
Be Cauntyrbery my way I ches ;   110
   Þere spak I wiþ þat dere.
Ryȝt weel gretes þee þat noble clerk, .
Þat mykyl can off Goddys werk :
   In þe world is non hys pere.
And also be Stane my way I drowȝ ;   115
Wiþ Egeland I spak inowȝ,
   And with þe countesse so clere.
Þey fare weel, is nouȝt to layne,
And boþe here sones.' Þe king was fayne,
   And in his herte made glad chere.   120

11

' Sere kyng,' he sayde, ' ȝiff it be þi wille,   [
To chaumbyr þat þou woldest wenden tylle,
   Counsayl for to here,

I schal þe telle a swete tydande,
Þer comen neuere non swyche in þis lande 125
   Off al þis hundryd ȝere.'
Þe kyngys herte þan was ful woo
Wiþ þat traytour for to goo;
   Þey wente boþe forþ in fere;
And whenne þat þey were þe chaumbyr withinne, 130
False lesyngys he gan begynne
   On hys weddyd broþer dere.

12

'Sere kyng,' he sayde, 'woo were me,
Ded þat I scholde see þe,
   So moot I haue my lyff; 135
For by hym þat al þis worl wan,
Þou hast makyd me a man,
   And iholpe me for to þryff.
For in þy land, sere, is a fals traytour;
He wole doo þe mykyl dyshonour, 140
   And brynge þe on lyue;
He wole deposen þe slyly,
Sodaynly þan schalt þou dy,
   Be Crystys woundys fyue.'

13

Þenne sayde þe kyng: 'So moot þou the, 145
Knowe I þat man, and I hym see?
   His name þou me telle.'
'Nay,' says þat traytour, 'þat wole I nouȝt,
For al þe gold þat euere was wrouȝt –
   Be masse-book and belle – 150
But ȝiff þou me þy trowþe wil plyȝt,
Þat þou schalt neuere bewreye þe knyȝt,
   Þat þe þe tale schal telle.'
Þanne þe kyng his hand vp rauȝte,
Þat false man his trowþe betauȝte; 155
   He was a deuyl off helle! [122 b]

124 a *inserted above line between* telle *and* swete   125 swyche *inserted
above line, in same hand* Z   142 deposē; poysoun þe Z; *see note*
152 schalt] chalt *has disappeared except for top of* t   bewreye] -eye
missing; cf. 670

14

'Sere kyng,' he sayde, 'þou madyst me kny3t,
And now þou hast þy trowþe me ply3t
   Oure counsayl for to layne :
Sertaynly, it is non oþir   160
But Egelane, þy weddyd broþir–
   He wolde þat þou were slayne ;
He dos þy sustyr to vndyrstande
He wole be kyng off þy lande,
   And þus he begynnes here trayne ;   165
He wole þe poysoun ry3t slyly,
Sodaynly þanne schalt þou dy,
   Be hym þat suffryd payne.'

15

Þanne swoor þe kyng be cros and roode :
'Meete ne drynk schal do me goode,   170
   Tyl þat he be dede ;
Boþe he and hys wyff, hys soones twoo,
Schole þey neuere be no moo
   In Yngelond on þat stede.'
'Nay,' says þe traytour, ' so moot I the,   175
Ded wole I nou3t my broþer se ;
   But do þy beste rede.'
No lengere þere þen wolde he lende :
He takes hys leue, to Douere gan wende.
   God geue hym schame and dede !   180

16

Now is þat traytour hom iwent.
A messanger was afftyr sent
   To speke with þe kyng.
I wene he bar his owne name :
He was hoten Athelstane ;   185
   He was foundelyng.
Þe lettrys were imaad fullyche þare,
Vnto Stane for to fare
   Wiþouten ony dwellyng,

To fette þe eerl and his sones twoo, 190
And þe countasse alsoo,
   Dame Edyue, þat swete þyng.

17

And in þe lettre ȝit was it tolde, [123 a]
Þat þe kyng þe eerlys sones wolde
   Make hem boþe knyȝt; 195
And þerto his seel he sette.
Þe messanger wolde nouȝt lette,
   Þe way he rydes ful ryȝt.

18

Þe messanger, þe noble man,
Takes hys hors and forþ he wan, 200
   And hyes a ful good spede.
Þe eerl in hys halle he fande;
He took hym þe lettre in his hande,
   Anon he bad hym rede:
'Sere,' he sayde also swyþe, 205
'Þis lettre ouȝte to make þe blyþe:
   Þertoo þou take good hede.
Þe kyng wole for þe cuntas sake
Boþe þy sones knyȝtes make—
   To London I rede þe spede. 210

19

'Þe kyng wole for þe cuntas sake
Boþe þy sones knyȝtys make,
   Þe blyþere þou may be.
Þy fayre wyff with þe þou bryng—
And þer be ryȝt no lettyng— 215
   Þat syȝte þat sche may see.'
Þenne sayde þat eerl with herte mylde:
'My wyff goþ ryȝt gret with chylde,
   And forþynkes me,
Sche may nouȝt out off chaumbyr wyn, 220
To speke with non ende off here kyn,
   Tyl sche delyueryd be.'

   216 syȝte] ȝ *not quite clear*   222 Tyll *Z*

20

But into chaumbyr þey gunne wende,
To rede þe lettrys before þat hende,
   And tydyngys tolde here soone.   225
Þenne sayde þe cuntasse : ' So moot I the,
I wil nouȝt lette tyl I þere be,
   Tomorwen or it be noone.

21

' To see hem knyȝtys, my sones fre,   [12?
I wole nouȝt lette tyl I þere be :   230
   I schal no lengere dwelle.
Cryst forȝelde my lord þe kyng,
Þat has grauntyd hem here dubbyng ;
   Myn herte is gladyd welle.'

22

Þe eerl hys men bad make hem ȝare ;   235
He and hys wyff forþ gunne þey fare,
   To London faste þey wente.
At Westemynstyr was þe kyngys wone ;
Þere þey mette with Athelstone,
   Þat afftyr hem hadde sente.   240

23

Þe goode eerl soone was hent,
And feteryd faste, verrayment,
   And hys sones twoo.
Ful lowde þe countasse gan to crye,
And sayde : ' Goode broþir, mercy !   245
   Why wole ȝe vs sloo ?
What haue we aȝens ȝow done,
Þat ȝe wole haue vs ded so soone ?
   Me þynkiþ ȝe arn oure foo.'
Þe kyng as wood ferde in þat stede ;   250
He garte hys sustyr to presoun lede –
   In herte he was ful woo.

---

237 Londone *Z, but I doubt whether the continuation of the* n *is intended for the* e-*contraction*   243 *in margin in same hand Z ; final* s *of* sones *invisible*   251 *word not readable ;* sustyr *Wr and Z*

24

Þenne a squyer, was þe countasses frende,
To þe qwene he gan wende,
   And tydyngys tolde here soone.   255
Gerlondes off chyryes off sche caste,
Into þe halle sche come at þe laste,
   Longe or it were noone.
'Sere kyng, I am before þe come
Wiþ a chyld, douȝtyr or a sone ;   260
   Graunte me my bone,
My broþir and sustyr þat I may borwe,
Tyl þe nexte day at morwe,
   Out off here paynys stronge ;

25

'Þat we mowe wete be comoun sent   265
In þe playne parlement . . .'
'Dame,' he sayde, 'goo fro me ;   [124 a]
Þy bone schal nouȝt igrauntyd be,
   I doo þe to vndyrstande.
For, be hym þat weres þe corowne off þorn,   270
Þey schole be drawen and hangyd tomorn,
   Ȝyff I be kyng off lande.'

26

And whenne þe qwene þese wurdes herde,
As sche hadde be beten wiþ ȝerde,
   Þe teeres sche leet doun falle.   275
Sertaynly, as I ȝow telle,
On here bare knees doun sche felle,
   And prayde ȝit for hem alle.
'A, dame,' he sayde, 'verrayment,
Hast þou broke my comaundement ?   280
   Abyyd ful dere þou schalle.'
Wiþ hys foot (he wolde nouȝt wonde)
He slowȝ þe chyld ryȝt in here wombe :
   Sche swownyd amonges hem alle.

266 playne *written twice*   268 igrauntyd] i *above line*   270 crowne Z

27

Ladyys and maydenys þat þere were,　　　　　285
Þe qwene to here chaumbyr bere,
　　And þere was dool inowȝ.
Soone withinne a lytyl spase
A knaue-chyld iborn þer wase,
　　As bryȝt as blosme on bowȝ.　　　　　290
He was boþe whyt and red;
Off þat dynt was he ded–
　　Hys owne fadyr hym slowȝ.
Þus may a traytour baret rayse,
And make manye men ful euele at ayse,　　295
　　Hymselff nouȝt afftyr it lowȝ.

28

But ȝit þe qwene, as ȝe schole here,
Sche callyd vpon a messangere,
　　Bad hym a lettre fonge,
And bad hym wende to Cauntyrbery,　　　300
Þere þe clerkys syngen mery
　　Boþe masse and euensonge.
'Þis lettre þou þe bysschop take,　　　　　[124 b]
And praye hym for Goddys sake
　　Come borewe hem out off here bande.　305
He wole doo more for hym, I wene,
Þanne for me, þouȝ I be qwene–
　　I doo þe to vndyrstande.

29

'An eerldom in Spayne I haue of land;
Al I sėse into þyn hand,　　　　　　　310
　　Trewely, as I þe hyȝt,
An hundryd besauntys off gold red.
Þou may saue hem from þe ded,
　　Ȝyff þat þyn hors be wyȝt.'
'Madame, brouke weel þy moregeue,　　>　315
Also longe as þou may leue:
　　Þerto haue I no ryȝt;

　295 at ayse *written as one word*　　303 whan *before* þou *marked for*
erasure

But off þy gold and off þy fee,
Cryst in heuene forȝelde it þe;
   I wole be þere tonyȝt. 320

30

'Madame, þrytty myles off hard way
I haue reden, siþ it was day:
   Ful sore I gan me swynke;
And for to ryde now fyue and twenti þertoo,
An hard þyng it were to doo, 325
   Forsoþe, ryȝt as me þynke.
Madame, it is nerhande passyd prime,
And me behoues al for to dyne,
   Boþe wyn and ale to drynke.
Whenne I have dynyd, þenne wole I fare. 330
God may couere hem off here care,
   Or þat I slepe a wynke.'

31

Whenne he hadde dynyd, he wente his way,
Also faste as þat he may,
   He rod be Charynge-cros, 335
And entryd into Flete-strete,
And seþþyn þorwȝ Londone, I ȝow hete,
   Vpon a noble hors.
Þe messanger, þat noble man, [125 a]
On Loundone-brygge sone he wan— 340
   For his trauayle he hadde no los—
From Stone into Steppyngebourne,
Forsoþe his way nolde he nouȝt tourne;
   Sparyd he nouȝt for myre ne mos.

32

And þus hys way wendes he 345
Fro Osprynge to þe Blee.
   Þenne myȝte he see þe toun
Off Cauntyrbery, þat noble wyke,
Þerin lay þat bysschop ryke,
   Þat lord off gret renoun. 350

333 way] ay *not readable*   338 hete] ete *not readable*   342 Steppyngebourne *two words MS.*   349 bysschop ryke *so Z*; *in MS. apparently*
one word

33

And whenne þey runggen vndernbelle,
He rod in Londone, as I ȝow telle :
   He was non er redy ;
And ȝit to Cauntyrbery he wan,
Longe or euensong began ;   355
   He rod mylys fyffty.

34

Þe messanger noþyng abod ;
Into þe palays forþ he rod,
   Þere þat þe bysschop was inne.
Ryȝt welcome was þe messanger,   360
Þat was come from þe qwene so cleer,
   Was off so noble kynne.
He took hym a lettre ful good speed,
And sayde : ' Sere bysschop, haue þis and reed ' ;
   And bad hym come wiþ hym.   365
Or he þe lettre hadde halff iredde,
For dool, hym þouȝte, hys herte bledde ;
   Þe teeres fyl ouyr hys chyn.

35

Þe bysschop bad sadele hys palfray :
' Also faste as þay may,   370
   Bydde my men make hem ȝare ;
And wendes before,' þe bysschop dede say,
' To my maneres in þe way ;
   For noþyng þat ȝe spare,
And loke, at ylke fyue mylys ende   375 [125
A fresch hors þat I fynde,
   Schod and noþyng bare ;
Blyþe schal I neuere be,
Tyl I my weddyd broþer see,
   To keuere hym out off care.'   380

---

352 rod *over* was, *the latter marked for erasure*   353 non er *written
close together ; a stroke put between the two words by another hand*   376
fresch *stroke through top part of* h

36

On nyne palfrays þe bysschop sprong,
Ar it was day, from euensong –
> In romaunce as we rede.
Sertaynly, as I ȝow telle,
On Londone-brygge ded doun felle   385
   þe messangeres stede.
' Allas,' he sayde, ' þat I was born !
Now is my goode hors forlorn,
   Was good at ylke a nede ;
Ȝistyrday vpon þe grounde,   390
He was wurþ an hundryd pounde,
   Ony kyng to lede.'

37

Þenne bespak þe erchebysschop, ·
Oure gostly fadyr vndyr God,
   Vnto þe messangere :   395
' Lat be þy menyng off þy stede,
And þynk vpon oure mykyl nede,
   þe whylys þat we ben here ;
For ȝiff þat I may my broþer borwe,
And bryngen hym out off mekyl sorwe,   400
   þou may make glad chere ;
And þy warysoun I schal þe geue,
And God haue grauntyd þe to leue
   Vnto an hundryd ȝere.'

38

Þe bysschop þenne nouȝt ne bod :   405
He took hys hors, and forþ he rod
   Into Westemynstyr so lyȝt ;
Þe messanger on his foot alsoo :
Wiþ þe bysschop come no moo,
   Neþer squyer ne knyȝt.   410
Vpon þe morwen þe kyng aros,
And takes þe way, to þe kyrke he gos,   [126 a]
   As man off mekyl myȝt.
Wiþ hym wente boþe preest and clerk,
Þat mykyl cowde off Goddys werk,   415
   To praye God for þe ryȝt.

39

Whenne þat he to þe kyrke com;
Tofore þe rode he knelyd anon,
   And on hys knees he felle :
'God, þat syt in Trynyte,   420
A bone þat þou graunte me,
   Lord, as þou harewyd helle –
Gyltles men ȝiff þat þay be,
Þat are in my presoun free,
   Forcursyd þere to ȝelle,   425
Off þe gylt and þay be clene,
Leue it moot on hem be sene,
   Þat garte hem þere to dwelle.'

40

And whenne he hadde maad his prayer,
He lokyd vp into þe qweer ;   430
   Þe erchebysschop sawȝ he stande.
He was forwondryd off þat caas,
And to hym he wente apas,
   And took hym be þe hande.
'Welcome ', he sayde, ' þou erchebysschop,   435
Oure gostly fadyr vndyr God.'
   He swoor be God leuande :
'Weddyd broþer, weel moot þou spede,
For I hadde neuere so mekyl nede,
   Siþ I took cros on hande.   440

41

'Goode weddyd broþer, now turne þy rede ;
Doo nouȝt þyn owne blood to dede,
   But ȝiff it wurþy were.
For hym þat weres þe corowne off þorn,   <
Lat me borwe hem tyl tomorn,   445
   Þat we mowe enquere,   [12
And weten alle be comoun asent
In þe playne parlement . . .

---

423 *thin stroke through* þat (*see note*); *apparently dots for erasure rubbed out*; ne *markèd for erasure before* be

42

' Who is wurþy be schent.
And, but ȝiff ȝe wole graunte my bone,   450
It schal vs rewe boþe or none,
     Be God þat alle þyng lent.'

43

Þanne þe kyng wax wroþ as wynde,
A wodere man myȝte no man fynde
     Þan he began to bee :   455
He swoor oþis be sunne and mone :
' Þey schole be drawen and hongyd or none—
     Wiþ eyen þou schalt see.
Lay doun þy cros and þy staff,
Þy mytyr and þy ryng þat I þe gaff ;   460
     Out off my land þou flee !
Hyȝe þe faste out off my syȝt ;
Wher I þe mete, þy deþ is dyȝt ;
     Non oþir þen schal it bee.'

44

Þenne bespak þat erchebysschop,   465
Oure gostly fadyr vndyr God,
     Smertly to þe kyng :
' Weel I wot þat þou me gaff
Boþe þe cros and þe staff,
     Þe mytyr and eke þe ryng ;   470
My bysschopryche þou reues me,
And crystyndom forbede I þe :
     Preest schal þer non syngge ;
Neyþer maydynchyld ne knaue
Crystyndom schal þer non haue ;.   475
     To care I schal þe brynge.

456 be oþis *transposed* Z

G

45

'I schal gare crye þorwȝ ylke a toun
Þat kyrkys schole be broken doun,
   And stoken agayn wiþ þorn.
And þou schalt lygge in an old dyke,   480
As it were an heretyke.
     Allas, þat þou were born!

46

'ȝiff þou be ded, þat I may see,
Asoylyd schalt þou neuere bee;
   Þanne is þy soule in sorwe.   485
And I schal wenden in vncouþe lond,
And gete me stronge men of hond;
   My broþir ȝit schal I borwe.
I schal brynge vpon þy lond
Hungyr and þyrst ful strong,   490
   Cold, drouȝþe, and sorwe;
I schal nouȝt leue on þy lond
Wurþ þe gloues on þy hond,
     To begge ne to borwe.'

47

Þe bysschop has his leue tan.   495
By þat his men were comen ylkan:
   Þey sayden: 'Sere, haue good day.'
He entryd into Flete-strete;
Wiþ lordys off Yngelond gan he mete
   Vpon a nobyl aray.   500
On here knees þey kneleden adoun,
And prayden hym off hys benysoun;
   He nykkyd hem wiþ nay.
Neyþer off cros neyþer off ryng
Hadde þey non kyns wetyng;   505
     And þanne a knyȝt gan say.

483 ȝyff Z   486 lond *cannot be read*; wende Z, *missing abbreviation*
500 aray *first* a *over line above* r

48

A kny3t þanne spak with mylde voys:
'Sere, where is þy ryng? where is þy croys?
   Is it fro þe tan?'
Þanne he sayde: '3oure cursyd kyng   510
Haþ me refft off al my þyng,
   And off al my worldly wan;
And I haue entyrdytyd Yngelond:
Þer schal no preest synge masse with hond,
   Chyld schal be crystenyd non;   515
But 3iff he graunte me þat kny3t,
His wyff and chyldryn fayr and bry3t:
   He wolde with wrong hem slon.'

49

Þe kny3t sayde: 'Bysschop, turne agayn;   [127 b]
Off þy body we are ful fayn;   520
   Þy broþir 3it schole we borwe.
And, but he graunte vs oure bone,
Hys presoun schal be broken soone,
   Hymselff to mekyl sorwe.
We schole drawe doun boþe halle and boures;   525
Boþe hys castelles and hys toures,
   Þey schole lygge lowe and holewe.
Þou3 he be kyng and were þe corown,
We scholen hym sette in a deep dunioun:
   Oure crystyndom we wole folewe.'   530

50

Þanne, as þey spoken off þis þyng,
Þer comen twoo kny3tys from þe kyng,
   And sayden: 'Bysschop, abyde,
And haue þy cros and þy ryng,
And welcome, whyl þat þou wylt lyng,   535
   It is nou3t for to hyde—
Here he grauntys þe þe kny3t,
Hys wyff and chyldryn fayr and bry3t;
   Again I rede þou ryde.
He prayes þe pur charyte   540
Þat he my3te asoylyd be,
   And Yngelond long and wyde.'

51

Hereoff þe bysschop was ful fayn,
And turnys hys brydyl and wendes agayn–
   Barouns gunne wiþ hym ryde–   545
— Vnto þe Brokene-Cros off ston;
Þedyr com þe kyng ful soone anon,
   And þere he gan abyde.
Vpon hys knees he knelyd adoun,
And prayde þe bysschop off benysoun;   550
   And he gaff hym þat tyde.
Wiþ holy watyr and orysoun,
He asoylyd þe kyng þat weryd þe coroun,
   — And Yngelond long and wyde.

52

Þenne sayde þe kyng anon ryȝt: 555
'Here I graunte þe þat knyȝt,
   And hys sones free,
And my sustyr hende in halle.
Þou hast sauyd here lyuys alle:
   Iblessyd moot þou bee.'   560
Þenne sayde þe bysschop also soone:
'And I schal geuen swylke a dome–
   Wiþ eyen þat þou schalt see–
Ȝiff þay be gylty off þat dede,
Sorrere þe doome þay may drede,   565
   Þan schewe here schame to me.

53

Whanne þe bysschop hadde sayd soo,
A gret fyr was maad ryȝt þoo,
   In romaunce as we rede–
It was set, þat men myȝte knawe,   570
Nyne plowȝ-lengþe on rawe,
   As red as ony glede.
Þanne sayde þe kyng: 'What may þis mene?'
'Sere, off gylt and þay be clene,
   Þis doom hem thar nouȝt drede.'   575
Þanne sayde þe good kyng Athelston:
'An hard doome now is þis on:
   God graunte vs alle weel to spede!'

54

þey fetten forþ sere Egelan –
A trewere eerl was þer nan –   580
   Before þe fyr so bryȝt.
From hym þey token þe rede scarlet,
Boþe hosyn and schoon þat weren hym met,
   Þat fel al for a knyȝt.
Nyne syþe þe bysschop halewid þe way,   585
Þat his weddyd broþer scholde goo þat day,
   To praye God for þe ryȝt.
He was vnblemeschyd foot and hand;
Þat sawȝ þe lordes off þe land,
   And þankyd God off hys myȝt.   590

55

þey offeryd hym with mylde chere   [128 b]
Vnto seynt Powlys heyȝe ɛwtere,
   Þat mekyl was off myȝt.
Doun vpon hys knees he felle,
And þankyd God þat harewede helle, —   595
   And hys modyr so bryȝt.

56

And ȝit þe bysschop þo gan say:
'Now schal þe chyldryn gon þe way
   Þat þe fadyr ȝede.'
Fro hem þey tooke þe rede scarlete,   600
Þe hosen and schoon þat weren hem mete,
   And al here worldly wede.
Þe fyr was boþe hydous and red,
Þe chyldryn swownyd as þey were ded;
   Þe bysschop tyl hem ȝede;   605
Wiþ careful herte on hem gan look;
Be hys hand he hem vp took:
   'Chyldryn, haue ȝe no drede.'

600 **hym** MS. hem *Z*   603 **and red** *seems to be over an erasure*
604 **ded**] ed *not visible*

57

Þanne þe chyldryn stood and lowʒ :—
'Sere, þe fyr is cold inowʒ.'   610
  Þorwʒout þey wente apase.
Þey weren vnblemeschyd foot and hand ;
Þat sawʒ þe lordys off þe land,
  And þankyd God off his grace.

58

Þey offeryd hem with mylde chere   615
To seynt Poulys hyʒe awtere ;
  Þis myracle schewyd was þere.
And ʒit þe bysschop efft gan say :
' Now schal þe countasse goo þe way,
  Þere þat þe chyldryn were.'   620

59

Þey fetten forþ þe lady mylde ;
Sche was ful gret igon with chylde,
  In romaunce as we rede—
Before þe fyr when þat sche come,
To Iesu Cryst he prayde a bone,   625
  Þat leet his woundys blede :
' Now, God, lat neuere þe kyngys foo
Quyk out off þe fyr goo.'
  Þeroff hadde sche no drede.

60

Whenne sche hadde maad here prayer,   630
Sche was brouʒt before þe feer,
  Þat brennyd boþe fayr and lyʒt.
Sche wente fro þe lengþe into þe þrydde ;
Stylle sche stood þe fyr amydde,
  And callyd it merye and bryʒt.   635
Harde schourys þenne took here stronge
Boþe in bak and eke in wombe ;
  And siþþen it fel at syʒt.

---

611 he MS. þey Z   612 hand] d *quite and* n *partly invisible*   615 hem *written above erased* þañe   616 þat hyʒe MS. ; Z *omits* þat ; cf. 592

61

Whenne þat here paynys slakyd was,
And sche hadde passyd þat hydous pas,   640
  Here nose barst on bloode.
Sche was vnblemeschyd foot and hand :
Þat saw3 þe lordys off þe land,
  And þankyd God on rode.
Þey comaundyd men here away to drawe,   645
As it was þe landys lawe ;
  And ladyys þanne tyl here 3ode.
Sche knelyd doun vpon þe ground,
And þere was born seynt Edemound :
  Iblessyd be þat foode !   650

62

And whanne þis chyld iborn was,
It was brou3t into þe plas ;
  It was boþe hool and sound.
Boþe þe kyng and bysschop free
Þey crystnyd þe chyld, þat men my3t see,   655
  And callyd it Edemound.
' Halff my land,' he sayde, ' I þe geue,
Also longe as I may leue,
  Wiþ markys and with pounde,
And al afftyr my dede—   660
Yngelond to wysse and rede.'
  Now iblessyd be þat stounde !

63

Þenne sayde þe bysschop to þe kyng :
' Sere, who made þis grete lesyng,
  And who wrou3te al þis bale ? '   665 [129 b]
Þanne sayde þe kyng : ' So moot I thee,
Þat schalt þou neuere wete for me,
  In burgh neyþer in sale ;
For I haue sworn be seynt Anne
Þat I schal neuere bewreye þat manne,   670
  Þat me gan telle þat tale.
Þey arn sauyd þorw3 þy red ;
Now lat al þis be ded,
  And kepe þis counseyl hale.'

      668 bour Z ; *see note*

64

Þenne swoor þe bysschop: 'So moot I the,   675
Now I haue power and dignyte
  For to asoyle þe as clene
As þou were houen off þe fount-ston;
Trustly trowe þou þervpon,
  And holde it for no wene: 680
I swere boþe be book and belle,
But ȝiff þou me his name telle,
  Þe ryȝt doom schal I deme:
Þyselff schalt goo þe ryȝte way
Þat þy broþer wente today,   685
  Þouȝ it þe euele beseme.'

The archbishop seems to be very powerful arm of god on earth

65

Þenne sayde þe kyng: 'So moot I the,
Be schryffte off mouþe telle I it þe,
  Þerto I am vnblyue—
Sertaynly, it is non oþir   690
But Wymound, oure weddyd broþer;
  He wole neuere þryue.'
'Allas,' sayde þe bysschop þan,
'I wende he were þe treweste man,
  Þat euere ȝit leuyd on lyue.   695
And he wiþ þis ateynt may bee,
He schal be hongyd on trees þree,
  And drawen with hors fyue.'

66

And whenne þat þe bysschop þe soþe hade
Þat þat traytour þat lesyng made,   700
  He callyd a messangere,   [13
Bad hym to Douere þat he scholde founde,
For to fette þat eerl Wymounde:
  (Þat traytour has no pere!)

696 *blotted mark above* bee   701–2 *indistinct at beginning of each line;*
b *of* bad *unreadable,* a *very faint*

'Sere Egelane and hys sones be slawe,   705
Boþe ihangyd and to-drawe.
   (Doo as I þe lere!)
Þe countasse is in presoun done;
Schal sche neuere out off presoun come,
   But ȝiff it be on bere.'   710

67

Now wiþ þe messanger was no badde;
He took his hors, as þe bysschop radde,
   To Douere tyl þat he come.
Þe eerl in hys halle he fand:
He took hym þe lettre in his hand   715
   On hyȝ, wolde he nouȝt wone:
'Sere Egelane and his sones be slawe,
Boþe ihangyd and to-drawe:
   Þou getyst þat eerldome.
Þe countasse is in presoun done;   720
Schal sche neuere more out come,
   Ne see neyþer sunne ne mone.'

repet: them.
Not effective
like in trial by fire
bt

68

Þanne þat eerl made hym glade,
And þankyd God þat lesyng was made:
   'It haþ gete me þis eerldome.'   725
He sayde: 'Felawe, ryȝt weel þou bee!
Haue here besauntys good plente
   For þyn hedyr-come.'
Þanne þe messanger made his mon:
'Sere, off ȝoure goode hors lende me on: 730
   Now graunte me my bone;
For ȝystyrday deyde my nobyl stede,
On ȝoure arende as I ȝede,
   Be þe way as I come.'

The signs of a
dramatic irony.

Echo of death of
horse of former
messenger.

69

'Myn hors be fatte and cornfed,   735
And off þy lyff I am adred,'
   Þat eerl sayde to hym þan;
'Þanne ȝiff myn hors scholde þe sloo,   [13●
My lord þe kyng wolde be ful woo
   To lese swylk a man.'   740

70

Þe messanger ȝit he brouȝte a stede,
On off þe beste at ylke a nede,
   Þat euere on grounde dede gange,
Sadelyd and brydelyd at þe beste.
Þe messanger was ful preste,   745
   Wyȝtly on hym he sprange.
'Sere,' he sayde, 'haue good day;
Þou schalt come whan þou may;
   I schal make þe kyng at hande.'
With sporys faste he strook þe stede;   750
To Grauysende he come good spede,
   Is fourty myle to fande.

71

Þere þe messanger þe traytour abood,
And seþþyn boþe insame þey rod
   To Westemynstyr wone.   755
In þe palays þere þay lyȝt;
Into þe halle þey come ful ryȝt,
   And mette wiþ Athelstone.
He wolde haue kyssyd his lord swete.
He sayde: 'Traytour, nouȝt ȝit! lete!   760
   Be God and be seynt Jhon,
For þy falsnesse and þy lesyng
I slowȝ myn heyr, scholde haue ben kyng,
   When my lyf hadde ben gon.'

743 *from* euere *to first* de *in* dede *written over an erasure*   759 swete]
te *beneath the line*   763 kyng *final* g *indistinct and squeezed against margin*

72

Þere he denyyd faste þe kyng,   765
Þat he made neuere þat lesyng,
    Among hys peres alle.
Þe bysschop has hym be þe hand tan ;
Forþ insame þey are gan
    Into þe wyde halle.   770
Myȝte he neuere with crafft ne gynne,
Gare hym schryuen off hys synne,.
    For nouȝt þat myȝte befalle.
Þenne sayde þe goode kyng Athelston :
‘ Lat hym to þe fyr gon,   775 [131 a]
    To preue þe treweþe wiþ alle.’

73

Whenne þe kyng hadde sayd soo,
A gret fyr was maad þoo,
    In romaunce as we rede –
It was set, þat men myȝten knawe,   780
Nyne plowȝ-lenge on rawe,
    As red as ony glede.
Nyne syþis þe bysschop halewes þe way,
Þat þat traytour schole goo þat day :
    Þe wers hym gan to spede.   785
He wente fro þe lengþe into þe þrydde,
And doun he fel þe fyr amydde :
    Hys eyen wolde hym nouȝt lede.

74

Þan þe eerlys chyldryn were war ful smerte,
And wyȝtly to þe traytour sterte,   790
    And out off þe fyr hym hade ;
And sworen boþe be book and belle :
‘ Or þat þou deye, þou schalt telle
    Why þou þat lesyng made.’

768 hym *above line and very scratchy*   770 þe *end of* e *only in out-*
line   776 in dede *MS.* wiþ alle Z ; *see note*   784 scol[d]e Z ; *see note*
787 doū *over erased* þer̄   792 sworē *over erased* saydē

'Certayn, I can non oþer red,   795
Now I wot I am but ded :
  I telle ȝow noþyng gladde–
Certayn, þer was non oþer wyte :
He louyd hym to mekyl and me to lyte ; <
  Þerfore enuye I hadde.'   800

75

Whenne þat traytour so hadde sayde,
Fyue good hors to hym were tayde,
  Alle men myȝten see wiþ yȝe–
Þey drowen hym þorwȝ ylke a strete,
And seþþyn to þe Elmes, I ȝow hete,   805
  And hongyd hym ful hyȝe.
Was þer neuere man so hardy,
Þat durste felle hys false body :
  Þis hadde he for hys lye.
Now Iesu, þat is heuene-kyng,   810
Leue neuere traytour haue betere endyng,
  But swych dome for to dye.
                              Explicit.

803 alle *above line and to right of* þat (*marked for erasure*)

NOTES

(Z = Zupitza, and notes taken mainly from his edition are indicated by his initial. References to the Introduction are by section; the Table of Contents gives the page of each section.)

1 ff. Such an invocation is frequent in tail-line romances, and *Emaré* (ii) enjoins such piety as the correct procedure for a minstrel. *Sir Gowther* (ed. K. Breul) is the closest to *Athelston*. For this and every other parallel of phrase and usage Z's notes (*Englische Studien*, XIII. 343–414) are a teeming mine of information. *most* could agree with *myȝtys* or with the subject of the sentence without affecting the sense very much. For the *is* referring to a vocative, cf. 420.

7–8 *it* repeats the idea of *falsnesse* and gives an arrangement useful for metrical purposes. *a man* is dative, *hym* reflexive. Tr.: 'Listen, my courteous lords, (to a tale) of unfaithfulness, and the fate it brings to any man who concerns himself with it.' For a similar use of *lede*, cf. *Havelok the Dane* 785 *þusgate Grim hym fayre ledde*, 'conducted himself, managed his affairs'. This theme of disloyalty is stated again at the conclusion of the poem, ll. 810–12, and is the chief part of the framework of the story.

9 *þerin* is not infrequently written *þrinne* and pronounced as one syllable.

10 *weddyd breþeryn* occurs only in *Athelston* for 'sworn-brethren': and since both here and in 23 the words overweight the line, it is tempting to substitute the usual expression, *wedbreþeryn* or *wedbroþer(s)*. This would not, however, suit 161, 691. The phrase with the two separate words may have arisen on the analogy of *weddyd wyff*.

11 MS. *wolden ... go dwel*. Z emends ingeniously, *þat wilen yn Yngelond go(n) dwel*, ' who once upon a time dwelt in England '. But since *wolden go dwel* does make sense, and since I feel that the material of this part of the poem may easily have been continental, I am not inclined to follow Z in disturbing the text. The phrase *of dyuers cuntre* 20 strengthens the idea of strangers from widely separated parts meeting and joining themselves in

brotherhood.   Z naturally (in his note to 20) says that *cuntre* means 'district'.   I think that the spirit in which the poem regards sworn-brotherhood seems to suit the dramatic and romantic union of absolute strangers; see the note to 22.   Of course, this interpretation involves us in the difficulty of having foreigners as English nobles; but is that any stranger than the method by which they earn their honours?   We are dealing with a romance.

12 Z emends *kynde* to *kynne* for the sake of the rhyme.   (In view of 221 I prefer the spelling *kyn*.)   It certainly would be quite easy for a scribe to substitute *kynde* for *kynne*, since the meaning of each is similar, and the sight of *kynde* in the next triplet may have influenced him.   Moreover, the following couplet from Robert Mannyng's *Handlyng Synne* seems to show that the phrase with *kynde* was the more usual one:

> Þe ner(e) syb she ys hys kynde,
> Þe more plyȝt shal he þere fynde.   (ll. 7371–2.)

That the connexion of *syb* and *kynde* is idiomatic is shown by the occurrence at l. 7444 of the adj. *sybkynd*, hitherto unrecorded. We may thus regard the *kynne* (suggested by Z) as a variant of the more usual phrase, and such variants occur elsewhere in this poem; see in particular the note to 716.   *sybbe*, adj. (OE. *sibb*) : tr. : 'who were not related by nature' (but by the man-made bond of sworn-brotherhood).

13 *messangeres* : both in the *chansons de geste* and in medieval life they were people of rank and importance.   In the *chansons de geste* (e.g. *Enfances Ogier* 2058) the same person frequently combined the functions of messenger and ambassador; hence the necessity of high birth.   If *Athelston* had a foreign original, the *messangeres* would have been people who could naturally assume the high offices they are given.   Line 339 *Þe messanger, þat noble man* seems to fit in with this idea.   But l. 41 *Þe pore man* seems to show that the writer of *Athelston* takes the popular minstrel's romantic view of a sudden rise to wealth and fame from obscurity.   See also the note to 362.   The re-arrangement of the words for metrical purposes gives the line a strange appearance; the sense-order is *þey were all foure* (in appos. with *þey*) *messangeres*.   On the rhyme *were : bere*, see Intro. 8 (3) and (10), and the note to 285.

14 *wolden* : according to Z, 'pflegten', i.e. 'were accustomed

to'; but it is rather 'wished', 'were intending to'. *Yngelond* has throughout the poem the spelling with *y* for the raised sound.

17 *wiþ*: 'over against'. Understand a relative ('which') before *stood*, and cf. 56 (probably), 253, 362 (note), 389, 725 (note), 763.

18 A piece of conventional landscape, frequent in the romances.

19 and 21 refer to an alleged original; cf. 29, 68, 383, 569, 623, 779. The fact that these references to originals (sometimes designated as French or Latin) became a habit is enough to show how derivative Middle English poetry was. These references developed into a convention ; but it is in the nature of things almost impossible to find out whether reference was ever made to a non-existent original. Zupitza, Gerould, and Beug suppose a French or Anglo-Norman original for *Athelston*; Miss Rickert, J. E. Wells, Miss Hibbard, and Albert C. Baugh think the poem is of English composition. I imagine that both sides are right (Intro. 5 and 7).

The presence of a large amount of conventional phraseology has been very generally accounted a good reason for slighting the tail-rhyme poems; but in my view the condemnation is often based on a misconception of what the poems pretend to do. I have attempted elsewhere (*Medium Ævum*, I. 3) to prove that conventional phraseology of various kinds was part of the purpose and of the excellence of the tail-rhyme poems; in this note, which concerns itself with representative conventionalisms of *Athelston*, I shall use the classification made in *Medium Ævum*, and refer the reader to it for the justification and the details. We have *expressions addressed to the audience*—7, 80 ; *comments on the nature of the actions*—150, 156, 168, 180, 374, 560, 578, 716 ; *epic compliments and alliterative ornaments*—45, 114, 413 ; 30, 36, 70-2 ; *references to sources and to oral tradition*—29, 68, 383, 569, 623 ; *generally useful expressions connected with the narrative machinery*—174, 228, 458, 563. On the outskirts of these classes of conventional expression lie what are more properly designated *tags*, e.g. 31, and the other expressions cited in the note to that line. But even these serve several artistic purposes which must be considered before they are dismissed as mere padding, a sign of the inefficiency or carelessness of the poet. These purposes are—(a) *to keep the stanza moving* 118 ; (b) *to make a good rhyme* 31, 390 (both (a) and (b) being connected with the musical element of the stanza); (c) *to give the diction a loose conversational texture* 184, 306. (For similar judgements about *tags*, see that most pregnant piece of literary criticism, the Introduction to Sisam, p. xxxix.) All these conventional expressions, especially the so-called tags, must be used with some discretion, and above all they must help the stanza to move and not clog it; but one soon learns to feel where the usages have been strained—384 (perhaps), 19 and 21 (taken together), 536. But these examples fail through *not* being conventional. Those who condemn the use of conventionalisms in tail-rhyme poems show that they have not really examined the poems; unless, indeed, like A. B. Taylor (*Introduction to Medieval Romance*, p. 158) they find nothing admirable in any of them. Since, however, that means a failure to perceive any value in *Amis and Amiloun, Athelston, Cleges*, and the *Sege of Melayne*, the attitude of these wholesale detractors may be safely disregarded. Cf. the notes to 94–6, 149–50, 545, 48, 31.

22 *þare* r. w. *mare* : *þore, more* is an alternative, but in view of 187 (*þare* : *fare*) *þare* seems to be the original form; see 187 (note). *here metyng* : Gerould (*E. St.* XXXVI. 193 ff.) is inclined to think that the *cros* suggested the oath. My opinion is rather that their uniting themselves is to be considered a spontaneous act prompted by sudden emotion—a romantic and artificial development from the real thing, to be compared with the perfect sworn-brotherhood of *Amis and Amiloun*. In the same way, I feel that the manner of this incident differentiates it from the ballad of *Adam Bell*, where men met by chance take the oath of brotherhood. As for the introduction of the *cros*, wayside crosses were common enough in the Middle Ages : cf. *Guy of Warwick* (tail-rhyme), stanza 142, ll. 11–12.

24 A slight re-arrangement would smooth the metre of the line : *In trewþe dede trewely hem bynde* with elision between *trewely hem*. For the alliterative combination, cf. 679 · in each line the alliteration provides effective emphasis of the idea in the verb. *dede bynde* periphrastic past tense, as in 372, 743. Tr. : 'united'.

25 Z, to mend the metre, suggests *everylkon*; but I should prefer to insert *broþer*; cf. 40, 43, 49. It would be very easy for a scribe to understand the idea from the end of the preceding stanza, and so miss out the noun itself.

26 Perhaps *hoten* for *hyȝt* ; cf. 185.

29 *I vndyrstood* : cf. the epic use of OE. *gefrægn*, as in *Judith* 246.

30 ' was closely related ', an unusual meaning for the phrase ; see note to 33.

31 *weel and fayr* may be considered a tag ; cf. *wiþouten ony dwellyng* 96, *boþe erly and late* 99, *is nouȝt to layne* 118, *so moot þou the* 145 and elsewhere, *on þat stede* 174, *at þe laste* 257, *þat þere were* 285, *whyt and red* 291, *I wene* 306, *as I þe hyȝt* 311, *hool and sound* 653, *in dede* 776 (MS.). These tags occur in all ME. romances ; but they vary from group to group. *Athelston,* for instance, has very few of the ' inclusive ' sort, like *blac and broun,* so frequent in *Havelok.* They are not, of course, to be taken literally, but it is not unprofitable to attempt to see by what course the phrase developed into a convention ; cf. the note on *blak or reed* (Chaucer, *Clerk's Tale,* ed. Sisam, p. 43). See note on l. 291 below. They are to be translated, if at all, with discretion ; for *weel and fayr* we might say ' as one would expect '. They are to be distinguished from phrases which though conventional are necessary to the meaning. *Athelston* is so full of conventional phraseology that it has little space for the odd tags ; Chaucer, on the other hand, who strives for individual phraseology, finds tags very useful in rhyme. See the excellent note of Sisam, *Clerk's Tale,* p. 45. See the notes to 19–21, 94–6, 149–50.

32 *hym dyyd* : Z says this must be an ethic dative but finds no parallel. Cf., however, Laȝamon's *Brut* (ed. J. Hall), l. 1747 *Þa Inne king was him dæd.*

33 i.e. ' fit to succeed him '. I leave out Z's comma at the end of the line. This and other conventional phrases are often used by the author of *Athelston* with a twist of meaning and significance—a process that is also very noticeable in the *Sege of Melayne.* This seems to me to be one of the signs of the comparative lateness of *Athelston,* since the twisting and refurbishing of well-worn phrases is always a sign of a decadent period in style ; cf. 30, 37, 42, 808.

33–4 To run on the lines over the triplet section is not usual in these tail-rhyme poems; it represents, I think, a late freedom; cf. 544, 678, and see Intro. 9 *b.* For the same phrase cf. 69, 114.

40 *eerl of Douere* ; that is, he was put in command of Dover Castle, just as Egeland was given the castle of *Stane* or *Stone.*

H

The best explanation for the choice of these honours seems to be that the author in adapting an older story or poem chose Stone and Dover because they were the best places along the Canterbury pilgrim-route to provide a habitat for his secular dignitaries, Dover and Stone both having well-known castles. *Stane* (r. w. *name* 43 ; see also 103, 115) must in this case be regarded as the Northern form of Stone ; so Z interprets it in his note to 43. Dover Castle was from very early times a place of immense strategical importance.

41 *couere* : this may be trans. or intrans. without affecting the sense ; cf. 331, 380.

42 *tour and toun* : this is, of course, a frequent expression for the whole of a city, originating, doubtless, from the two aspects of the early Norman town, the lord's castle and the establishment of the townspeople protected by the lord. Since there are signs, however, that the author of *Athelston* does manipulate these phrases, I think it worth suggesting that he may have had in mind the nature of Dover, which was distinctly a town *and* a castle, both famous.

48 Any literal translation of this tail-line will fall short of giving its significance. It belongs to a class of conventional expressions for which I have suggested the term *emotional comment*. It is intended to call up the quality of the situation mentioned. It might be taken to mean : ' that was a solemn and splendid occasion '. *Solempnitee* occurs as a variant in other tail-rhyme poems (e.g. *Amis* 336, 432, *Octavian* (Camb. MS.) 1053, *Ottuell* 612) ; and it is noteworthy as showing the foundations of Chaucer's verse that he often uses *devocioun* in this manner, and (very significantly) uses *solempnitee* several times, always after the prep. ' with ' and always with the tail-rhyme significance (twice *wedded with greet solempnitee*). Cf. note to 31.

50 Cf. 101 (note), 113, 415.

54 Z thinks that the parallel of 348 settles the meaning of *wyke* as town (OE. *wīc*) ; but it may well equal OE. *wīce*, ' office, duty, function '. Cf. the following quotation from the *N.E.D.*: Laȝamon 29752, *Austin . . . haveð his cantel-cape on of Gregorie þan pape, and mid wurðscipe mucle haldeð his wike.*

56 A relative understood after *clerk* ; so Z.

58 *broþer* pl. = OE. *brōþor* ; so Z ; but it may be taken as sg. referring to Alryke and by implication to the other brothers.

58-9 *gras* r. w. *was*: Is the *a* long or short? Cf. 639-40, 651-2. Other instances occur in ME. which suggest that a vowel nominally long in French did not sound so to English ears; cf. *Havelok the Dane* 1331-2, *doute* r. w. *noute* (OFr. *doute*, OE. *hnŭtu*). See note to 64-5.

61 *eerl* two syllables; see Intro. 9 *b*.

63 *was trewe*: for the method of narration, see Intro. 3 *b*, and cf. 580.

64-5 *gras* r. w. *countas*: there are other instances in Middle English (e.g. in *Cursor Mundi*) of final *a* for *e* before *s* in words borrowed from French. An interesting example is *Amadace* (Ireland MS.) 294, *burias* (OFr. *burgeis*) r.w. *was, mas* (OE. *mæsse*), *lasse*, the Edin. MS. having *masse* (for *messe*) r.w. *plese* v., *burges*. This is quoted from Behrens (*Beiträge zur Geschichte der französischen Sprache in England*, I. 90), who suggests no explanation.

67-8 *þat on, þat oþer*: 'the one, the other'. *men* 'one' (OE. indef. *man*). On the sudden growth of the children, see Intro. 3 *a* in the account of *Amis and Amiloun*.

70-2 This accumulation of well-worn phrases seems almost to achieve beauty. *off here colour* 'in hue'. See note to 291. Cf. *Amis* 452-3.

77 *to boure and to halle*: literally 'to private and public counsel' (so French and Hale), but probably here implying 'on numerous occasions'.

78 Such inversions are frequently brought about in fitting the sense to the rhyme; but I think they often point also to the early state of English verse and language, in which the first half-line strongly stressed held an important unit of the sense.

79 On the name *Wymound*, see the Intro. 6 *a*.

81 *he was . . . woo*: cf. 133 (orig. OE. constr. with dat.), 127 (dat. or nom.), 739.

82 To insert *loue* would improve the metre and the sense; cf. 86 for the idea and the two syllables in *loue*, which in 82 could be taken as an old feminine genitive. I would have no hesitation at all in suggesting this emendation, were it not that the number of syllables in the poss. pl. *here* is doubtful (cf. 22, 69). French and Hale have a footnote: *for here sake*, i.e. 'for their ruin'.

83 Cf. 131, 664, 700, 724, 766.

84 'In order to cause them to be burnt to death': a conventional punishment, especially of women, in the French *chansons*

de geste, and, since it differs from the 'drawing and hanging' with which the offenders are later threatened, it may point to confusion of an old tale with a newer one. Perhaps, however, *brenne* is a glance forward at the ordeal. The best way to explain the construction is to suppose an indefinite 'one' as subject to the dependent verbs; cf. the modern German use of *lassen.* Cf. 163, 269, 308.

85 *hym beþouȝte*: 'reflected', *hym* reflexive, different from *hym þouȝte* 367, 'it seemed to him'.

87 If one takes *wurd* as 'word', Z's suggestion for the line seems as good as can be got. Wymound by a word (conversation) with the king will set about the business of sowing dissension between him and Egeland. Acting on Z's suggestions, we may explain thus : ' By means of speech (*þorwȝ wurd*) our business (that of ruining Egeland) may begin to go forward (*sprynge*).' French and Hale translate : ' A rumour will forward our plan '. Why *oure*? Possibly from the idea of his communing with himself. A suggestion, to which I do not attach much weight, is that of transposing *wurd* and *werk*; we should then have the well-known idiom *wurd may sprynge,* and translate 'By immediate action we shall become famous '. Miss Rickert translates : 'And the fame of our doing may be spread through the world', apparently taking *wurd* as ' world'. The evidence of his purpose, *to speke* 90, and the importance which is always given in these traitor stories to the original lying conversation both support the first suggestion made above. As to the form *wurd*, which occurs again at 273, Jordan (*Handbuch,* § 35, anm. 2) explains it as 'Verdumpfung von *o* > *u* nach Labial und besonders vor *r* ', and shows that the form is not confined to one area, although the evidence appears to be chiefly Eastern.

93 *he*: ' the king '. The confusion of pronouns is frequent and a sign of primitive style. See note to 437.

94–6 These lines have unabashed conventional expression— *soone anon, wiþouten ony dwellyng*—of the kind that critics are wont to call ' tags ' or ' filling-up ' phrases; but the latter belongs to a recognizable class of conventional expressions like *I schal no lengere dwelle* 231, *For noþyng þat ȝe spare* 374, which convey the urgency of the situations, and which help to give tail-rhyme poems (with their stanzaic arrangement) something quite different from the mere consecutive narration proper to the couplet. Such expressions occur usually in the tail-line, and the added expressiveness they afford was undoubtedly one of the chief reasons for the popularity of the stanza. This passage (94–6) is a good example of the dilution of sense, of which Sisam (Intro., p. xxxix) speaks ; but from his apologetic manner (to the 'modern standards') he surely overlooks the fact that, in tail-rhyme poems, there is no diminution of meaning, but an increase of (poetical) meaning. The wielders of these 'modern standards' might be reminded that a minstrel singing to the harp would be burdened by close-packed sense, and that these expressions would be exactly what the musician would require to give his phrasing the light and shade which is the essence of musical progression. That is the supreme merit of the tail-rhyme stanza, that it has a predestined fitness for the expression one finds in it.

95 *igon* : 'come'.

97–8 *ouʒt* : 'at all', 'perchance' : most common in questions (Z). The comment of French and Hale on this couplet is indeed *mery* : 'The monks of St. Augustine's in Canterbury were reputed to be gay fellows and good singers.' And what about those of Ely ?—

> Merie sungen þe munaches binnen Ely,
> Þer Cnut ching reu þer by.

The *mery* refers, surely, not to a drunken carousal, but to the pleasant effect of the chanting of the services. The rhyme *mery* : *Cauntyrbery* was conventional : cf. the note to 291. See the note of Skeat on Chaucer, *Cant. Tales*, B 2023.

99 *erly* : three syllables. An 'inclusive' tag, 'throughout the day', or perhaps in view of 302 with a glance at Matins and Evensong.

101 *on Goddys werk* : 50 has *off*. *On* appears to have been almost interchangeable with *of* : cf. *Havelok* 870 *Sprongen forth so sparke on glede*. *Athelston* 141 has *brynge þe on lyue* for *of lyue*; the shortened form *o* standing for either preposition contributed to the confusion. Dr. C. T. Onions suggests that here and at ll. 50, 113, 415, *Goddys werk* = *opus dei* of the Benedictine Rule ; also *opera dei* = *Goddes werkes* of *Seven Sages* 3509.

104 *wane* r. w. *stane* ; *wan* 512 r. w. *tan* ; *wone* 755 r. w. *Athelstone* are to be regarded as the same word, from ON. *ván*. See the note to Tolkien and Gordon's *Sir Gawayne and þe Grene Knyʒt* 257.

108 For the omission of *and* where we should now require it, cf. 172, 204, 606, 661. But it seems more awkward and un-idiomatic where it leaves a single noun unjoined (108, 172) than a clause (204, 606), the latter being quite usual in later English poetry. The levelling in *wat(e)* is notable.

112 An interesting textual point: *he* marked for erasure. The scribe having the general sense and the connexion from the previous line proceeded to put in *he* as subject; then noticed later the subject after the verb and deleted the *he*.

116 *inowȝ*: not 'sufficient' or 'much'; rather, like the col-loquial 'quite a lot'.

117 Perhaps omit *with* for the metre.

120 Omit *his*, cf. 252, and scan possibly, *And in hért(e) made glád chér(e)*. Cf. 401. See Intro. 9 *b*.

122 *to . . . tylle*: since *tyl(le)* is in ME. the Northern equiva-lent of *to*, we have in this sentence a repetition of the preposition. *Tylle*, convenient here for the rhyme, is to be regarded as an adverbial use of the preposition, very common in Old Norse, where the preposition is separated from its connexion, and placed at the end of the sentence. The rejection of *-est* in *woldest* and *-(e)n* in *wenden* as the work of a Southern copyist would bring this line nearer a reasonable scansion. Since, how-ever, awkward constructions like this of 122 are foreign to the poem, it is possible that we have a trace of a northerly reviser who added the *tylle*; there are other signs of corruption in this stanza, at 124. I suggest for the original:

> 'Sere kyng,' he sayde, 'ȝif (it) þi wille be
> To chaumbyr þat þou wolde(st) te . . .'

The *N.E.D.* shows that *te(n)* = OE. *tēon*, 'draw', 'proceed', is a common Eastern verb, and very popular in rhyme. Compare for the first line *Orfeo* 384 and Sisam's note.

124 MS. *a swete tydande* (with *a* written above the line). If the MS. *swete* is retained, it would have to be taken ironically, and I agree with Z that this can hardly be assumed. It is pos-sible that the *a* had displaced a *u* from which the stroke on top has been missed. A *u* could easily be mistaken for an open *a*, and *unswete* would give the sense required, 'unpleasant'; cf. *Tristrem* (ed. Kölbing) 968:

> Tristrem, y telle it þe,
> A þing, is me vnswete.

In the similar situation in the accounts of Richardis' ordeal, the traitor uses an expression which seems to be the exact equivalent of *unswete*. Z's *a swyche* is feeble, and, in any case, is rare, and was probably obsolete by this date (see *N.E.D. such* I. 1 d.) Omit *þis* 125 for metre and idiom.

134 *þat*: 'if '.

135 *lyff* acc. and *þryff* inf. r. w. *on lyue* and *fyue*. Have the last three the unvoiced sound or the first the voiced sound? Assonance with *f* and *v* does not occur. Phonetically the last three might have *f*, if one supposed that the early loss of the final vowel in the North allowed the consonant to be unvoiced; *fyue* could also go back to OE. *fīf*. Recorded spellings seem to show that the unvoiced sound existed in these words at a later date. The *N.E.D.* has the following: *c.* 1375 *Sc. Leg. Saints* xxv 'thryfe'; *c.* 1500 *Debate Carpenter's Tools* 'to þryffe'. For 'alive', *c.* 1500 *Partenay* 4204 'on lif '; *c.* 1440 *Morte Arthure* 'olyfe'. The unvoicing in words like *wardrop* (OFr. *warderobe*) is attributed by Jordan (*Handbuch der mittelenglischen Grammatik*, § 158) to loss of stress.

136 *worl*: 'world'. There is no need to assume that the form is incorrect, because the most various forms do result from the *-rld*, both in English and in the cognate languages. Z quotes a *worle* from Laȝamon 23081; *Havelok* 1349 has a *worde*; and modern German shows the other alternative, to lack the 'r ', *welt*. *worl* is probably disyllabic; see Intro. 9 *b*.

137 *makyd me a man*: 'ensured my fortunes '. This instance of the phrase is much earlier than any recorded in the *N.E.D.*

139 As regards the syntax I think Z's idea is feasible, that the writer had in mind a general sense from the first six lines of ' There is danger to you ', and then proceeded with *for* to give the reason. It may be simply that *for* means ' since ', and then one would punctuate with a comma after *traytour*. The omission of *sere* would improve the metre; a minstrel could very easily and naturally insert such titles. It may be noted that the version of *Bevis* in MS. Caius Coll. Camb. 175 has many unnecessary *sere*'s.

141 *brynge on lyue* = *of lyue* ' out of life '; but there is no need to suppose that *on* is merely a scribal error or misunderstanding. Z's citations (n. to 141), and the material of the *N.E.D.* (*on* prep. 27; *of* prep. xvi. 55) indicate that *on* was really used instead of *of*. Cf. note to 101.

142 MS. *deposen*; Z proposes *poysoun þe* on account of the parallel in 166–7. He may be right, and one thing in his favour is that with *deposen* the *-en* of the infinitive is needed for the metre. But in view of 164 *He wole be kyng off þy lande*, I propose to leave *deposen*. As far as the argument from the parallelism is concerned, the parallel is not complete, and I think that the word *slyly* of itself might suggest the addition of *Sodaynly . . . dy*.

145 Cf. 666, 675, 687.

149–50 Cf. 681, 792. These lines really look like 'padding', but before one condemns one should understand. The defect— if defect it be—has arisen from the fact that the poet has used in the second line of the couplet a perfectly legitimate asseveration expressed in the form of a conventional phrase, and then in the next line a conventional, semi-musical (or, as I have said elsewhere, *sotto-voce*) tail-line. *Horn Childe*, st. iv, shows a precisely similar example. The latter of the two lines should be connected, not so much with the line immediately preceding, as with the whole of the surrounding passage. The method of writing the tail-line (as in Brit. Mus. MS. Addit. 31042) attached to the side of the couplet by a bracket may point to some such feeling about the tail-line. One must take this fact into account in reading the lines, and in judging them; they are not merely two successive 'filling-in' lines; each of them has a different status in the stanza. One can see also that they serve a rhythmical purpose; the check in the forward movement gives more emphasis not only to the entry of the Condition 'But ȝiff . . . plyȝt' in the seventh line, but to the whole of the rest of the stanza. Musically considered, one may think of the lines as a cadenza, or a 'flourish' comparable to ll. 70–2. That this is no *ad hoc* explanation may be seen from the similar occurrences in *Guy of Warwick* (stanzas 64, 74), and in *Amis and Amiloun* (451–3, 655–7). Cf. the notes to 19–21, 94–6.

154 An ancient and modern method of taking an oath. The custom is mentioned frequently in romances: *Guy of Warwick* (Caius MS. 8436):

> The sowden behyght me his land
> And therto he held vp his ryght honde.

See J. Grimm, *Deutsche Rechtsalterthümer*, I. 194, II. 555–6. Originally the man taking the oath placed his right hand on some sacred object, the sword-grip (heathen), or the sacred relics (Christian). In later times this was simplified to raising the right hand, which is still the legal practice of some countries.

155 *þat false man*: dat.

156 Cf. 180, 296, 692, 812. This abuse of the villain, especially of the 'false man', is a constant habit of medieval narrators, including Chaucer.

160–1 Cf. 690–1.

166 *þe poysoun*: see note to 142. Poisoning was popular both in poems (as the *chanson, Parise la Duchesse*), and in real life, as a means of getting rid of enemies, but it seems to have been less used in England than elsewhere. See T. Wright, *Domestic Manners and Sentiments of the Middle Ages*, pp. 279–80.

170 i.e. 'I shall not eat or drink'; cf. *Melayne* 1192 *Ne mete ne drynke my hede come in, The city of Melayne or we it wyn.* As an asseveration it is derived from the French *chansons*. This particular form of words seems to belong to the East Midlands. *Ne . . . ne* are OE. correlatives, and the omission of the first member in ME. is not uncommon; cf. *Havelok* 548.

172–4 On the punishing of the wife and children, see Intro. 5.

174 A tag, 'there', useful for rhyming, very frequent in tail rhyme poems and varied with *plas*. See 652 (note).

176–7 On the ethics of Wymound's attitude, see Intro. 4.

177 The meaning is obviously: 'Do as you think best'. A more usual and frequent expression is 'to do by someone's rede'. The nearest parallel would seem to be the *Do þi best* of *Orfeo* 126 (ed. Sisam, II), which is used with the suggestion of 'washing one's hands' of an affair. The connotation of *Athelston* 177 might be conveyed by a translation: 'But please yourself!'

179 *gan wende*: 'went'. Cf. *is iwent* 181 = 'has gone'.

182 *was afftyr sent*: 'was sent for'. Cf. *Minot*, ed. J. Hall, 3, 49 f.: *schipmen sone war efter sent*: so Z, who gives examples of similar arrangements with other verbs and prepositions.

185–6 This curious and unusual detail would seem to show, as Miss Rickert suggests (*Romances of Friendship*, Intro., p. xvii), that the English author of *Athelston* must have been using an original, since he could not invent such a piece of information.

But French and Hale give a reference to *Celtic Myth and Arthurian Romance* by R. Loomis, who (p. 333) shows that Old Celtic tales have just this feature of a foster-child being named after the father who adopted it. It is a fact, also, that tail-rhyme romances, for example, *Launfal*, *Amadace*, and *Cleges*, do draw on deep-seated layers of folk-lore and popular story. Nevertheless, I think Miss Rickert's suggestion is justified.

187 *lettrys*: a letter, esp. a formal letter. On *þare* r. w. *fare*, see Intro. 8 *a*.

192–3 On the division of the stanza, and the six-line stanzas in general, see Intro. 9.

193–4 *tolde* r. w. *wolde*: perhaps from Angl. *talde*, and Anglian or Northern *walde*. But even Chaucer occasionally rhymes $\bar{\varrho}$ and $\bar{\varrho}$, so that OE. *wolde* will serve.

195 *knyȝt* may be pl.: 209 has *knyȝtes*. Z cites *Guy of Warwick* (Auchinleck MS.) 1947 *Lordinges, kniȝt* (r. w. *diȝt*).

200 Cf. 406, 712. Z suggests that in 406 (and perhaps 712) *take* means 'spur', since at 406 the bishop has not dismounted. But 712 must be emended, and I do not know that we need press accuracy so far as to reject the ordinary meaning of 'taking horse' in 406. The rhyme in this line necessitates a quick change from historic pres. (*takes*) to past (*wan*) and back to pres. again (*hyes*).

210 *þe*: cf. 539 *þou*: in 210 it is not possible or necessary to say whether *þe* goes with *rede* or *spede*.

211–12 This linking of stanzas by repetition is not uncommon in tail-rhyme romances. It is a device of narration such as we find in all writers who use a stanza for narrative, rather than the technical verbal linking of *Pearl*. Cf. 229, 766.

215 Probably taken from the *Sege of Melayne*; see Intro. 6 *d*.

219 *forþynkes*: impers. vb. without the substitute pron. 'it'. Cf. 249, 328, 367.

221 *non ende off here kyn*: parallels to this phrase are in *A peniworþ of witte* (MS. Camb. Ff. II. 38) l. 106; Sisam XVI (*York Play*) 232; *Sawles Warde* (ed. J. Hall, *Early Middle English*, 120/117): *ba mi feader 7 mi moder ant al þe ende of mi cun*. Tolkien, in his *Glossary* to Sisam (s.v. *ende* n.), explains *vttiremeste ende of . . . kynne* as 'the furthest point (to which one can go back) in your ancestry'. But the other occurrences of the phrase suggest the meaning 'part' or 'portion' for *ende* (*N.E.D.* end sb. 5 c), as in *Harold ofsloh mycelne ende þes folces*

(Peterborough Chronicle 1052). *Ende of kynne* seems to be an idiomatic phrase meaning simply 'member of one's kindred'. Hall has much the same explanation. The parallel in *A peniworþ of witte* (*E. St.* VII. 113) is interesting on other grounds than that of meaning:

> Say, in my chaumbyr y lye sore syke ;
> Owt of hyt y may not wynne
> To speke with none ende of my kynne.

The couplet is repeated at ll. 127–8 ; and the suggestion that the author knew and imitated *Athelston* is supported by other similarities, not common to tail-rhyme poems (e.g. *The marchaund swore be seynt Anne* 61), as well as by its sharing much the same dialectal peculiarities. The Camb. version of *A peniworþ of witte* is minstrel's work, with the characteristic virtues and defects, and it is significant that wherever one thinks to see likeness to *Athelston*, the Camb. version differs from the early Auchinleck MS. References, direct or indirect, to *Athelston* being very difficult to find, the parallel with *Penniworþ of witte* is the more valuable.

224 *þat hende*: 'the lady'

228 Cf. 258 : the expression is conventional, but must mean here before midday, and is not without importance in fixing the time of the various events.

229 *fre*: a conventional epithet, common in romances; but its use in *Athelston*, as at 424, 654, suggests imitation of the *Sege of Melayne*, where *free* is a frequent epithet of the bishop, Turpin.

235 Cf. 88, 371 ; and see Glossary.

238 Cf. 755. *at Westemynster ... wone*: this piece of localization is usual in ME. romances, when the king is introduced. See e.g. *Tristrem* (ed. Kölbing) 2234 (note), where the English version has *Westminster* for the scene of the ordeal before King Mark, while the German has *Karliune*.

246 *ʒe* is often used to a superior, and twice repeated as it is here, it may indicate Edyff's attitude of humility in appealing to the king for mercy. The *ʒe* of 450 (despite Z's note), and the *ʒoure* of 730, 733, seem to be merely used for *þu* and *þyn*.

251 Cf. 428, 477, 772 (note). For the construction, 84.

253 Understand rel. pron. *Squyer* has two syllables.

256 'A favourite occupation of the ladies in the Middle Ages

was making garlands and chaplets of flowers' (Wright, *Domestic Manners and Sentiments*, pp. 288–90). 'The cherry, indeed, appears to have been one of the most popular fruits in England during the medieval period' (p. 299). The idea of the gesture was, I think, borrowed from the *Sege of Melayne*.

259–63 On the assonances, see Intro. 9 *b*. *come* r. w. *sone*, either OE. *cuman* and *sunu* with *o* written for *u*, or, in view of 721, *ō* lengthened from *ŭ*.

261 is repeated at 268, 450, 522, 731 : this looks less like mere poverty of vocabulary when we realize the extremely conventional nature of tail-rhyme diction.

262 Z in his note to 264 gives examples to show that *borwe* has the weakened general sense instead of the technical one (from OE. *borg*) of ' bail '. But the word certainly has something of the technical meaning in *Amis and Amiloun*, whence the idea was probably taken for *Athelston*.

265–6 A coincidence (if it is mere coincidence), for which I should like to find the explanation, is that something has gone wrong with the text immediately after the word *parlement* both here and at 448, here the sense, and at 448 rhyme-scheme and perhaps the sense also. At 266 there are other signs of trouble : it is the end of a column and of a page, and the adj. *playne* has been inadvertently repeated. The mention of Parliament points to English political habits; see Sisam's note to *Orfeo* 216. *playne parlement* ' full (OFr. *plein*) Parliament ', the meeting of all the Estates, with full deliberative and judicial powers. See 'Memoranda de Parliamento 1305' (Rolls), p. 293 : *Memorandum quod dominus Rex in pleno parliamento*, &c. The word *parlement* at this time meant merely a ' consultation ', of a special kind.

269 Tr.: ' I will have you know '.

280 Z punctuates with a comma, and takes the clause as a condition. I put a question mark, which seems to give a better rhetorical effect.

281 *abyyd* : a very early example of the word in the sense of ' aby ' (Z). See C. T. Onions, *Shakespeare Glossary*, *aby*.

282–3 Gerould suggests (*E. St.* XXXVI. 193 ff.) that such behaviour is reminiscent of Angevin cruelty; and Albert C. Baugh (*P.M.L.A.* XLIV. 377) thinks he finds a source in Walter Map. But this sort of treatment of women was common in the Middle Ages. ' The chevalier de la Tour Landry tells his daughters of the story of a woman who was in the habit of contradicting her husband in public (like the queen in *Athelston*), for which he knocked her down and kicked her in the face. The good "chevalier" makes no remark on the husband's brutality' (Wright, *Domestic Manners*, p. 275). As for the special circumstance of a woman with child being violently ill-treated, it occurs in *chansons* like *Parise la Duchesse*, and in English romances like *Sir Eglamour*. Moreover, 274 seems to show that the poet's mind is running on the routine punishments for peccant wives. *he wolde nouȝt wonde*: 'he would not hesitate', 'showed no compunction'. A conventional expression highly characteristic of E.-Mid. tail-rhyme romances; cf. *Amis and Amiloun* 1611, *For noþing wold sche wond*: where it is a case of the sick Amiloun being turned away by his wife.

285–6 *were* r. w. *bere* = Anglian *wēron*: *bēron* (pa.), different from *were*: *bere* 13–14.

288–9 *spase* r. w. *wase*: a favourite species of rhyme in the East-Mid. romances; see note to 58–9. The spelling in *wase* is to make the rhymes look alike.

291 The colours of flesh and blood respectively: a conventional expression for describing a goodly external appearance. This passage is very like *Sir Eglamour* 968 ff. Shakespeare uses the expression beautifully in *Twelfth Night*, I. v. 242–3 (Camb.):

> Tis beauty truly blent, whose red and white
> Nature's own sweet and cunning hand laid on.

French and Hale in their note say 'the colours of the aristocracy', with *blac and brown* (*Havelok* 1008) for the plebeians, as if Providence wisely decided to keep the classes distinct from birth. Their explanation seems to me to be another example, as in 97–8, of the danger of the literal interpretation of conventional phrases; it does not, for instance, cover the other uses of *blac and brown* in *Havelok* itself.

294–6 This anticipation of trouble from the treachery is exactly similar to the habit of the French *chansons*, as adopted also by other English romances like the *Sege of Melayne*.

294 *baret*: a word frequent in the West-Mid. poems, but not in the East; in *Athelston* its use is, I think, due to the *Sege of Melayne* 178 ff., where it is employed in this same situation. The West-Mid. (*Gawayne* 353) *baret is rered* employs the OE. cognate for the ON. *reisa* used here.

298–9 Cf. 701–2.

303 This sudden change to direct speech is quite in the manner of popular romance and primitive style, as in the Icelandic Sagas, or *Anglo-Saxon Chron.* (Parker MS.), ann. 755. Other instances are at 370 (a notable case), 705, 725; and reverse example at 364. See note on 437–40.

309 *in Spayne*: this is puzzling. Miss Rickert mentions Eleanor of Castile, wife of Edward I; and, from the latter half of the fourteenth century, when the poem must have been written, Constance of Castile, second wife of John of Gaunt. I make an alternative suggestion that it may be a detail taken over from a French original. In the *chansons* dealing with the *Enfances* of Charlemagne, his wife whom he ill-treats, and who needs a rescuer, is a Spanish princess. That an English author would feel no incongruity in this geographical mixture, one may see from the concluding part of the English *Bevis*.

313 *þe ded*: 'death', a variant (usually Nth.) of *deþ*. An attempt is made by A. B. Taylor (*Floris and Blanchefleur* 46) to explain it as a development from the OE. *to dēadan* (adj.) *dǣdun* ('did'), the adjective being mistaken for a noun.

315 This use of *brouke* (OE. *brūcan*) in refusing a proferred gift is exemplified in *Amadace* (ed. Robson, 61. 1 ff.): *Broke wel thi londus brode—Of hom kepe I riȝte none* (Z). For the more usual idiom, cf. *Havelok* 2544: *I shal don hengen hem ful heye, so mote ich brouke my rihte eie*; and Chaucer, *Hous of Fame* 273–5.

318–19 For *forȝelde off*, cf. *Degrevant* 859 *Of this gret gentyl rede, God forȝelde the.* The *it* seems to be a cognate object corresponding to the use of *lēan* as obj. after *forgieldan* in OE.: *Guthlac* 560 *We ðe nu willaþ womma gehwylces lean forgieldan.*

324 Z proposes *fyffti* on account of the distance, and, of course, numbers are peculiarly subject to corruption; but I wonder whether MS. *ffyue and twenti þertoo* might be taken to mean five-and-twenty added to thirty, which is almost exactly the distance required.

325 Two syllables in *hard* for scansion; cf. 577.

326 *me þynke = me þynkes*, cf. *me þynkiþ* 249. This form of the expression (see *N.E.D. methinks* impers. v. γ. *methink*) is probably to be connected with ON. *þykki mér*.

328 John Bull wants his dinner. For a similar anxiety see Chaucer, *Shipman's Tale* B. 1394 ff. On the times of dinner, cf.

the following from Wright, *Domestic Manners*, p. 155 : ' An old proverb :

> Lever à cinq, diner à neuf,
> Souper à cinq, coucher à neuf,
> Fait vivre d'ans nonante et neuf.'

Another version has six and ten for the hours; either would suit here.

329 More French than the old beer-drinkers of *Beowulf*.

332 *slepe a wynke*: the noun is rare at this time, occurs only in this phrase, and rhymes with *drynke* (as in *Handlyng Synne*, E.E.T.S. 123, l. 9146). This touch most likely came from the *Sege of Melayne* 1352–3.

334 Cf. 370. A conventional expression; to Z's examples add a highly typical one, *Horn Childe* 161.

335 *Charynge-cros*: ' a fair piece of work—made by command-ment of Edward I in the twenty-first year of his reign in memory of Eleanor, his deceased queen' (Stow's *Survey*, p. 168).

336 *Flete-strete*: according to J. E. B. Gover, *Place-names of Middlesex*, the name Fleet-street is first recorded in 1280. He suggests OE. *flēot*, ' channel', but since the metre at 336 indi-cates two syllables, we may suppose a weak form, which is recorded.

340 *Loundone-brygge*: the original bridge was built in A.D. 994. Wat Tyler and his followers entered the City from Kent over this bridge at about the time our poem was written.

341 *los*: with Z, mod.E. 'loss', and not, with French and Hale, ' praise' (OFr. *los*). The meaning ' praise' gives no sense; whereas ' loss' provides us with just such an expression as medieval popular poets loved—the restatement of a fact in a negative form. This is one of the very early occurrences of the noun ' loss', and it may be here a variation of the phrase *laboure lost* which does occur at this time, e.g. in *Piers the Plow-man*, B. Prologue 181. There is something remarkable about each of the four rhyme-words in this sequence, 335 ff. *Cross* must have ŏ (ON. *krŏss*), while in 508 we have *croys* (OFr. *crois*); *hors* must be pronounced ' hoss ', now common dialectally, but in Middle English (Jordan § 166) a non-northern feature; *mos* has its OE. meaning of ' bog'. Curiously enough, the other member of the alliterative expression *myre* has an OE. cognate *mēos*, meaning ' moss '.

342 See the Intro. 6 *e*. According to Hasted (II. 384), Stone

takes its name from its stony situation; the high road from
London crosses it. If *Egeland* may be supposed to have command of Stone Castle, it is a quite suitable place for including
in a story in the fourteenth century. According to Matthew
Paris, it had legendary stories attached to it; and Hasted
mentions repairs carried out at Stone during the fourteenth
century. The Bishops of Rochester frequently rested here on
their journey to and from London. *Steppyngebourne* (Sittingbourne?): Hasted (VI. 152) says: 'The principal support of it
has always been from the inns and houses of reception in it for
travellers.' Chaucer, *Cant. Tales*, D 847, mentions *Sidingborne*.

344 Omit *nouȝt* for the metre; cf. 170.

346 Perhaps change *to* to *into*; cf. 342. *Osprynge*: Hasted
has: 'In Ospryng-Street there is a tolerable inn, and the remains of the Maison-Dieu on each side of the high road' (VI. 499).
This Maison-Dieu is still pointed out to-day. Ospring is more
like what it must have been in the fourteenth century than any
of the other stopping-places on the route. See Skeat's note to
Cant. Tales, G 555, where evidence for Ospringe as a resting-
place on the Canterbury pilgrim-route is assembled. It is curious
that the name missing in the *Cant. Tales* should be supplied in
Athelston. *þe Blee* was 'anciently a forest of Blean, and later
called The Blean'. At its foot on the west is Boughton-under-
Blee (*Cant. Tales*, G 556). Dean Stanley in his *Historical
Memorials of Canterbury*, p. 237, refers to the impression which
the view of Canterbury from the Blee made on Erasmus when
he was being conducted thither by Dean Colet. See also Skeat's
notes to *Cant. Tales*, G 556 and H 2.

349 *bysscop ryke*: in MS. as one word. Z must be right in
suggesting that, in view of 350, *ryke* is to be taken separately
as an adj.

351 *vndernbelle*: perhaps about 10 a.m.

353 *non er*: a rare combination; the *N.E.D.* (*ere*, adv. 2)
records another example from the Paston Letters, like *Athelston*,
of East-Anglian origin.

362 An adj. clause which syntactically goes with *qwene*, but
from one point of view perhaps best with *messanger*; cf. 339, and
see the note on 13.

365 A notable instance of the capacity of Middle English for
confused reference of pronouns, here complicated by the omission of the subject of *bad*, which is probably 'the messenger'.

366–8 See Intro. 6 *d* on similarity of *Athelston* and the *Sege of Melayne*. As a metonymy for 'face', *chyn* must have come into use from its connexion with *cheke* in the alliterative combination of *chyn and cheke*; cf. *Gawayne and the Grene Knyȝt* 1204: 'With chynne and cheke ful swete'.

374 Probably an independent adhortative sentence, comparable to the French use of 'que + subjunctive'. Z in his note to l. 374 gives numerous parallels, e.g. *Sir Torrent of Portyngale* 'Ordeyn swith among you all, For nothing þat ȝe spare'. French and Hale isolate the expression by dashes; but I think it better to leave the comma, since the other examples show that the sentence was regarded as parallel with the accompanying imperatives. Cf. 421. This use of *spare* (as of *wond* 282) is highly characteristic of tail-rhyme romances; Chaucer, also, is fond of *spare* in this sense: e.g. *Cant. Tales*, A 192 *for no cost wolde he spare*, D 1543 *Hayt, Brok, hayt, Scot! what spare ye for the stones?*, and numerous other examples.

375 *loke* is a return to the imperative after the other unusual construction needed for the tail-line. Tr.: 'Spare no possible effort to see that I find a fresh horse at each five-mile stage'.

375–6 *ende* r. w. *fynde*: this same rhyme occurs in *Torrent*, stanza 1: *wynde* (n.), *ende, lende* (v.), *ffynde*. The explanation may possibly lie in a pronunciation of *ĕ* for *ĭ* before certain combinations of sounds; cf. *stille, duelle* (*King Horn* 373–4), *kende, defende* (*Ipomadon* 7973), *lyste, kyste, wyste, brest* (*Ipom.* 7550). The matter is complicated by the fact that many of the examples are with words and in areas where south-eastern influence might operate. A spelling *fende* (OE. *findan*) occurs several times, e.g. *Guy* (tail-rhyme), stanzas 40 and 43, *Torrent* 1395; and it may have been used originally in this line 376 of *Athelston*. See Morsbach, *Mittelenglische Grammatik*, p. 150, and p. 167 (note 2); but the whole question of what rhymes were permissible in Middle English needs proper investigation.

377 *noþyng bare*: i.e. saddled. Z quotes ON. 'ríða berum hestum' = 'ríða berbakt'.

382 The inversion is necessitated by the rhyme.

384 As a minstrel's trick the phrase is mimicked in *Sir Thopas*, Cant. Tales, B 1918.

385 The scansion of this line with *Londone-brygge* must be exactly similar to 340.

390–2 A neat example of the difficulties of composition in

I

the twelve-line form. The meaning to be expressed was, ' I
have lost a valuable horse '. ' He was wurþ a hundryd pounde ',
a conventional phrase, immediately suggested itself. What
was to go before, and what after ? ' Upon the grounde ' was
adopted because it had an association with horses in the phrase
' gange on grounde ', as in 743. What to follow ? Something
to rhyme with rede—stede—nede. The difficulty was sur-
mounted by the inversion, and the use of *lede* ' carry '. Similar
complications confronted the author in nearly every stanza.
Ony kyng to lede: either—governed separately by *wurþ*: ' worthy
to carry any king '; or—*ony kyng* (dat.) *to lede* (gerund. inf. =
' for carrying '): ' to any king for a mount '.

394 In the *Early South English Legendary* (E.E.T.S. 87,
p. 136) Becket is made to say : ' Also dignete of þe preost, herre
þan þe kyngus is, *and is gostliche fader ich am* '. Cf. 436, 466.

402–4 I should like to omit *and* (402) which could easily have
been inserted by a minstrel or a copyist. The omission improves metre and logic, the latter because the sentence beginning *þy warysoun* is the *reason* for the messenger's being *glad*,
and this is disguised by the connective *and*. Line 403 can be
taken either (1) ' if God (shall) have granted thee to live '; or
(2) ' and I (shall) have goods granted thee so as to live '. The
first seems preferable. The sense of the three lines then is :
' I shall give thee thy reward (which will be sufficient) even if
God grants thee to live till thou art a hundred years old '.

405–6 See notes to 200 and 712.

407 *lyȝt* : ' nimbly ', ' in haste '.

412 Z's note is, ' to þe kyrke steht ἀπὸ κοινοῦ '. Kellner,
Historical Outlines of English Syntax, has an excellent paragraph
(111) on the evolution of the ἀπὸ κοινοῦ construction. What
makes the situation rather queer in this instance is that the
verbs before and after *þe kyrke* have the same meaning. French
and Hale punctuate with a stop after *kyrke* and none after *gos*.
I should be against this as too sophisticated, were it not that
the *Sege of Melayne* makes just such a use of conventional
phrases and run-on lines. The *kyrke* would be the chapel
within the Abbey of Westminster. On the rhyme *aros*: *gos*
see Intro. 8 *a*.

416 Cf. 587.

423 Z in his critical apparatus says, *ȝiff* is written over an
erased *þat*; but though the line through *þat* is still there, the

dots beneath have, I think, been rubbed out. Some word is needed for the metre; I therefore restore *þat* to the text. This six-line unit shows a skilful management of the rhythm in the accommodation of a quite complex sentence to the verse-structure without violence to either. The short line 425 is turned to good account in the subordinate phrase *Forcursyd ... ʒelle*; the *ʒiff* of 423 is caught up again in the *and* ('if') of 426, and both sense and rhythm combine to emphasize the actual request which begins on the strongly accented *Leue*. Stanza 64 gives another example of this same sort of metrical skill, and such stanzas are a guarantee that there was nothing wrong with the tail-rhyme measure as such, and that, when we get really feeble passages as in stanzas 46, 53, corruption may well be suspected. It is unnecessary to stress the fact that tail-rhyme poems being minstrel poems were peculiarly subject to the accidents of transmission.

424 *presoun free*: Is this an extreme instance of the conventional use of *free*, or has the phrase a special legal significance? Z notes without comment two exs. of *fre presoun* from *Guy* (Auchinleck MS.) 5876 and 5882. French and Hale say 'on parole', but this is not consistent with *feteryd faste* (242), or with 425. I believe *presoun free* means loosely, 'strong prison'.

426 *clene* r. w. *sene* (OE. *gesēne*): see Intro. 8 (3) (*b*).

427 The meaning of this line seems to be determined by the following quotation from *Amis and Amiloun*, 1565–6:

> þou wreche chaitif,
> Wiþ wrong þe steward les his liif,
> & þat is on þe sene;

where the meaning is that Amiloun's hideous disease is a punishment for his slaying the steward wrongfully. The only difference between *Amis* and *Athelston* is that in the latter one must not interpret the *sene* quite literally. I should translate: 'Grant that their sin may be visited on them'. This is a good example of that manipulation of conventional phrases which is characteristic of *Athelston*; see note to 33.

429 *prayer*: two syllables, r. w. *queer* (OFr. *cuer*); cf. 630, r. w. *feer*. The abbreviation mark here placed above the *p* seems to be merely a conventional sign; I have written *ra* because of the *ra* spellings in *prayer* in the rest of the poem. It is not the sign for *re* which is used in *presoun* 708, 720.

436 Cf. note to 394.

437–40 There may be corruption here (see Intro. 8 *a*) ; but, taking the text as it stands, one has a difficulty of interpretation. Who is the ' he ' of 437, and to whom belong the lines 438–40 ? Z wishes to give 438–40 to the king for two reasons, (1) that they fit him better, and (2) that only if he speaks them is there any explanation of the causal connexion implied in the *for* of 439. Taking this view he is obliged to reject the obvious meaning of 440 (' Since I became archbishop '), and to attempt, without much success, to attach the line to the king. But I deny Z's premisses. I think that the words are much better as coming from the archbishop, and also that there are quite plain indications that they are intended for him. He has an urgent case, and has referred to it in 397 (*mykyl nede*) in exactly the same phrase as he uses to the king in 439. As soon as the king has greeted him, he makes his appeal vehemently (*He swoor...*). At the beginning of the next stanza, he specifies his request, with the excellent touch of the added endearment, *goode*. Unless the archbishop speaks 438–40, the opening of the next stanza is too abrupt. This interpretation allows the natural meaning for 440 ; and with regard to the *for*, there is no advantage in giving the words to the king rather than the archbishop ; moreover, we are rid of the awkwardness of having two welcomes from the king and none from the archbishop. The only difficulty is in making *he* of 437 refer to the archbishop ; and that is really not a difficulty in ME. usage ; it is, indeed, exactly paralleled at 93. I think, therefore, that *he* of 437 refers to the archbishop and that the words which follow are his.

441 *turne þy rede* ; ' change thy mind '. Z quotes from *Otuel* 1159 *ȝit I rede, þou turne þi mood*.

443 *wurþy* : this might be considered parallel to *wurm* (written *worm*) from *wyrm* ; but this change is not Anglian. *wurþy* seems to be an extension of the Anglian *wurþ*, from *weorþ* (Orm *wurrþ*). The *N.E.D.* makes a separate word of *wurthe*, from OE. *wyrþe* (apparently an illustration of the sound-change mentioned above) ; but the Anglian *wyrþe* gives *wirþe* in the East Midlands, as in Robert Mannyng (Jordan, *Handbuch*, § 70). The possibilities are hard to pin down in a word which has OE. forms *weorþ*, *wurþ*, *wierþe*, and includes the consonants *w* and *r*.

447 *asent* is probably for the aphetic *sent* as in 265. It is to be noted as another discrepancy in the poem that, when the prisoners are forfeited to Alryke, he makes no motion to refer the case to Parliament, but appoints the ordeal.

448 See note to 265-6.

449-52 Following Z I print these lines as a fragment on account of the break-down of the rhyme-scheme. It will be observed, however, that the only objection to carrying the sense on from 448 to 449 is the occurrence of *alle* as an object to *weten*. If one took *alle* as an adverb, the objection would be removed. French and Hale print the twelve lines as one stanza. Clearly, some corruption has taken place. These four lines are feeble, and may represent the effort of a scribe or a minstrel to fill a gap he found at this point.

449 For the construction with the *to* omitted, Z compares *Bevis* 1684, *þow were worþi ben hanged and drawe*.

453 *wax wroþ . . . wynde*: the alliteration is a reminder that the *w* in *wroþ* was still sounded in the fourteenth century. This expression with the three alliterating words does not otherwise occur in the tail-rhyme poems, although one finds *wax wroþ* (*Amis* 1588) and *wrathe as winde* (*Ipomadon* A 7292). The West Midlands use the phrase with the three words, e.g. *Gawayne and þe Grene Knyȝt* 319.

456 Miss Rickert says: ' There is a reminiscence of paganism in this oath ', and she refers to, and Z quotes, *Kyng Alisaunder* 1750 *He laughwith and swerith by the sonne*.

457 *or none*: here vaguely, ' in the morning '.

458 The line is conventional; cf. 563, 803, and also 483, 655. In its strictly conventional form the phrase is used in *situations which may be regarded as spectacles*; a clear instance is in 803. In 563 the original conventional expression, with its idea of drawing attention to a remarkable fact, has become more metaphorical. In the original it is equivalent to ' You shall see it with your own eye ', in its developed form to ' make no mistake about it '.

459-60 The archiepiscopal insignia, three articles not four. For the king either to appoint or dismiss a bishop in this fashion was of course impossible; such an action belongs to the style of poetry, and of popular poetry. See *Heinrich Massing, op. cit.*, p. 135, for similar action in the French *chansons*.

461 An effective use of the initial stressed syllable, which can be paralleled in all the tail-rhyme poems in this position, that is, at the beginning of the tail-line.   It occurs in *Athelston* at ll. 311, 422, and with a line of five instead of six syllables at 123, 246, 258, 392, 467, 509.   Its effect is partly to give emphasis, and partly to strengthen the rhythmical unity of couplet and tail-line.   Cf. the *Sege of Melayne* 439–41 :

> I darre lay my lyfe full ryghte
> þat of hym selfe he hase no myghte
> Owte of this fire to wyn.

Gervase of Canterbury tells of King John, when the monks refused to reject Stephen Langton : ' Iratus rex iuravit quod nec unus ex eis . . . in Anglia remaneret '.

463 *þy deþ is diȝt* : a popular and widespread alliterative phrase, to be found in WMid., Northern, and EMid. poems. *Diȝt* ' prepared ', and so ' certain '.

464 Rhetorical emphasis by negative statement ; in positive terms, ' That is exactly what will happen '.   Tr. : ' Expect no better fate '.   Z (in his note) quotes several examples of the phrase, mostly from EMid. texts and including *Cleges* 315 (in the tail-line).   Cf. *Piers Plowman*, B-text, Passus VI, l. 182.

465–6 repeat 393–4.   The points of comparison between *Alryke* and Bishop William Bateman are, to say the least of it, extremely interesting.   The date of his episcopate is just right— 1344–53—to suggest him as a model for *Alryke* in the poem. He was a champion of the Church, and an opponent of the kingly power.   Though his quarrels were local to East Anglia, with Lord Morley and the Abbot of St. Edmunds, the latter case especially became one of national importance, for Blomefield tells us that his conduct was condemned in Parliament ' as being in defiance of the King '.   His dealings with Lord Morley (Intro. 6 *d*) brought about a scene very like what we are told of in the poem at stanza 51.   The parallel becomes more striking when we observe that particular circumstances added to the central idea of a defiant bishop are such as could well have been suggested by the character and conduct of Bishop Bateman.   *Firstly*, the loss of property (*Athelston* 512) : the *Victoria County History* (II. 240) says : ' He was threatened with arrest, his temporalities were seized, and his goods and cattle distrained ' ; and, though offending bishops often lost temporalities, the question of worldly goods was more prominent in his case, because for years he defeated the efforts of the King's

council to distrain on his property for a fine of £10,000.
Secondly, the threat to raise foreign forces (*Athelston* 486) : it
is remarkable that during most of his episcopate he was often
employed on the king's service in negotiations with France and
the Pope; hence, he could easily be credited with influence
abroad. *Thirdly*, the display of tenderness (*Athelston* 605 ff.) :
Blomefield says, ' Though he was a zealous assertor of the rights
of his church, yet his constant affability and generosity,
morality, and diffusive charity, was such that he was also
admired and beloved by the generality of those that knew him.'
Fourthly, though this is rather fanciful—the reconciliation with
the king : it is a fact that ' the action had been taken against
him by the justiciars in the absence of the king, with whom
he was on sufficiently good terms to be appointed by him in
that year ambassador for negotiations between France and
England '. *Lastly*, we may observe in him that ' English '
quality which has been noted (*Medium Ævum* I. 2) as characteristic of tail-rhyme romances; for dying at Avignon ' he
desired to be buried in England, either among his ancestors, or
in the Cathedral '. When we add that Bishop Bateman was
very well known at King's Lynn, near which the poem of
Athelston, as we now have it, may well have been written,
I consider that the case for bringing fact and fiction into
connexion is as good as can be got in such a matter. I do not,
of course, assert that *Alryke* was Bishop Bateman : the very
nature of the poem forbids any such assumption ; *Alryke* was,
I doubt not, some one before the Conquest, he was Becket,
he was Langton, and the result of the working of the poet's
imagination on all these. But *Alryke* does impress us by his
air of reality, and such a lively portrait, unlike the mere
chanson-type in *Wymound*, almost presupposes some immediate
model, just as Shakespeare could not have drawn his great
Roman political figures without having Englishmen of similar
greatness before his eyes. And that hold on reality is a marked
quality of the tail-rhyme poets, who wove strands from the life
around them into the pattern of romantic story. (The historical
material for this note is taken from Blomefield's *History of
Norfolk*, III. 506 ff.)

471–2 For the use of the dramatic contrast in a precisely
similar situation, see the *Sege of Melayne*, stanza 56. On the
Interdict, see Intro. 6*d*.

473 *per* is expletive, as also in 475, and being unstressed is spelt without the final -*e*; contrast 111, 617.

474 Unexampled severity. Roger of Wendover (Rolls) on the Great Interdict: 'Cessaverunt itaque in Anglia omnia ecclesiastica sacramenta—*praeter baptisma parvulorum*.'

478-9 In the *Annales de Dunstaplia* (Rolls), p. 314, we have a reference to an interdict of 1284, following the murder of one Laurence Duket in the Church of St. Mary-le-Bow: 'Dicta vero ecclesia per archiepiscopum fuit interdicta, et ostium et fenestrae spinis obturatae.' Cf. also *Cronique de London* (Camden Society), p. 19. *Stoken* would represent *obturatae*. The difficulties in the way of this interpretation are in getting a meaning for *agayn*, and in connecting the line with the previous one. Z suggests that 480 indicates that access to churchyards is to be denied, and Miss Rickert translates *stoken* by 'choked'. The line would then mean that the sites of the churches would become wilderness again.

480 Gervase of Canterbury (Rolls): 'Mortuorum quoque corpora, cuiuscumque fuissent ordinis vel religionis, non in cimiteriis Deo dicatis sed in locis turpibus et profanis sepulta sunt.'

483-94 There is an unusual repetition of the same rhymes in this stanza. The tail-rhymes could be accounted for by the absence of fitting rhymes; but the repetition of *lond* points either to carelessness or tampering. The curious thing is that in both metre and expression the stanza is a good one.

483-4 The cases I have referred to in the Intro. 6 *d* are mentioned in *Monumenta Ritualia Ecclesiae Anglicanae* (ed. W. Maskell), II. clxxviii.

487 *stronge ... of hond*: the connotation of the phrase is 'men ready for violence'. One may compare a practically contemporaneous reference in a *Petition from the Folk of Mercerye*, London, 1386, wherein a complaint is made that a certain mayor intended to procure his election 'with stronge honde', 'thourgh debate and strenger party a-yeins the pees' (*Rotuli Parliamentorum*, III. 225). See *N.E.D.*, *strong hand*, given as a separate word, with the meaning 'use of force', the examples beginning with Wyclif.

490-1 The combination of terrors threatened here seems to recall some of the threats of the Old Testament, for example, Deut. xxviii. 16 ff., or Ps. lxxviii. 44-50. Z remarks, 'Der erzbischof denkt hauptsächlich an die folgen des göttlichen zornes '.

492 *nouȝt* : 'nothing '; the expression of these three lines is very racy.

496 The archbishop's retinue may be supposed to cover the journey from Canterbury at a more nearly normal pace. On the rhyme *ylkan* : *tan*, see Intro. 8 *a*.

497 *haue good day* : frequent, but usually given at parting, as at 747.

498-9 On the historical background, see Intro. 6 *d*.

503 *nykkyd...with nay* : ' said no to (them) '. This expressive phrase is a widespread alliterative combination, especially frequent in the West Midlands.

505 Reduced from OE. *nānes cynnes*, a genitive phrase with adjectival force, ' of no kind '. For a full discussion of the development of the expression, see Kellner, *Historical Outlines of English Syntax*, §§ 167-172.

511-12 That is, he was deprived, as was usual with offending bishops, of his temporalities ; see note to 465-6.

513 *entyrdytyd* : I suggest *entyrdyt* (*Promptorium Parvulorum* : interdyte : *interdictus*) which improves the metre. An exactly similar instance of the *-yd* of this word overloading the line is in *Le Morte Arthur* (E.E.T.S., E.S. 88), where at l. 2268 we have :

> or Ynglande entyrdyted shulde bene,

while a little later at l. 2284 :

> Or Yngland enterdyt shuld bene.

514 As Z notes, and as his abundant quotations prove, the phrase *with hond*, after beginning, doubtless, with actions (like fighting or blessing) in which the hand played the chief part, was extended to other activities. The conjunction of *synge* and *hond* is amusing ; but both phrases are conventional, and *synge masse with hond* means merely ' celebrate Mass '. The convenience of *hand* for rhyming increased the frequency of the phrase. For the bizarre collocation of words in the phrase, one might perhaps cf. *presoun free* (424).

520 *off þy body* : ' of thee ', ' of thy presence ', cf. 808, where however, *body* is more of a metonymy. The usage is, of course, well-known in the modern dialects, especially Scottish.

523 *broken*, not ' destroyed ' but ' violated ' (Z).

524 *hymselff* is dat. ; the two datives exactly as in Old English.

535 There is no question of *welcome* being regarded as a noun, object of *have*. Understand ' be '.

536 'It is not to be hidden': a rather weak tag, as used here. Syntactically *for to* is 'to'; *hyde* is Gerundial Inf. It was a very popular stock expression, occurring in nearly every one of the tail-rhyme poems, and in some of them, especially *Horn Childe*, very often. It had an obvious fitness as marking an important piece of information, a confidence to be divulged. The best practice in regard to this and other similar conventionalisms did not favour their use in the sixth line unless sense and rhythm were strong enough to carry them. Stanza 43 is an instance of the thing well done; but this stanza (50) is in general not a good one, and may be corrupt.

537–8 repeat 516–17. This trick of economically repeating whole sentences is frequent in the latter part of *Athelston*; it is a feature also of *Emaré*, which, like *Athelston*, is a fairly late poem. *here*: 'at this point in affairs'.

540–2 *Roger of Wendover* on King John's absolution: ' Rex autem venit obviam illis (the archbishop and his followers), cecidit pronus in terram ad pedes eorum, lachrymis profusis obsecrans ut de se ac regno Angliae misericordiam haberent '.

542 *Yngelond* is the second subject of *myȝte asoylyd be*.

✗ 545 This line is an interesting example of a developed (and late) use of what I have called (in the note to 149–50) the *sotto-voce* tail-line, because, although it contains part of the sense, it is still felt as accessory. From the point of view of sense it may be considered parenthetical, but its real significance is only seen when its rhythmical (and musical) basis is grasped. As I have remarked about 21, it is impossible to punctuate such lines adequately; but Z's brackets are certainly better than the sophisticated manner of French and Hale in running the sense straight on. An interesting development of the *sotto-voce* tail-line is represented by the following from the *Sege of Melayne* 1417–22 :

> Haue guddaye, Charls, in this stede,
> For þou sall neuer gyffe me brede,
> *Ne in thy burdynge say*
> If I be pore of golde and fee,
> þat I fro this grete Journee
> Fayntly fledde away.

This tail-line is a neat development from early uses where it was employed to make a formal announcement of a speaker, like the use of *mapelode* in OE. epic ; see for these early examples *Amis* 267, 387, 591.

546 Z, taking 498 to mean that Alryke came into Fleet Street and no farther, is compelled to look for his *brokene cros* between Fleet Street and Westminster.   But since a place called The Broken Cross actually did exist at the time when our poem was written, since it was near St. Paul's, and known as a place of assembly, as I have shown in the Intro., I do not really think (I prefer not to think) that Stanza 47 is strong enough to upset this identification. In the *Memorials of London in the thirteenth, fourteenth, and fifteenth centuries,* by H. T. Riley, there are several references to The Broken Cross : on p. 435, for the year 1379—' Also the different stations about Le Brokenecros were on the same day let to divers persons ' . . . (Footnote : The Broken Cross or the ' Cross at the North Door ' of St. Paul's. It was erected by the Earl of Gloucester, temp. H. III, and on its removal in 1390, these Stationers, who dealt in various small wares, probably retired into Paternoster Row). A document of 1390 (p. 521) refers to its removal. Another of 1344 (p. 220) refers to it as the ' Stone Cross, in the high street of Chepe '. There are two other references on pp. 250 and 347. Maitland's *London* knows of ' the ancient Stone Cross, denominated the Old Cross ' ; and Stow's *Survey,* p. 100, refers to the ' Old Cross ' at the west end of West Chepe, and draws a careful distinction between the ' Eleanor ' cross, which was also in Cheapside, and the cross to which we refer. It is thus clear that we have a stone cross, well known in London records, called the ' Stone Cross ' about 1350, ' Le Brokenecros ' by 1379, and removed in 1390.

551 For the omission of the *it*, Z quotes the following parallel : *Guy of Warwick* (MS. Univ. Lib. Camb.), 5707 :

> He toke a mantell of ryche colowre,
> And caste on Gye for his honowre.

pat tyde, ' then ' is very frequent in romances, sometimes with *on* or *in*.

553–4 Roger of Wendover : ' Videntes ergo archiepiscopus et episcopi tantam regis humilitatem illum de terra levaverunt . . . et illum absolverunt '.

558 *hende in halle*: Z's note is: '*hende in halle* ist gewissermassen der gegensatz . . . zu *bryʒt in boure*'; and it is a fact that both phrases are characteristic of EMid. tail-rhyme poems as against others that employ alliteration. The phrase occurs in the opening of *Isumbras* (and elsewhere) as a term of compliment not for ladies only, but for the general company.

564–6 The syntax is a little confused; but the sense is clear: 'The accused persons will sooner confess than face the ordeal.' *Schewe* appears to be an inf. gov. by *drede*: 'they will fear the ordeal (*doome*) more than showing &c. (*schewe*)' (Z).

567 ff.: almost exactly repeated in stanza 73.

572 It is to be noted that this conventional simile, which is very feeble here applied to *it = fyr*, is quite in place referring to ploughshares. But I do not see any chance of getting behind what is stated here, that the ordeal was by 'fire'. On the meaning of the *nyne plowʒ-lengþe* (*plowʒ-lenge* 781) see the Intro. 5.

574 '*and*': 'if', and written by the same sign as for the copula.

575 'They need (*thar* = OE. *þearf*, impers.) not fear this judgement'.

577 We should say simply, 'This is a severe judgement'; the *one* is an indefinite pronoun. Cf. the *Sege of Melayne* 1078 *A felle stroke Sir Charls gafe hym one* (Z). The construction is favoured in tail-rhyme poems by the suitability of *ān* (*ǭn*) for rhyme.

579 *Egelan*: r. w. *nan*: see Intro. 6 *a*.

582 Cf. 600. It is said of Queen Emma in the Legend of the Ploughshares: 'Subtrahuntur reginae calcei et caligae; et posito peplo et reiecto chlamyde . . . .' *scarlet* r. w. *met*: cf. 600–1; *met* (OE. *gemǣte*, 'fitting') perhaps short like mod.E. *wĕt* from OE. *wǣt*, the final *e* of *gemǣte* being lost early in the North. With regard to the ordeal, Miss Hibbard finds evidence of 'palpable ballad-like quality' in the fact that we are given three lots of ordeal, which, she says, is due to the well-known ballad preference for the number three. In proof of this claim she quotes 582–3; but this couplet is only repeated *twice*, and, unless we have a threefold repetition of the *words*, there is no case for comparing the passage with the ballads. As I have shown, repetitions are a feature of certain of these tail-rhyme romances, and the three ordeals are three because husband, sons, and wife are to be tested. *scarlet* (600 *scarlete*): 'rich cloth of bright red colour, usually for clothes'; so *N.E.D.* In our poem the word is used for the clothes themselves, a use not exactly recorded in the *N.E.D.* Wyclif has the phrase *reed scarlet* (Rev. xviii. 16). For a similar development in meaning, cf. *bleaunt*, and the note in Tolkien and Gordon's *Gawayne* 879.

584 *al* adv.; *fel . . . for*, 'befitted' (see Z's parallels).

591 *mylde chere*: 'with gentle bearing', 'reverently'. I do not know quite what is meant by *offeryd*. I have made two suggestions in the course of the Introduction, (1) that it is connected with the final act in the 'ordeal' ceremony, and (2) that it is a bad adaptation of the 'offering' as 'dedication' in the *Sege of Melayne.*

592 On St. Paul's, see the Intro. 6 *d* and *e.* There is a good illustration of the exterior of medieval St. Paul's in Maitland's *History of London.* The high altar was famous for its rich adornment. There is an excellent note on St. Paul's as a civic centre in the Middle Ages in Sisam's *Nun's Priest's Tale*, p. 27, note to l. 14.

593 An exceptionally feeble tag; but this part of the poem is corrupt.

600 ff. repeats 582 ff. MS. *hym*; on the confusion of the pronouns, see notes to 611 and 625.

606–11 A delightful little picture, neatly touched in.

606 *careful*: 'full of care', i.e. anxiety or concern.

609 *stood and lowȝ*: probably, 'laughed as they stood there'.

611 MS. *he.* Z alters to *þey*, arguing (in his note to 611) that, since *he* is not otherwise used as a plural in the poem, this instance must be a mere scribal error. But if *he* in 625 is taken to mean 'she' (which it may well do), the degree of probability for the southern *he* for *þey* in 611 is increased.

615 Cf. 591.

617 *schewyd*: this word, with regard to a miracle, is commonly used both in chronicle and poetry (e.g. *Sege of Melayne* 478) of the action of God in showing, declaring his *miraculous* power. This sense will not hold here, if we accept the text as it stands. I have come across another use of *schewe* in this connexion which would be rather more satisfactory: Trevisa, *Polychronicon* (Rolls), VIII. 251; 'Of hym (Simon de Montfort) greet fame telleþ þat he dede many myracles; but þey were nouȝt *i-schewed* for drede of þe kyng'. We may suppose perhaps some ceremony of thanksgiving for the successful outcome

of the ordeal.   As to the repetition of the rhyme of the couplet
(-*ere*) in the tail-line, we could get rid of it by supposing that
þere : *were* had been substituted by the southern scribe for
þare : *ware* (or þore : *wore*), forms proved for the original by the
rhyme at 22–3.

625 ff. : 630 states that *sche*, i.e. Edyff, made a prayer, but the
prayer in the previous stanza is one which *he* (presumably the
archbishop) *prayde* (625).   On general grounds the prayer should
belong to the accused lady, because in the three outstanding
examples of ' ordeal ' stories, those of Richardis, Kunigund, and
Emma, the queen makes such a protestation of innocence just
before she undergoes the ordeal.   Emma says : ' Invoco hodie
Deum testem in corpus meum, ut peream, si quid horum quae
mihi imposita sunt vel mente commiserim.'   Then, if we give
this prayer to Edyff, we must suppose that *he* 625 is either
a mistake or the southern form for ' she '.   Z objects (in his
note to 625) that only if some one other than the queen utters
the words of 627–8 is there proper sense to be made of 629.
But this argument is not valid.   If *þeroff* 629 be taken to refer
to the fire, and not to the prayer, then 629 becomes a comment
of the poet on the fearlessness born of innocence which the lady
showed, and the line is, I think, more dramatic if so interpreted.
Of course, it is possible to regard the *prayer* as corresponding to
the ' Oratio ' which the ecclesiastic presiding at the ordeal used
to pronounce ; and if that is done, then the prayer of the queen
may have been contained in the three lines which seem to be
missing from the end of stanza 59.   If, however, one did give the
prayer to the queen, and suppose a southerly reviser at work,
one could find in this section of the poem several confirmatory
circumstances.   (1) The rhyme *prayer* : *feer* (OE. *fӯr*) ; (2) the
apparent necessity of the *i* of the past part. in 651, and the
possibility in 622, not to mention the spellings of 650 and 662 ;
(3) the irregular stanzas of this section of the poem, especially
when taken in conjunction with the marked change to a better
and more vigorous style at stanza 63 ; (4) the many repetitions
of the passage ; (5) the confusion of pronouns referred to above ;
(6) the possibility that the section was inserted or remodelled
to get in the reference to St. Edmund ; and (7) a similar feeble-
ness of style in a section of *Bevis* (in the same MS. as *Athelston*),
which expands with a display of ' London ' knowledge similar to
that in *Athelston* the ' London' scene towards the end of the poem

(*Bevis*, ed. Kölbing (E.E.T.S.), ll. 4294 ff.). These considerations do not make out a case for this hypothetic southern reviser : one very weighty objection is that throughout the poem we are prepared to see the whole family of Egeland punished. It remains, nevertheless, remarkable that such a number of circumstances indicative of a southerly (i.e. SE.Mid.) reviser should mass themselves in the one section of the poem. See Intro. 8 *a*.

630–1 *prayer* r. w. *feer* : see Intro. 8 (4) and *a*.

633–4 On my suggested interpretation of this line, see Intro 5. The rhyme *prydde* : *amydde* is widespread and popular from an early date; it occurs, for instance, in Laȝamon's *Brut* (ed. J. Hall) l. 19. The fact is interesting because it makes a possibility that 633 has become difficult through the necessity of bringing in *prydde* as the rhyme for *amydde*.

636 *schourys* : since I have no contribution to make towards solving the problem of the semantic development of this word, I refer the reader to the *N.E.D.*, and to Z's note on l. 9206 of *Guy of Warwick* (E.E.T.S., E.S. 25–6), where there is a collection of material English and Germanic.

638 I can make nothing of this line. I cannot believe that Z is right when he says (in his note to 638) : ' It fel at syȝt bedeutet wohl " es geschah, dass sie seufzte " '.

639 *paynys . . . was* : the sg. verb, doubtless, for the sake of the rhyme.

640 *pas* : ' passage '.

641 *on bloode* : the same phrase occurs in the tail-rhyme *Guy* xxiv. 9 *Hir fingres brast o blode* (Z). The phrase = the modern *a-bleeding*, the *a-* being descended from the *on* as used here.

642 Cf. 588, 612.

645 Z is certainly right when he says (note to 645) that, if *here* is ' her ', it must be due to a scribal misunderstanding of the original; for there can be no doubt about the real meaning, since the impropriety of a man beholding a woman in travail is often remarked upon in romances, as also in ballads, e.g. the ballad of *Leesome Brand* (Child, I, p. 182), *Fair Janet* (Child, III, p. 108), and others. Kölbing has a long note on this matter in his edition (E.E.T.S., E.S. 46, 48, 65) of *Sir Beues*, l. 3630. *drawe* is thus an intrans. verb, ' move ', ' go '. *Here* might be taken as the adverb ' here ' without prejudice to the required meaning; but since it overweights the line, I think that *here* represents a scribal misunderstanding.

652 *into þe plas*: Miss Rickert and French and Hale both take this *plas* as ' open square ', and this translation would suit well my view of the topography of the poem. But instances of *plas* meaning ' square ' are, according to the *N.E.D.*, either earlier (from Lat. *platea*) or later (1585) from OFr. *place*. I think that *into þe plas* might mean ' thither ' just as *in þe* (or *þat*) *plas* is used for ' there '. It is a recognized tag, especially in EMid. poems : *Guy of Warwick* (Auchinleck) 223 ' And seþþe she asked him *in þe plas* ', which in the Caius MS. is ' And than she asked him *in that place* '. Along with *in þe* (*þat*) *stede* (*Ath.* 250), of which the above phrase may be regarded as a variant, it is frequently pleonastic, being brought in for the sake of rhyme ; so in 174 of *Athelston*, ' *In Yngelond on þat stede* '. With this phrase in mind, I suggest that possibly l. 9 of Chaucer's *Sir Thopas* contains an example : ' at Popering *in the place* '. *Place* is explained by Skeat as ' manor-house ' ; but it would be good mimicry of the tail-rhyme style if *in the place* were intended by Chaucer as this tag—in usage exactly like 174 of *Athelston*.

655 *þat men myʒt see*: although conventional, this phrase probably points to the gathering of people looking on ; cf. notes to 458 and 803.

657 Omit *he sayde* for the sake of metre.

660 The line is two syllables short and the syntax is weak. I suggest two words after *al*, equivalent to ' my welthe '. *Yngelond* is then co-ordinate without the *and*, as at 108.

667 *for me* : ' as far as I am concerned '. The idiom is frequent ; cf. *York Plays* XIII, 59 ff. : ' She is a clene virgine, for me ' ; *Sege of Melayne* 406 ff. : ' Bot goddis forbode and þe holy Trynytee, þat ever Fraunce hethen were for mee ' (Z).

668 *in burgh* : this expression I take to mean ' in public ', ' among the people ' (cf. Sisam, XIV. 4), and *in sale*, ' in private '. Z's emendation of *burgh* to *bour* seems unnecessary.

669 *sworn* : two syllables for the metre. *seynt Anne* r. w. *manne* : for the rhyme, cf. the *York Play of The Osteleres*, l. 37 :

IV Angelus. Hayle ! þe doughtir of blissid Anne,
　　　　　　þe whiche consayued thurgh þe holy goste,
　　　　　　And þou brought forthe both god and manne.

The cult of St. Anne was very popular in the east of England after 1378, when the Feast of St. Anne was introduced into England. (See Intro. of *Life of St. Anne*, E.E.T.S. 174.)

673 A word of two syllables is wanted in this line, perhaps a noun after *þis*.

674 *hale*: the northern form of *hole* (OE. *hāl*), 'whole', 'entire', i.e. 'undivulged'.

✗ 676–8 From what has the king to be absolved? Z suggests, from the sin of breaking his oath to his sworn-brother. That seems right; for then the first half of the stanza deals with the results of his confessing, and the latter half with what will happen if he does not confess. Tr.: 'Now I have power and authority (as an archbishop) to make thee as pure (free from sin) as if thou wert just baptized', i.e. as innocent as a new-born babe. The idea and expression are similar to *Melayne* 908–9:

> ȝee are als clene of syn, I plyghte,
> Als þat day borne were ȝee.

677 Scan with elision.

678–9 *fount-ston* r. w. *þerevpon*: *vpon* as a prep. placed after its object might have a lengthened vowel; cf. *Havelok* 1051–2. The form *fount* (= 'font'), either singly or in compound, has not been accorded recognition as a separate word, either by the *N.E.D.* or by *Bradley-Stratmann*. *funt* itself is widespread: the *N.E.D.* gives among others 1175 *Cott. Hom.* 241, 1447 Bokenham *seyntys* (Roxb.) 111, 1523 Lord Berners; *funnt* is regular in Orm, and *ffunt* is in *Promptorium* (E.E.T.S.). But whether by accident or not the combination is chiefly evidenced from the East Midlands: *funtstane* (*Pr. Conscience*); *fount-stone* (a four-teenth-century account-book in East Dereham, Norfolk, church), *funt-fat* (*Bestiary* 108 in the *OE.Miscellany*). There is an ON. *funt-r*, OSw. *funt*; but possibly ONFr. *funt* lies behind all the forms.

679–80 On this collection of conventional phrases, see the note to 149–50.

683 By taking *þe* as the pronoun we avoid the difficulty of having the weak adj. *ryȝte* with unstressed syllable in 684 and without it in 683. *ryȝt(e)*, 683 'just', 684 'exact'.

689 *vnblyue*: this word is not recorded in the *N.E.D.* The positive *blyve*, properly an adv. 'quickly', is used sometimes as an adjective; see *N.E.D.* 'belive' adv. 4 as adj. 'eager', 'glad' (perhaps by confusion with *blīþe*); examples from 1400 to 1651. The compound *vnblyue* would give the sense required,

K

'unwilling', a similar meaning to that of 797. But the very
common assonance with -*ive* and -*iþe* in these E-Mid. tail-rhyme
romances makes it possible that *unblyþe* of the original was
altered to *unblyue* by a scribe who wished to make the four
rhymes alike. It is rather a remarkable situation that we should
have two different words interchangeable in meaning and
as rhyme-words. I append some material bearing on the
question: *Amis and Amiloun* 53 *þryue, lyue, fyue, bliþe*;
King of Tars 777 *lyue, wyue, discryue, blyue* (Vernon MS.), 784
bliþe, fiue (Auchinleck MS.) = 748 (Vernon MS.) *blyue, fyue*;
Cleges 151–2 *blyth, swyth* (Auchinleck MS.), *blyth, blyue* (Ash-
mole MS.)

696 *and*: 'if'.

697–8 *trees þree . . . hors fyue.* Why the numbers? *Trees
þree* probably refers to the two uprights and cross-bar of the
gallows (so French and Hale). The *Triple Tree of Tyburn*, so
named from the triangular form of the gallows, is first recorded
in 1571. *fyue*, on the other hand, is nothing more than a popular number as a rhyme-word. The legal 'drawing' was by *one*
horse (illustration facing p. 90 of *Tyburn Tree* by Alfred Marks),
and the 'drawing' of the *chansons* was by *four* horses (*Chanson
de Roland*, ed. J. Bédier, ll. 3964–5). For another amusing
instance of a pointless *fyue*, cf. *Havelok the Dane* 212–13. By
assuming the syllabic *r* in *hors* we may regard it as the OE. pl.
form of the neuter noun.

699 The rhyme *hade*: *made* (on which see Intro. 8 *a*) can
scarcely be regarded as parallel to the *was*: *plas* of 651–2, because the long vowel of *made* is undoubted. The rhyme occurs
several times in the *Sege of Melayne* and many times in *Sir
Perceval*. The long vowel may have been due to the loss of the
f before the assimilation to the *d* took place.

702 For the asyndeton, which is characteristic, cf. 299.

704 I think it better (as against Z's direct speech) to regard
this line as an *emotional comment* (cf. 156, 180) of the narrator.
It is very unusual, also, to begin a speech in the sixth line.

707 I assume that the admonition is a reply to the surprise
which the messenger would show on being instructed to convey
false news. This is an excellent instance of the dramatic aware-
ness of these tail-rhyme poets, and of the way in which 'the
tail-rhyme stanza acted as a spur to the imagination'; see
Medium Ævum I. 106.

709 The line being too long, *off presoun* is probably an insertion, in view of 721.

711–12 *badde* r. w. *radde*: Z's method of dealing with these two lines is not satisfactory. He does cite what seems to me a proper parallel:

> Wyth the knythe was none abad;
> He buskyd hyme forth and rade. (*Degrevant* 129.)

But he ignores the difficulty of the spelling with -*dde*, and the fact that in his own quoted parallel and in the similar places of *Athelston* (357, 405) the second verb is from OE. *rīdan*. If we take *badde* as equivalent in sense to *bod* of 405, and the *abod* of 357 and 753—and there is no warrant for doing anything else— then we may regard it as an aphetic form of the *abad* found in *Degrevant*, corresponding to the mod.E. 'abode', and having the vowel *ā*. But *radde*, past tense of *rǣdan*, cannot possibly have a long vowel. Moreover, if we keep *radde* (from *rǣdan*) we have to give an unusual meaning to *took his hors*. Therefore I think the original rhyme must have been *bād* : *rād*, that somehow the *rād* was changed to *radde*, the line altered to suit the word as from *rǣdan*, and *bad* then changed to *badde* to make the rhymes look alike. This seems a very complicated change; but *bad(de)* (from *biddan*) and *rad(de)* (from *rǣdan*) were often associated in rhyme: e.g. in *Peniworþ of Witte* (Auchinleck) 156–7:

> To don so þeldman him badde
> & so bifore haþ him radde;

and elsewhere in Eastern poems, e.g. *King Alisaunder*.

716 MS. *wone*; Z *wonde*, on the evidence of 282; but there are two objections to the change; (1) that assonances with *n* (or *m*) and *nd* are rare, occurring only in *Ipomadon* (ed. Kölbing, Intro. clxiv); (2) that *wonde* does not give the meaning required, which is 'delay' rather than the 'hesitate' proper to 282. There are two alternatives. The first is to accept *wone* (from OE. *wunian*) in the sense of 'dwell', 'delay', the change *ŭ > ō* being exhibited by 720–1. The phrase *wiþouten wone* occurs several times, and it would be quite in the manner of the *Athelston* author to bring the corresponding verb into service for his phrase. Alternatively, I would read *hone*, which in the sense 'delay' is quite well evidenced, though rare. Moreover, it occurs in just the required sense in the *Sege of Melayne*.

Confusion between *hone* and *wone* could come about because they are alike in form and meaning; l. 23923 of *Cursor Mundi* shows the following rhymes in the four manuscripts : *hon—wone—hone —hon*.   But I do not really think it necessary to change *wone*.

717 ff. repeat 705 ff.

725 Possibly omit *it*, and cf. 362.

726 *weel þou bee* : a salutation. For the evolution of the construction, see *N.E.D. well*. a. I. a. b. c.

731 a good instance of a *sotto-voce* tail-line : see note to 149– 50.   The half-stanza from 729 to 734 is an example of allowable diffuseness in narration ; cf. 94–6 (note).

733 *ʒoure arende* : ' your business '.   The journey of the messenger to Canterbury and back—to which the reference here must be—might be designated Wymound's business in a double sense (*zweideutig*, says Z).   It was concerned with Egeland's imprisonment which Wymound brought about ; and, again, the expression might have some ironical humour since the ' business ' is to end in Wymound's death.   The messenger, in effect, asks to be rewarded for putting Wymound's neck in the noose. See note to 753.

735 ff. This stanza seems also to have a humorous tone : Wymound tries to get off by bestowing flattery instead of the more substantial gift.

741 *þe messanger* : dat.

743 *dede gange* : ' went ', ' walked '.

745–6 Is the messenger anxious to be off so as to make sure of his gift ?

749 Apparently, ' I shall cause the king to be at hand ', but this does not agree with his waiting at *Grauysende*.

751 *Grauysende* : ' the high road from London to Dover went formerly through the town of Gravesend.   Here are several good inns, taverns, and other such houses for travellers ' (*Hasted*, III. 319 ff.).   The only reason for mentioning *Grauysende* seems to be that the author wished to bring in another well-known place on the Canterbury route.

752 The meaning of *fande* is ' try ', ' test '.   The *N.E.D.* mentions this meaning, but the conventional usage is not exactly recorded.   Syntactically, it is a gerundial inf. ' in the trying ', ' if one tests it '.   The phrase occurs especially in alliterative combinations with *fayre* and *free*, hence frequently in describing

women, e.g. *Duke Rowlande and Sir Ottuell*, 1284 *þat mayden faire to fande*. The *-ande* was also useful for rhyming, and the *Athelston* poet has made good use of the tag because he has got his alliteration with *fourty*, completed his fourth rhyme of the difficult tail-line scheme, and given a certain freshness to the tag by applying it to the description of a hard journey. Even in the use of tags, there are degrees of skill. The distance from Dover to Gravesend is actually just on 50 miles.

753 This contradicts 749. We may perhaps understand it as deliberate deceit, in keeping with the messenger's conduct in cajoling a steed from Wymound. Possibly, Wymound is to be given the comic ill-treatment meted out to villains in the Miracle plays. The name of Wymound, as I have shown in the Intro., was associated with the character of a low fellow who receives rough treatment. It is to be noted (see *Medium Ævum*, J. 2, pp. 105–6) that tail-rhyme poems have a prominent strain of humour.

754–5 Cf. 768–9.

757 *þe halle*, 770 *þe wyde halle*: the Great Hall of Westminster. ' This hath been the principal seat and palace of all the kings of England since the Conquest . . . for here have they in the great hall kept their feasts of coronation . . . and other solemn festivals. In the year of 1224 (Henry III) it was agreed that there should be a standing place appointed where matters should be heard and judged ' (Stow's *Survey*, p. 174). *þe halle* of the first mention (757) indicates the place where the king would be found with his barons, perhaps at table; but *þe wyde halle* clearly refers to Westminster as a place of justice.

760 This device, of the stern greeting, is used several times in the *Sege of Melayne*, e.g. stanza 48.

764 *hadde ben gone*: past subjunctive.

765 ff. I think there is a case for placing 768–70 before 765–7. There is something wrong with the transmission at this point, for, according to the rhymes, we have a nine-line section followed by one of fifteen lines. The transposition I suggest seems to bring events into a better order, and to clarify the sense of some lines. At 768–70 the company goes *into þe wyde halle*, where the trial is held and Wymound pleads ' not guilty ', *among hys peres alle* (which is good law). The *crafft ne gynne* of 771 refers naturally to the denial with which he seeks to escape from the consequences of his unfaithfulness. That such

an error in transmission is possible is shown in this same MS., where in stanza 43 of *Sir Ysumbras*, ll. 1–3 appear behind 4–6, altering, as the other texts show, the obviously correct order.

765–6 For the negative in both clauses, Z cites many good examples, including *Havelok*, 249 ff. :

> Þe riche erl *ne* foryat nouth,
> Þat he *ne* dede al Engelond
> Sone sayse.

768 On the rhyme *tan* : *gan*, see Intro. 8 *a*.

772 *schryuen*, at the hands of the archbishop, as Athelston for a similar offence had been; see 553, 677. If inf. *schryuen* would require the *-en* for the metre; but may it not be a past part., 'got hymself shriven'?

776 Z substitutes *wiþ alle* for MS. *in dede*, 'weil so das metrum auf die einfachste weise in ordnung kommt'. Although, as I have maintained in the Intro. 9, I do not think such emendation worth while, I adopt his suggestion here because it is convenient for the text, and is a pleasant example of his unfailing ingenuity.

777–8 Both these lines are short, although *makyd* (cf. 137) would help the second one. Perhaps, however, they were badly adapted from 567–8.

784 *schole* : Z alters to *scholde*, but one may presume that the vowel has been levelled from the plural. Z's emendation disregards the fact that the sequence of tenses in the two parallel passages is different: *halewid* 585, *halewes* 783.

786 Cf. 633 and note.

797 We may presume *gladde* : *hadde* to have been originally *glade* : *hade*; cf. 723–4.

801–2 *sayde* r. w. *tayde*: the rhyme may not be original; the author may have written:

> Whenne þat traytour hadde sayd(e) so,
> Fyue goode hors were tayd(e) hym to . . .

For the first line compare 567, 777; and rhymes like *so* : *to* are very popular in tail-rhyme romances, e.g. *Amis* 603, 1165, 1491, 2082; *Guy*, stanzas 68, 75, 112. This emendation would give us another example of $\bar{\varrho} <$ OE. $\bar{a}$; see Intro. 8 *a*.

803 *alle men*: i.e. the citizens of London, a neat use of a conventional phrase.

804–5 Compare the following account of the execution of William Wallace from *Flores Historiarum* (Rolls), III. 124: ' Primo per plateas Londoniae ad caudas equinas tractus (this was the ' drawing '), usque ad patibulum altissimum sibi fabricatum quo laqueo suspensus.' Another account in *Annales Londonienses* (Rolls), p. 141 says: ' a palatio Westmonasterii usque Turrim Londoniarum et a turri usque Allegate et sic per medium civitatis usque Elmes.' Such cases as this undoubtedly lie behind our poem. *þe Elmes*: Z quotes Stow's *Survey*, p. 142 *a*, where he mentions the ' west part of Smithfield, in a place then called Elmes, for that there grew many elm-trees; and this had been the place of execution for offenders '. I have suggested in the Intro. 6 *e* that Tyburn is the more likely site; see in general Alfred Marks, *Tyburn Tree, its History and Annals*. In 1196 William Fitzosbert was executed ' ad furcas prope Tyburnam ' (*Chronicle of Ralph de Diceto* (Rolls), II. 143); ' ad ulmos ' (*Gervase of Canterbury* (Rolls), I. 533–4). In 1222 the Sheriff of London, Constantine Fitz-Athulf, was spirited away and executed ' ad ulmos ', whither he was taken by way of the Thames (Matthew Paris, *Chron. Maj.* (Rolls), III. 71–3). To have hanged him at Smithfield would have been a challenge to a riot: and Smithfield could not possibly be reached by water (*Athenaeum*, Sept. 7, 1907). Several chronicles mention the *Elmes* as the place of execution of Roger Mortimer by Edward the Third, and the interesting thing is that the word *Elmes* now makes its way unchanged into the Latin text, for example in the *Chron. Murimuth* (Rolls), p. 62: ' Fuit dictus comes Marchiae suspensus apud Elmes '; *Chron. Avesbury*, p. 285: ' apud Elmes per unam leucam extra civitatem '. The distance of one league from London is far too much for Smithfield, and about correct for Tyburn, whose site was roughly where Edgware Road joins Bayswater Road. We are safe in concluding that *þe Elmes* in *Athelston* means Tyburn. The use of the name ' The Elms ' for a place of execution may have been affected by two circumstances: (1) that in Old French the elm was particularly associated with the administration of justice; Littré (s.v. *orme*) cites the phrase *juges de dessous l'orme*, meaning ' judges without tribunal '; and (2) that elm trees were used for hanging malefactors (*Athenaeum*, Sept. 7, 1907).

807–8 Prohibition against the removal of the body was sometimes a feature of the punishment of notable criminals. An

Anglo-Norman poem (*French Chronicle of London*, Camden Soc. 28; Appendix, pp. 100–1) on the execution of Sir Thomas Turberville says:

> Nul home ne l'deit enterrer
> Tant cum son cors porra durer.

felle: Z thinks that *felle = fele*, from OE. *fēolan* in the sense of Gothic *filhan*, 'bury', and thus a nonce-usage. I imagine it is merely a rather forced use of *fell*, causative of *fall*, its usual sense being 'to strike down'. The word is popular in north-eastern and northern poetry, especially in the combination *fande to felle*.

810–12 The conventional piety of the conclusion is usual in Middle English romances, especially of the tail-rhyme species, and the special condemnation of the traitor and of unfaithfulness marks not only the poems, but also the Chronicles, which can find no terms bad enough for an offender like William Wallace. There was no romantic worship of rebels in the feudal society of the Middle Ages. French and Hale suggest that *dome* may be an error for *dede*, 'death'; but *dome* in the sense of 'death' is just such a graphic expression as came naturally to tail-rhyme poets, and, in fact, by Shakespeare's time the use is well established. Apparently critics do not admit that tail-rhyme poems should be poetical.

APPENDIX

Grammar

I GATHER here the chief characteristics of the grammar, adding forms only where they have not already been given, as, for instance, in the section on the phonology of the poem.

NOUNS. Final -e is probably silent in the oblique cases: *on lyue* 141. The inflexion of the gen. sg. of masc. nouns is syllabic: *Crystys woundys* 144.

Uninflected datives are: *a man* 9, *þat false man* 155, *hymselff* 524.

PLURALS. The inflexion of the plural of the noun was pronounced in disyllabic words: *knyʒtes* 209, *wurdes* 273, but *teeres* 275, 368 might be monosyllabic. In trisyllables more often silent: *tydyngys* 225, *besauntys* 312.

Weak plurals: *eyen* 458, *hosyn, schoon* 583.

Uninflected plurals: *wyntyr* 67, *knyʒt* 195, *pounde* 391, *ʒere* 404, *þyng* 511, *hors* 698, *myle* 752.

ADJECTIVES. It is possible that final -e was silent except in the weak form. *þat* is used for the definite article, 67, 68. *þis* 126 and *þese* 273 are the plural forms.

PRONOUNS: 1 sg. always written *I*, 2 sg. *þou, þe*, but *ʒe* 246, *ʒoure* 510; 3 pl. *þey* 23, *hem* 23, *here* 15. Reflexive: *hymselue(n)* 59; *hymselff* 524 (not reflexive in meaning); *hym* 723, 772. Demonstrative: *þis* acc. 364. Relative: *þat* nom. 61, acc. 460. Indefinite: *men* 68.

VERBS: inf. forms with *-en* are found, but never in rhyme: *weten* 447. No infs. with prefixed *y-* (OE. *ge-*).

PRES. INDIC.: 1 sg. *graunte* 556, *swere* 681 are to be noted, since a syllabic scansion would give them two syllables; 2 sg. *knowest* 102, *hast* 137, *reves* 471; 3 sg. with *-es, -s* is proved by rhyme; and such forms predominate in the text; but *me þynkiþ* 249, *me þynke* 326, *haþ* 511.

Pl. without ending; but *syngen* 98.

PRET.-PRES. VERBS: 2 sg. levelled under 1st and 3rd: *schalle* 281, *moot* 145: but *schalt þou* 143. Pl. similarly levelled: *we may* 6; but *we mowe* 265; *ʒe schal* 63; *þay may* 565. To note— *þou wil* 151, *he wole* 140, *wole ʒe* 246, *we wole* 530.

Past Tense: weak verbs: 2 sg. *wente þou* 105, *þou madyst* 157 ; 3 sg. : the pronunciation of the *-e* is uncertain ; some forms are—*neyʒyd* 30, *told* 68, *louede* 74, *ferde* 250, *swownyd* 284, *callyd* 298, *lokyd* 430, *nykkyd* 503, *deyde* 732.

Pl. without ending ; but *prayden* 502, *fetten* 579.

Strong Verbs : 2 sg. *þou gaff* 468. Some forms of 1 and 3 sg.: *spak* 111, *drowʒ* 115, *gat* 65, *gan* 244, *sprong* 381, *sawʒ* 431, *barst* 641, *strook* 750, also—*ches* 110, *fande* 202, *felle* 277, *fel* 583, *fyl* (pl.) 368.

Pl. without ending ; but *comen* 125, *runggen* 351, *spoken* 531, *token* 582, *drowen* 804.

Subjunctive Mood. The final *-e* being generally silent, it is sometimes difficult to determine whether a verb is in the indicative or the subjunctive. Forms certainly subjunctive are : *be* 121, *graunte* 421, *were* 528, *telle* 682, *beseme* 686, *deye* 793, *geue* 180, *forʒelde* 232, *slepe* 332, *fynde* 376 ; pl. *spare* 374.

Imperative : *telle* 147, *take* 207, *bryng* 214, *lat* 396, *þynk* 397, *flee* 461 ; pl. *lystnes* 7, *wendes* 372.

Past Participle : for the forms with *i-* see the Glossary. Some weak forms are : *makyd* 137, *maad* 429, *forcursyd* 425, *asoylyd* 484, *ateynt* 696, *tayde* 802. Strong forms : *slayne* 162, *drawen* 271, *broke* 280, *reden* 322, *born* 387, *stoken* 479, *comen* 496, *houen* 678.

Present Participle : *leuande* 437.

Verbal Noun ; *lettyng* 215, *menyng* 396.

Adverbs : *þare* 22, *lengere* 178, *fullyche* 187, *þer* (expletive) 215, *welle* 234, *weel* 315, *þedyr* 547.

Conjunctions : *þere* (for *where*) is usual, but *wher* once, 463. Many conjs. have *þat* added : *ʒiff þat* 108, *tyl þat* 171, &c. To note—*or* (before) 228, *ar* 382 (cf. *er* adv. 353), *þe whylys þat* 398.

Syntax : Points of general interest : datives without preps. 9, 155 ; cognate accs. 198, 812 ; omission of subject 365 ; continuance of the weak adj. 241 and elsewhere ; omission of the indef. art. 186 ; relative pron. omitted 17, 253, 362, 389, 752, 763 ; paratactic arrangement 427, 796.

Dialectal complexion of the text

I give a list of selected forms, Northern, Midland, or Southern, which reflect the dialectal quality of the whole text as we have it.

NORTHERN : *lystnes* 7, *ledes* 3 sg. 9, *telles* 19, *sendes* 38, *gaff hym tyl* 46, *fares* 106, *þou wate* 108, *mekyl* 101, *gretes* 112, *tydande* 124, *nay* 148, *dos* 163, *dede* (death) 180, *hyes* 201, *forþynkes* 219, *weres* 270, *wete* inf. 265, *fro me* 267, *born* 387, *nerhande* (adv.) 327, *wendes* imper. 372, *ar* conj. 382, *kyrke* 417, *dyke* 480, *tan* 495, *nykkyd with nay* 503, *with wrong* (ON. phrase) 518, *prayes* 540, *þedyr* 547, *geuen* (if *ē* < *i*) 562, *swylk* 562, 740, *knawe* (r. w. *rawe*) 570, *Egelan* (r. w. *nan*) 579, *brennyd* 632, *hale* 674, *hedyr-come* 728, *felawe* 726, *gange* r. w. *sprange* 743.

MIDLAND (here are included those common to Midland and South) : *holy* 5, *hys owne* 47, *werk* r. w. *clerk* 50, *lyche* 57, *world* 57, *is* 114, *þey fare* 118, *ouȝte* 206, *wone* n. 238, *we mowe* 265, *clerkys syngen* 301, *behoues* (not *bus*) 328, *seþþyn* 337, *abod* r. w. *rod* 357, *teeres fyl* 368, *ȝelle* 425, *wot* 468, *goo* 586, *hool* 653, *may leue* 658, *leuyd* 695, *on hyȝ* 716, *wone* 755, *strete* 804, *hongyd* 806.

SOUTHERN : *breþeryn* 38, *sustyr* 47, 251, *chyldren* 66, 598, *þere* 98 and many other places, *faryth* 100, *knowest* 102, *woldest* 122, *goþ* 218, *þynkiþ* 249, *hast þou broke* 280, *hadde be beten* 274, *brygge* 340, *wurþ* 391, 493, *morwen* 411, *þat syt* 420, *bysschopryche* (and other such spellings) 471, *we scholen* 529, *þey spoken* 531, *þou wylt* 535, *hosyn, schoon* 583, *gon* 598, *it haþ gete* 725, *feer* (SE.) 631, *swych* 812, several past participles with prefix *i-*, for which see the Glossary.

PROBLEMATIC FORMS (on which see notes) : *wyke* 54, *countas* 65, *wurd* 87, 273, *þryff* inf. 138, *worl* 136, *ded* n. 313, *me þynke* 326, *los* 341, *fynde* v. 376, *wurþy* 443, 449, 104, *mete* adj. 601, *fount-ston* 678, *vnblyue* adj. 689, *badde* n. 711, *wone* v. 716, *felle* v. 808.

The Spelling

The spelling is moderately regular : different spellings generally indicate different pronunciations. The unaccented vowel of an inflexion if not itself final is generally written *y* : *myȝtys* 1, *lettrys* 14, *goddys* 58, but *sones* 229.

Final *-e* of the dative is usually written : *mylde* 217, *chylde* 218, *herte* 252, 606 ; but it was certainly not uniformly pronounced, and sometimes not written, *gret* 48. Some unwarranted *-e*'s appear : *heuene* 6, *doome* 565. The inf. is generally written with *-e*, in most instances not pronounced. In inflexional syllables ending with a consonant *e* is written, though seemingly not pronounced, *ledes* 9, *begynnes* 165, *gerlondes* 256. *o* is written for *u* : *schole* 521 ; but *sunne* (OE. *sunne*) 456, *gunne* 223.

An extensive use is made of doubled vowels to indicate length, and there is no distinction between the writing of $\bar{e}$ and $\bar{ę}$, or $\bar{o}$ and $\bar{ǫ}$.   Examples are: *meete* (OE. *mete*) 170, *soones* 172 (but *sones* 229), *imaad* 187, *soone* 248, *woo* 252, *teeres* 275, *leet* 275, *abyyd* 281, *caas* 432, *weel* 438, *swoor* 456 (but *sworen* pl. 792). According to Jordan, pp. 35–6, spellings like *caas* and *maad* are not very frequent in ME. texts, and are to be found mainly in the period immediately after the middle of the fourteenth century and in London charters.

Final *-e* appears to be used as a sign of length: *loke* 375, *soþe* 699, *dome* 812.   *Red* (mod.E. 'red') is so spelt at 291, but *rede* 600.

i is written *y* in all positions; but *his* 154, *is* 160, *wiþ* 414, *igon* pp. 622, and so all other participles with prefix.

ȝ is used regularly; *þ* also, except in *thee* (OE. *þēon*), and a few isolated words, e.g. *thar* 575.

Some of the double *f*'s are: *leff* 18, *gaff* 39, *þryff* 138, *wyff* 236, *hymselff* 296, *halff* 366.   Other spellings with double consonants are: *bysschop* 55 and elsewhere, *runggen* 351, *syngge* 473, *fatte* adj. 735.

GLOSSARY

THE Glossary gives all words, and all forms, but not explanations of all of them. Etymologies are given only exceptionally. The references, though not complete, are sufficient for any purposes of study. References grouped by semi-colon but without separate gloss indicate different (but obvious) classes of meaning in the same word (e.g. þat *conj.*). An asterisk marks a note. A word followed by *conv.* is indicated as conventional, a fact which frequently influences meaning. Abbreviations which may not be self-explanatory are : *a.* = adjective ; *tr.* = transitive ; *pt.* = past ; *pr.* = present ; *prec.* = preceding word. As to arrangement, **u** and **v** are together, under **v** ; þ and rare **th** follow **t** ; ʒ follows ġ ; **y** is always treated as **i**. An Index of Names is given at the end of the Glossary.

a

a *interj.* 279.

a(n) *a.* 312 ; *indef. art.* 9 ; **a swyche** (?) 124*.

abyde *v. intr.* 548 ; *imper.* 533 ; **abod** *pt.* 357 ; *tr.* **abood** 753 ; **abyyd,** pay for 281.

adoun *adv.* 501, 549.

adred *pp.* r. w. **cornfed** 736.

affter *adv. and prep.* 38, 240 ; **afftyr sent** sent for 182.

aġayn *adv.* again 479 ; back 519, 539.

aʒens *prep.* against 247.

ayr *n.* heir 32. See **heyr.**

ayse *n.* at ayse 295.

al, alle *a.* 13, 136, 278 ; *as noun* 660*.

al *adv.* 82, 328, 584.

ale *n.* 329.

allas *interj.* 387, 482.

also(o) *adv.* as well 191, 408 ; **also . . . so** 70 ; **also . . . as** 316, 658 ; **also swyþe** as quickly as possible 205.

amydde *prep.* (*after noun*) 634, 787.

among *prep.* 767 ; **amonġes** 284.

and *conj.* 19, 31 ; if 426, 574, 696.

anon *adv.* at once 204, 418 ; **soone anon** 94 (*N.E.D. anon* 4d) ; **anon ryʒt** 555.

apase *adv.* 433, 611

ar *conj.* 382. See **or.**

aray *n.* 500.

are *v. ind. pl.* 424 ; **arn** 249.

arende *n.* errand 733.

aros *v. pt. sg.* 411.

as *conj.* 15, 19, 63 ; as if 250, 274, 678.

asent *n.* agreement 447* ; **sent** (aphetic) 265.

asoyle *v.* absolve 677 ; **asoylyd** *pt. sg.* 553 ; **asoylyd** *pp.* 484, 541.

at *prep.* 31, 238, 638*.

ateynt *pp.* proved guilty 696.

avaunsyd *v. pt. sg.* promoted 58.

away *adv.* 645.

awtere *n.* altar 592, 616.

b

badde *n.* probably for *bād* staying, delay 711*.

bak *n.* 637.

bale *n.* misery 665.

bande *n.* bondage 305. Cf. Sisam, XIV. *c* 47.

bare *a.* 277; without harness 377.

baret *n.* strife, trouble 294*.

barouns *n.* 545.

barst *v.* burst 641.

be *v.* 164; *subj.* 171, 222 (*auxil.*); **ben** *ind. pl.* 7.

be *prep.* 18, 95, 97; **by** 16.

befalle *v. inf.* 773.

before *adv.* 372; *prep.* in front of 224, 624.

begge *v. inf.* 494.

begynne *v.* 131; **begynnes** 3 *sg.* 165; **began** *tr.* 455; *intr.* 355.

behoues *v.* me behoues 328.

belle *n.* 150, 681, 792.

benysoun *n.* blessing 502, 550.

bere *n.* bier 710.

bere *v. inf.* 14; **bar** *pt. sg.* 184; **bere** *pl.* 286*; **born** *pp.* 387; **iborn** 651.

besauntys *n. pl.* gold coins 312, 727.

beseme *v. subj.* 686.

bespak *v. pt. sg.* spoke (with some notion of objection and remonstrance) 393, 465.

beste *a.* 177; *for noun* 744.

betau3te *v. pt. sg.* entrusted 155.

beten *pp.* 274.

betere *a.* 811.

beþou3te *v. pt. sg. reflex.* reflected 85.

bewreye *v. inf.* betray 152, 670.

bydde *v. imper. pres.* 371; **bad** *pt.* 3 *sg.* 88, 204, 299, 369.

bynde *v. inf.* 24.

bysschop *n.* 55, 349, 405, 543; as *dat.* 303.

bysschopryche *n.* 471; see note to 349.

blede *v. inf.* 626; **bledde** *pt. sg.* 367.

blyþe 206, 378; **blyþere** *compar.* 213. See 689 (note).

blood(e) *n.* kin 28, 442; **barst on bloode** 641*.

blosme *n.* 72*, 290.

bod *v. pt. sg.* delayed 405.

body *n.* person 520*, 808.

bone *n.* boon 261, 421, 522, 731.

book *n.* 21; of ritual 56; Bible 681.

borwe, borewe *v.* go surety for 262*, 399; borrow 494.

boþe *a. and pron.* 119, 195, 209; **boþe . . . and** 5, 99, 632, 653.

boure *n.* lady's bower 77; **boures** *pl.* 525.

bow3 *n.* bough 290.

brenne *v.* burn; **brennyd** *intr. pt. sg.* 632; **don . . . brenne** 84*.

brere *n.* briar 72.

brydyl *n.* bridle 544.

brydelyd *pp.* 744.

brygge *n.* Londo(u)ne-brygge 340, 385.

bry3t *a.* 72, 107, 290, 635.

brynge(n) *v. inf.* 400, 476; **bryng** *imper. sg.* 3, 214; **brou3t** *pp.* 631, 652; **bryng on** (=of) **lyue** 141*.

broke(n) *pp.* 280, 478, 523*.

broþir, er (only from suspension) 40, 43, 132, 685; **broþer** *pl.* 58*; **breþeryn** 10, 23, 38.

brouke *v.* use, enjoy (formal) *imper. sg.* 315*.

but *conj.* except 34; **oþir, er ' . . . but** 161, 691; **but 3iff**

unless 151 ; 522 ; **but ȝet** and yet 297 ; however 177.

c

caas *n.* circumstance 432.
calle *v. inf.* 76 ; **callyd** 635, 656, 701 ; **callyd vpon** i.e. for aid 298.
can *v.* know *pr.* 3 *sg.* 101, 795 ; **cowde off** *pt.* 50 ; **cowde on** 56.
care *n.* misery 331, 380.
careful *a.* anxious 606.
caste *v. pt. sg.* 256.
castelles *n. pl.* 526.
certayn *adv.* assuredly 795.
charyte : **pur charyte** 540 ; more usually *par charyte*.
chaumbyr *n.* 122, 130, 220, 223, 286.
chere *n.* demeanour 591 ; **glad chere** rejoicing 120, 401.
ches *v. pt. sg.* chose ; **ches my way** took my way 110.
chyld *n.* 260, 283, 515, 651 ; **chylde** *dat.* 218, 622 ; **chyldryn** *pl.* 517, 604.
chyn *n.* 368*.
chyryes *n. pl.* cherries 256.
clene *a.* spotless 677 ; free from (guilt) 426, 574.
clere, cleer bright, radiant (*conv.*) of women 117, 361 ; of gold 36.
clerk *n.* an ecclesiastic 49, 56, 100, 414 ; **clerkys** *pl.* 98.
cold *a.* 610 ; *as noun* 491.
colour *n.* 71.
comaundement *n.* 280.
comaundyd *v. pt. pl.* 645.
come *v. imper. sg.* 305 ; **come** *pt. 2 and 3 sg.* 91 (r.w. **sone** *adv.*), 97, 103, 624, 751 ; *subj. sg.* 713 ; **come** *pp.* 259 (r. w. **sone**) ; **comen** 496.
comoun *a.* 265, 447.

cornfed *pp. or a.* 735.
corowne *v. inf.* 36.
c(o)rown(e), coroun *n.* 270, 444, 528, 553 ; metre against pronunciation of first **o**.
cosyn *n.* 27.
couere *v.* recover 41* ; *tr.* 331. See **keuere**.
counsayl, counseyl *n.* 78, 123, 159, 674.
countesse, countasse *n.* 117, 191, 244, 619 ; r. w. **gras** (OFr. *grace*) 65* ; **countasses** *gen.* 253 ; **cuntas** *gen.* with **sake** 208, 211.
crafft *n.* deceit 771.
crye *v. inf.* 244, 477.
cryst(e)nyd *v. pt. pl.* 655 ; *pp.* 515.
crystyndom *n.* 472, 475, 530.
croys *n.* (r. w. **voys**) 508.
cros, *n.* 17, 169, 440*, 459* ; **Charynge-cros** 335 (see 341*) ; **Brokene-cros** 546*.
cuntre *n.* 20*.
cursyd *pp.* excommunicated or (more likely) execrable 510.

d

day *n.* 263, 322, 586, 784.
Dame as title 47, 267. See **Madame**.
ded *a.* dead 134, 176, 248, 483, 604, 673, 796 ; **dede** 171.
ded(e) *n.*[1] death 180, 313*, 442, 660.
dede *n.*[2] deed 564.
deep *a.* 529.
deliueryd *pp.* 222.
deme *v.* award 683.
denyyd *v. pt. sg.* 765.
deposen *v. inf.* 142*.
dere *a.* 27, 66, 132 ; *as noun* 111 ; *as adv.* 281.

derelyng *n.* 93.
deþ *n.* death 463.
deuyl *n.* deuyl of helle (*conv.* term of abuse) 156.
deuocioun *n.* 48*.
dy(e) *v. inf.* 143 (r. w. slyly), 167, 812; deye *subj. pr. sg.* 793; dyyd *pt. sg.* 32*; deyde 732.
dignyte *n.* status 676. See *N.E.D. dignity* sb.²
dyȝt *pp.* prepared 463*.
dyke *n.* ditch 480; back-stop k proved from rhyme with heretyke; usual form in *Gen. and Exod.*
dyne *v.* 328; dynyd *pp.* 330.
dynt *n.* blow 292.
dyshonour *n.* 140.
dyuers *a.* different 20.
dome, doom(e) *n.* judgement 562, 575, 683; penalty 565, 812*.
do(n), doo *v.* 84, 306; dos 3 *sg. pr. ind.* 163; doo *imper. pr. sg.* 442, 707; dede (OE. dǽd-, dēd-) *pt. sg.* 743; as *auxil.* 24, 372; don .. brenne 84; doo to vnderstand give (one) to understand 163, 269; done (*pp.*) in presoun 708.
dool *n.* grief 367; lamentation 287. Mannyng (*Chron.* 165) has the form *doole.*
douȝtyr *n.* 260.
doun *adv.* 275, 277, 459.
drawe *v. tr.* 525; *intr.* 645*; drowȝ *pt. sg.* 115; drowen *pl.* 804*; drawen *pp.* 271, 457, 698; to-drawe (r. w. slawe) 706.
drede *v.* 565, 575.
drede *n.* 608, 629.
drynk *n.* 170.
drynke *v.* 329.
drouȝþe *n.* drought 491.

dubbyng *n.* conferring of knighthood 233.
dunioun *n.* dungeon 529.
durste *v. pt.* 3 *sg.* 808.
dwel(le) *v.* 11, 231, 428.
dwellyng *n.* wiþouten ony dwellyng without delay (*conv.*) 96*.

e

eemes *n. gen.* uncle's 29, 34.
eerl *n.* 40, 43, 61*, 73; eerlys *gen. sg.* 194.
eerldom(e) *n.* 309, 719.
efft *adv.* again 618.
eke *adv.* 470, 637.
eldest(e) *a.* 25, 40.
ende *v. intr. inf.* 8.
ende *n.* end 375*; part 221*.
endyng *n.* death 811.
endure *v. inf.* 86.
enquere *v. inf.* inquire 446.
entyrdytyd *pp.* placed under interdict 513*.
entryd *v. pt. sg.* 336, 498.
enuye, envye *n.* 79, 800.
er *adv.* earlier 353*.
erchebysschop *n.* 393.
erly *adv.* 99*.
euele *a.* euele at ayse (cf. *ille at ayse*) 295.
euensong(e) *n.* 302, 355, 382.
euere *adv.* 149.
euermare *adv.* 23.

f

fadyr *n.* 2, 293, 394, 599.
fayne *a.* glad 119; fayn off 520.
fayr *a.* 107; fayre perhaps wk. 214.
fayr *adv.* weel and fayr as one should expect (*conv.*) 31*.
falle *v. inf.* 275; fel *pt. sg.* 787; felle 277, 419; fyl *pl.* 368; fel for appertained to

584; **fel** of a benefice, to revert to a superior (*N.E.D. fall* v. 41a) 53.

fals(e) *a.* 83, 131, 155; in **fals traytour** the *conv. a.* from OFr. for the villain of the romances untrue to obligations, feudal or other 139.

falsnesse *n.* treachery 8, 762.

fande *v. inf.* try 752*.

fare *v. inf.* 89, 188, 236; **faryth** *pr.* 3 *sg.* 100, **fares** 106; **fare** *pr. pl.* 118.

faste *adv.* securely 242; **fast** 237, 462; **also fast as þay may** (*conv.*) 370; cf. 334.

fatte *a.* 735.

fee *n.* 318.

felawe *n.* 726.

felle *v. inf.* cut down 808*.

ferde *v. pt. sg.* behaved (sense rare; cf. *Havelok* 2411) 250.

fere *n.* 129: see **in fere**.

ferþe *a.* fourth 49.

feteryd *pp.* 242.

fette *v. inf.* fetch 190, 703; **fetten** *pl.* 579, 621.

fyfftene *a.* 67.

fyffti *a.* 324*.

fynde *v. inf.* 454; **fynde** *ind. pl.* 21; **fynde** *subj. pr. sg.* 376; **fand(e)** *pt. sg.* 202, 714.

fyr *n.* 568, 581, 603, 610; **feer** 631*.

fyue *a.* 698*; MS. **ffyue and twenti** 324*.

flee *v. imper. sg.* 461.

folewe *v. ind. pr. pl.* 530.

fonge *v. inf.* 299.

foo *n.* 249, 627.

foode *n.* child 650.

foot *n.* 282, 408; **foot and hand** (OE. *fōtum and handum*) 588, 612, 642.

for *prep.* 22, 23, 149, 416, 667*; **for to** 4, 324, 812.

for *conj.* 136, 139*, 732.

forbede *v.* refuse *ind.* 1 *sg.* with *dat. of person* 472.

forcursyd *pp.* condemned 425; rare, only two instances in *N.E.D.*, from Peterborough Chronicle and Cursor Mundi.

forest *n.* 16.

forȝelde *v.* requite *subj.* 3 *sg.* 232, 319.

forlorn *pp.* done for 388.

forþ *adv.* 200, 579; forward 129, 769.

forþynkes *v. impers. pr.* repent 219.

forwondryd *pp.* amazed 432; perhaps a northerly word; examples in *N.E.D.* from Orm, Cursor Mundi, Barbour.

founde *v. inf.* hasten 702.

foundelyng *n.* 186*.

fount-ston *n.* baptismal font 678*.

foure *a.* 10, 13.

fourty *a.* 752.

fraynyd *v. pt. sg.* asked 94.

free *a.* good (*conv.*, often in rhyme) 229, 424, 654.

frende *n.* 253.

fresch *a.* 376.

fro *prep.* 267; **fro þe lengþe** 633*, 786.

from *prep.* 313, 382*.

ful *adv.* 81, 92, 198, 323.

fullyche *adv.* 187.

ġ

ġan *v. auxil. pt. sg.* 41, 76, 131, 323, 606, 671; **ġan** *pl.* 16; **ġunne** *pl.* 223, 236, 545.

ġange *v.* **on ġrounde** (allit. phrase for 'live') 743.

ġare *v.* **ġarte** *pt. sg.* 251; *pl.* 428; **ġare cry** cause (men) to 477; **ġare hym schryuen** 772*.

ġate *n.* way 105.
ġerlondes *n. pl.* 256 ; the spelling perhaps on analogy of
lond, land.
ġete *v. inf.* 487 ; ġetyst 2 *sg.*
719; ġat *pt.* 65; ġete *pp.* 725.
ġeue(n) *v. inf.* 402, 562 ; ġeue
ind. pr. 1 *sg.* 657 ; ġeue *subj.*
pr. 3 *sg.* 180 ; ġaff *pt. sg.* 39,
46, 54, 460.
ġylt *n.* 426, 574.
ġylty *a.* 564.
ġyltles *a.* 423.
ġynne *n.* trickery 771.
ġlad(e) *a.* ġlad chere 120, 401 ;
made hym (*reflex.*) ġlade
723 ; ġladde *adv.* 797.
ġladyd *pp.* 234.
ġlede *n.* burning coal (*conv.*)
572*, 782.
ġloues *n. pl.* 493.
ġod *n.* God 180, 403* ; ġoddys
gen. sg. 50, 58, 101.
ġold *n.* 149, 312, 318.
ġon *v. inf.* (r. w. ston) 775 ;
ġoo 78 ; ġos (r. w. aros)
pr. 3 *sg.* 412* ; ġoþ 218 ;
ġoo *imper. sg.* 267 ; ġon
(r. w. ston) *pp.* 764 ; iġon
come (r. w. anon) 95 ; ġan
(r. w. tan) 769* ; ġoo þe way
586, 598, 684 ; ġoþ with
chylde 218, 622.
ġood *a.* 60, 201, 207, 727 ;
ġoode (hors) *pl.* 730 ; do me
ġoode be beneficial to 170.
ġost *n.* holy ġost 2.
ġostly *a.* spiritual 394, 436, 466.
ġrace, ġras *n.* in religious
sense 4 ; þorwȝ ġoddys
ġras (*conv.* expression of
piety) 58*, 64*.
ġraunte *v. imper. sg.* 731 ;
subj. pr. sg. 421 ; ġrauntyd
pp. 233, 403*.
ġret *a.* 45, 48 ; with chylde
218, 622 (*perhaps adv.*).

ġretes *v. pr.* 3 *sg.* 112.
ġround *n.* 648 ; on ġrounde
(*conv.*) on earth 743 ; vpon
þe ġrounde 390*.

ȝ

ȝare *a.* ready 88, 235, 371 ;
only in phrase make hem
ȝare.
ȝe *pron.* 63 ; ȝow *dat.* 10 ;
ȝoure *poss. a.* 510 ; for *sg.*
450, 730, 733 ; to a superior
246*, 248, 249.
ȝede *v. pt. r. w.* wede 599, 605,
733 ; ȝode r. w. foode 647.
ȝelle *v. inf.* shriek 425.
ȝerde *n.* stick 274.
ȝere *n. pl.* years 126, 404.
ȝiff *conj.* (usually with *subj.*)
483, 564 ; ȝiff þat 108, 314,
399, 423* ; but ȝiff 151, 450.
ȝistyrday *adv.* 390 ; ȝystyrday 732.
ȝit *adv.* moreover 193 ; none
the less 278 ; even now 488 ;
all the same 741 ; *conj.* and
ȝit 618 ; but ȝit 297.

h

hale *a.* keep counseyl hale
preserve confidence entire
674 (r. w. tale).
halewes *v.* 3 *sg.* 783 ; halewid
pt. sg. 585.
halle *n.* 77*, 202, 757*.
halff *a.* 657 ; *adv.* 366.
hand *n.* 154*, 203 ; took cros
on hande 440* ; stronge
men of hond doughty men
487* ; make þe kyng at
hande 749*.
hongyd *v. pt. pl.* 806 ; *pp.* 457,
697 ; hangyd 271 ; ihangyd
706.

hard *a.* 321, 325*, 577 ; **harde**
pl. 636.

hardy *a.* bold 807.

harewyd *v. pt.* 2 *sg.* only in
phrase **harewyd helle** 422 ;
harewede 3 *sg.* 595.

haue *v. inf.* 135, 475 ; **I haue**
669 ; **þou hast** 137, 158 ;
haue we 247 ; **hadde** *pt. sg.*
79 ; **hade** (r. w. **made**) 699*,
791 ; **haue** *imper. sg.* 727 ; *pl.*
608; **haue good day** a salutation 497*, 747.

he *pron.* 30, 37 ; **hym** *acc.* 35 ;
reflex. 9, 32*, 723, 772 ; *dat.*
46, 54 ; **hymseluen** *reflex.*
59 ; **hymselff** *nom.* 296 ;
dat. 524 ; **hys** *poss. a.* 29.

hede *n.* heed 207.

hedyr-come *n.* (r. w. eerldome) coming hither 728.

heyȝe, hyȝe *a.* high 592, 616,
806 (r. w. yȝe, lye, dye).

heyr *n.* heir 763. See **ayr.**

helle *n.* 156, 595.

hende *a.* courteous, gracious
pl. 7 ; *as noun* **þat hende**
224* ; **hende in halle** 558*.

hent *pp.* 241.

here, hem *prons. used as poss.
and dat.* (*or acc.*) *of* þey ;
here 15, 22, 69, 75, 501 ;
hem *dat.* 25 ; *acc.* 74 ; *reflex.*
23, 88, 235.

here *pron. fem. acc.* 636 ; *dat.*
225, 255 ; **here** *poss. a.* 277,
630.

here *adv.* 537 ; **hereoff** 543.

here *v. inf.* 123 ; **herde** *pt. sg.*
273.

heretyke *n.* 481.

herte *n. dat.* 81, 120, 217,
606.

hete, hyȝt ; **I ȝow hyȝt** I as-
sure you (*conv.*) 311 ; **hete**
337, 805 ; **hyȝt** *pp.* called
26 ; **hoten** 185. For the

vowels see Tolkien's *Glossary*
to Sisam.

heuene *n.* 6 *acc.* ; 319 *dat.* ;
heuene-kyng either OE.
heofoncyning or *heofona cyn-
ing* 810.

hyde *v.* **nouȝt for to hyde**
(*conv.*) 536*.

hydous *a.* awful 603.

hyȝ *n.* **on hyȝ** in haste 716.

hyȝe *v.* hasten ; **hyes** 3 sg. 201 ;
hyȝe þe *imper.* 462.

holde *v.* **holde it for no wene**
do not doubt it 680.

holewe *a.* 527.

holy *a.* holy 2, 5, 552.

hom *adv.* homewards 181.

hool (*a.*) **and sound** 653.

hors *n.* 200, 314, 338, 376 ;
hors *pl.* 698*, 730, 802.

hosyn, en 583, 601.

hou *adv. interrog.* 8, 100.

houen *pp.* raised 678*.

hundryd *a. or n.* 126, 312.

hungyr *n.* 490.

i

I *pron.* 10, 440 ; **me** *acc.* 137 ;
dat. 19, 133 ; *with impers.
verbs* 219, 249, 323, 328 ; **my**
poss. 93 ; **myn** 234, 735.

iblessyd *pp.* 560, 650, 662.

iborn *pp.* 289, 651.

igon *pp.* 95, 622.

igrauntyd *pp.* 268.

yȝe *n.* eye 803 ; **eyen** *pl.* 458,
563, 788.

ihangyd *pp.* 706.

iholpe *pp.* helped 138.

ylkan *pron.* (r. w. tan *pp.*) each
one 496* ; **ylkon** 25*.

ylke *a.* 20, 375 ; **ylke a** 477,
742, 804.

imaad *pp.* 187.

in *prep.* 17, 57, 120, 250, 352,
756 ; **yn** 11.

in fere together 129 · see
N.E.D. yfere adv.
inne *adv. (or post-prep.)* 359.
inowȝ *adj.* much 287 ; *adv.*
enough, quite 116*, 610.
insame *adv.* together 754, 769.
into *prep.* 53.
iredde, *pp.* read 366.
is *v. sg.* 1*, 181, 720.
it *pron.* 8 ; *anticipating subj.*
15, *clause* 193, 427 ; *pleonas-*
tic 325 ; *impers.* 228, 322 ;
indef. 686.
iwent *pp.* gone 181.
iwreten *pp.* written 21.

k

kepe *v. imper. sg.* 674.
keuere *v. inf. tr.* recover 380 ;
see **couere.**
kyn *n.* 12*, 221 ; **kynne** *dat.*
362.
kynde *n.* proper occupation
15 ; see *N.E.D.* kind sb. 2b.
MS. **kynde** 12*.
kyng *n.* 32, 392* ; **kyngys** *gen.*
sg. 27, 28 ; **kyng** *dat.* 765.
kyrke *n.* 5 ; *dat.* 412, 417 ;
kyrkys *pl.* 478.
kyssyd *pp.* 759.
knaue *n.* boy 474.
knaue-chyld *n.* male child
289 ; **-chyldren** *pl.* 66.
knawe *v. inf.* 770, 780 ; **knowe**
I *ind.* 146 ; **knowest þou**
ind. 102.
knees *n. pl.* 277, 419, 501,
549.
knelyd *v. pt. sg.* 418, 549, 648 ;
kneleden *pl.* 501.
knyȝt *n.* 106, 410 ; **knyȝt** *per-*
haps pl. 195. ·

l

lady *n.* 621 ; **ladyys** *pl.* 285,
647.

lay *v. tr. imper. sg.* 459.
layne *v. inf.* hide ; (it) **is nouȝt**
to layne (*conv.* in tail-rhyme
poems) 118.
land *n.* 657 ; **landys** *gen.* 646 ;
lande, land *dat.* 125, 139.
laste *a. for n.* **at þe laste** 31,
257.
late *adv.* 99*.
lawe *n.* 646.
lede *v. inf.* 251, 392*, 788 ;
ledes *ind.* 3 *sg.* 9.
leff *n.* leaf 18*.
lende *v. inf.* remain (cf. *Egla-*
mour (Camb. MS.). 609) 178 ;
lende *imper. sg.* give 730.
lene *v. imper. sg.* 4 ; **lent** *pt.*
sg. 452.
lengþe *n.* 633*, 786.
lere *v. pr.* 1 *sg.* instruct 707.
les *n.* falsehood ; **wiþouten**
les (*conv.*) truly 109.
lese *v. inf.* lose 740.
lesyng *n.* lie 700, 724, 762 ;
lesyngys *pl.* 83, 131.
lete *v.* ; **leet** *pt.* 3 *sg.* 275, 626 ;
lat *imper.* 627, 673, 775 ; **lat**
be cease 396 ; **lete** *imper.*
desist 760.
lette *v. intr.* delay 197, 230.
lettyng *n.* delay 215*.
lettre *n.* 193, 203, 206, 299 ;
lettrys *pl.* 14 ; *as sg.* 187* ;
224.
leuande *pres. part.* r. w. **hande**
living 437.
leue *n.* leave 179, 495.
leue *v.*¹ *inf.* 492.
leue *v.*² allow ; *imper. sg.* 427,
811.
leue *v.*³ live ; *inf.* 316, 403,
658 ; **leuyd** *pt. sg.* 695.
lyche *a.* like 57.
lye n. 809.
lyff *n.* 74, 135* ; **lyuys** *pl.*
559 ; **on lyue** alive 695 ; **on**
(=of) **lyue** 141*.

lygge *v. intr.* 480, 527 ; **lay** *pt.*
  sg. dwelt 349.
ly3t *adv.* nimbly 407.
ly3t *adv.* brightly 632.
ly3t *v. pr. pl.* alight 756.
lylye-flour *n.* 70.
lynde *n.* lime-tree (*conv.*) 18*.
lyng *v. inf.* remain 535 ; r. w.
  ryng ; = *Eglamour* (Cotton
  MS.) 606 ; from ON. *lengja.*
lystnes *v. imper. pl.* 7.
lyte *adv.* 799.
lytyl *a.* 288.
long *a.* **long and wide** in
  length and breadth 542,
  554.
longe *adv.* 316, 355 ; **lengere**
  compar. 178, 231.
lord *n.* 42, 104 ; (the) Lord 1 ;
  lordys *pl.* 499.
lordyngys *n. pl.* often used by
  minstrels 7.
look *v. inf.* 606 ; **loke** *imper. sg.*
  375 ; **lokyd** *pt. sg.* 430.
los *n.* loss 341*.
loue *v. inf.* 5 ; **louede** *pt. sg.*
  74 ; **louyd** 799.
lowde *adv.* 244.
lowe *a.* 527.
low3 *v. pt. pl.* (r. w. **inow3**)
  laughed 609.

m

madame *n.* as title 315.
make(n) *v. inf.* 35, 88, 206 ;
  made *pt. sg.* 40, 43, 55, 664 ;
  madyst 2 *sg.* 157 ; **made**
  pp. r. w. **glade** 724 ; **maad**
  429, 630, 778 ; **makyd me
  a man** 137*.
may *v. ind. and subj.* ; 86, 220 ;
  2 *sg.* 213 ; *pl. pr.* '370, 565 ;
  we mowe 265 ; **my3te**
  pt. sg. 347, 454, 771 ; *pl.*
  570 ; **my3t** 655 ; **my3ten**
  780.

maydenys *n. pl.* 285.
maydynchyld *n.* 474 ; OE.
  mægdencild.
man *n.* 20, 45, 137*, 199 ;
  men *pl.* 88 ; *impers.* 68,
  570, 655, 780 (possibly).
maneres *n. pl.* manors 373.
manye *a.* 295.
markys *n. pl.* coins 659.
masse *n.* Mass 302.
masse-book *n.* 150.
meete *n.* food 170*.
mene *v. inf.* signify 573.
menyng *gerund*, complaining
  396.
mercy *n.* as exclamation 245.
merye *a.* 635 ; **mery** *adv.* 98*,
  301.
messanger(e) *n.* 182, 197, 199,
  701 ; **messanger** *dat.* 741 ;
  messangeres *pl.* 13*.
met(e) *a.* appropriate 583*,
  601.
mete *v. inf.* 16 ; **I mete** *pres.
  for fut.* 463 ; **mette** *pt. sg.*
  92 ; *pl.* 239, 758.
metyng *n.* 22.
my3t *n.* 590 ; 1* (on which see
  Z's parallels, p. 343).
mykyl *a.* 113, 140, 397 ;
  (*Prompt.*) ; **mekyl** 50, 101,
  400 ; (Lydgate).
mylde *a.* gentle 217, 591, 621 ;
  mylde chere humble demeanour 507*.
myle *n. sg. for pl.* 752 ; **mylys**
  pl. 375 ; **myles** 321.
myracle *n.* 617*.
myre *n.* mire 344 ; see note to
  341.
mytyr *n.* 460, 470.
modyr *n.* 596.
mon *n.* complaint ; **made . . .
  mone** (*conv.*) 729.
mone *n.* moon 456.
moo *a. for n.* more 409.
moo *adv.* 173.

moot *v.*may 1 *sg.*135; 2 *sg.*145,
438, 560 ;3 *sg.* 427. Common
in strong asseverations, as **so
moot I the** 175.

more *a. for n.* 306.

moregeue *n.* morning-gift 315;
properly, the gift from husband to wife on wedding
morning, sometimes dowry.

morwen n. 411.

mos *n.* bog 344 ; note to 341.

most *a.* 1*.

mouþe : schryffte of mouþe
688.

n

nay *adv.* 148 ; used as noun
with **nykkyd** 503.

name *n.* 44, 51, 682.

nan, non *pron.* 33, 57, 125,
580* (r. w. **Egelan**).

ne *adv.* nor 170*, 771.

nede *n.* 397, 439, 742 ; **good
at nede** 389.

ney3yd *v. pt. sg.* approached ;
ney3yd . . . **nere** was closely
related 30*. ONorthumb.
(ge)nēhwiga; Gothic *nēhwjan*.

neyþer *adv.* 474, 722 ; **neyþer**
. . . **neyþer** 504 ; **neþer** (so
spelt) . . . **ne** 410.

nere *adv. compar.* 30.

nerhande *adv.* nearly 327 ; a
northerly word.

neuere *adv.* 125, 152.

nexte *a. perhaps wk.* 263.

nykkyd *v. pt. sg.* ; . . . **with
nay** said no to 503* ; see
Tolkien's *Glossary*.

nyne *a.* 381, 571.

no *adv.* 231.

no *adj.* 215 ; **non** (before vowel)
464.

noble *a.* noble 362 ; mostly a
conv. epithet of compliment
100, 106, 338, 339 ; **nobyl**
500, 732.

nolde *v. pt. sg.* 343.

non *(adv.)* **er** no earlier 353*.

noone, none *n.* noon *(conv.)*
228*, 258, 451.

nose *n.* 641.

noþyng *adv.* not at all 357, 377,
797.

nou3t *n.* nothing 492, 773.

nou3t(e) *adv.* 35, 86, 760*.

now *adv.* 37, 181, 324, 627.

o

of(f) *prep.* 1 ; 8, 10, 50* ; 20,
45, 272, 362 ; 28 ; by 432,
by means of 292 ; for 736 ;
praye off (Fr. *prier de*) 502.

offeryd *v. pt.* 3 *pl.* 591*, 615.

offtensyþe *a.* often 76. See
N.E.D. often adj. and adv. C,
with nouns denoting time.

old *a.* 67, 480.

on *prep.* 72, 101*, 132 ; 56,
174 ; **on lyue** alive 695, out
of life 141* ; **on bloode**
641*.

on *pron.* 577, 730 ; **þat on** the
one (opposed to 'the other')
67.

ony *a.* any 96, 189.

or *conj.* 260.

or *prep.* before 451 ; *conj.* 228,
355 ; **or þat** 332, 793.

orysoun *n.* 552.

oþer, ir *a.* 43 ; *pron.* 160 ;
non oþir nothing different
464 ; **þat oþer** the other 68.

oþis *n. pl.* oaths 456.

ou3t *adv.* at all 97, 102.

ou3te *v. pt. sg.* 206.

ouyr *prep.* 368.

out *adv.* 3, 220.

owne *a.* 47, 442.

p

payne *n.* 168 ; **paynys** *pl.* 264,
639.

palays *n.* 358, 756.

palfray *n.* 369 ; **palfrays** *pl.* 381.

parlement *n.* Parliament 266*, 448.

pas *n.* path 640.

passyd *pp.* 640 ; *impers.* 327.

pere *n.* 33, 69, 704 ; **peres** *pl.* 767.

playne *a.* full 266*, 448.

plas *n.* 652*.

plente *n.* good plente in great abundance 727.

plyȝt *v.* 151, *pp.* 158.

plowȝ-lenȝe 781 ; see next.

plowȝ-lengþe *n.* a distance, the length of a plough (or ploughshare), 571*.

poysoun *v. inf.* 166.

pore *a.* poor 41.

pounde *n. pl.* 391, 659.

power *n.* 676.

praye *v. inf.* 416, 587 ; *imper. sg.* 304 ; **prayes** 3 *sg.* 540 ; **prayde** *pt.* 3 *sg.* 278 ; **prayden off** *pl.* begged for 502.

prayer *n.* 429, 630* (note to 625).

preest *n.* 414, 473.

presoun *n.* 251, 424, 523, 708.

preste *a.* ready 745.

preue *v.* prove 776.

prime *n.* first division of the day; **passyd prime**, i.e. from about 9 a.m. to 10 a.m. 327 ; see note to 328.

pur (charyte): 540 ; cf. OFr. *pour*; see *N.E.D. par* prep. b.

q

quyk *a.* alive 628.

qweer *n.* choir 430.

qwene *n.* 254, 273, 286, 307.

r

rayse *v. inf.* 294*.

rauȝte *v. pt. sg.* stretched 154.

rawe *n.* row ; **on rawe** (*conv.*) in succession 571, 781.

red *a.* 71, 291*, 312 ; **rede** 582, 600.

rede, read *v. inf.* counsel 539 ; **wysse and rede** (cf. *Havelok* 104) direct 661 ; read 56, 204, 224 ; **we rede** *ind.* 383, 569, 623 ; **radde** 712* ; **i-redde** *pp.* 366.

red(e) *n.* counsel, plan 441,672 ; **do þy beste rede** 177* ; **can non oþer red** see nothing else for it 795.

redy *a.* 353.

renoun *n.* **off gret renoun** (*conv.*) 45, 350, and others.

reues *v. ind. pr.* 2 *sg.* deprivest 471 ; **refft** *pp.* 511.

rewe *v. impers.* 451.

ryche, ryke powerful 60, 349*.

ryde *v. inf.* 324, 545 ; **he rydes** 198 ; **ryde** *imper. sg.* 539 ; **rod** *pt.* 3 *sg.* 335, 352, 406 ; *pl.* r. w. **abood** 754 ; **reden** *pp.* 322.

ryȝt *n.* right 317 ; justice 587.

ryȝt *a.* **ryȝt doom** 683 ; **ryȝte** (wk.) way exact 684.

ryȝt *adv.* 112, 166 ; 198 ; 283, 326.

ryng *n.* 460, 470, 534.

roode, rode *n.* the Cross 169, 418 ; **on rode** 644.

romaunce *n.* 383, 569, 623, 779 ; see note to 19.

rose *n.* 71.

runggen *v. pt.* 3 *pl.* 351.

s

sadele *v. inf.* 369 ; **sadelyd** *pp.* 744.

say *v. inf.* 372 ; **says** 3 *sg.* 148 ; **sayde** *pt. sg.* 93, 145 ; **sayden** *pl.* 497, 533 ; **sayd(e)** *pp.* 777, 801.

sake *n.* **for here sake** 82*;
for þe cuntas sake 208.

sale *n.* hall 668*.

saue *v. inf.* 313; **sauyd** *pp.*
559, 672.

scarlet(e) *n.* of clothes 582*,
600.

schal *v.* 1 *sg.* 124; **schalle**
(r. w. **alle**) 2 *sg.* 281; **schalt**
143, 480; **schal** 3 *sg.* 153,
schole 784*; **schal** *pl.* 598;
schole 173, 271, 527; **schol-**
en 529; **scholde** *pt.* 134, 586,
702, 763.

schame *n.* disgrace 180; ig-
nominy 566*.

sche *pron. fem.* 216, 220, 256,
622.

schent *pp.* confounded 449.

schewe *v. inf.* 566*; **schewyd**
pp. 617*.

schod *pp.* 377.

schoon *n. pl.* 583, 601.

schourys *n. pl.* labour-pains
636*.

schryffte off mouþe auricular
confession 688.

schryuen *pp.* 772*.

se(e) *v. inf.* 134, 229, 347;
semely to se (*conv.*) 37;
see *ind. pr.* 1 *sg.* 146; **saw3**
pt. sg. 431; *pl.* 589, 612.

seel *n.* of a letter 196.

seynt *n.* 592, 649, 761.

semely *a.* 37 (*conv.*).

sene *a. as pp.* 427*.

sent *n.* 265 *see* **asent**.

sent(e) *pp.* 182, 240.

sere *n.* Sir 62, 85.

sertaynly *adv.* 160, 384, 690.

sese *v.* put in legal possession,
generally of land 310.

sette *v. inf.* 529; **sette** *pt.* 3 *sg.*
196; **set** *pp.* 570, 780.

sybbe *a.* related 12*.

sy3te *n.* 216, 462, 638*.

syngge *v. inf.* sing (in Divine

service) 473; **syngen** *pr. pl.*
98, 301.

synne *n.* 3, 772.

syt *v.* 3 *sg.* [OE. (WS) *sitt* <
sitþ] 420.

siþ *conj.* since 322, 440.

syþe *n. as pl.* 585; **syþis**
783.

siþþen, seþþen, yn *adv.* afterwards 638, 754, 805.

slakyd *pp.* slaked 639.

slepe *v. pr.* 1 *sg.* 332.

slyly *adv.* 142*, 166.

sloo *v.* slay; *inf.* 84 (r. w. **woo**),
246; **slon** (r. w. **non**) 518;
slow3 *pt. sg.* 283, 293, 763;
slayne (r. w. **layne**) *pp.* 162;
slawe (r. w. **to-drawe**) 705.

smerte *adv.* 789; **smertly**
467.

so(o) *adv.* 4, 567; 135; 36, 117,
248; 70.

sodaynly *adv.* 143, 167.

sone *n.* son 2, 29, 34, 260;
sones *pl.* 75, 107; **soones**
(14th cent. form; see *N.E.D.*)
171.

sone, soone immediately 92,
225, 523; **soone anon** 94;
so soone 248.

sore *adv.* grievously 323.

sorrere *a. compar.* more
grievous 565.

sorwe *n.* 400, 491, 524; **soule**
in sorwe in torments (of
Hell) 485.

soule *n.* 485.

sound *a.* 653.

soþe *n.* truth 699; **forsoþe**
326, 343.

spare *v.* **for noþing þat ye**
spare (*conv.*) spare for nothing 374*; **spared he nou3t**
for myre ne mos went as
fast as he could 344.

spase of time 288.

spede *v. inf.* fare 785; in

asseverations 578 ; **weel
moot þou spede** well met
438.

spede n. speed, only in adv.
phrase ; (a) **ful good speed**
201, 363 ; **good spede** 751.
From OE. spēdum (dat.)
fēran, go speedily, the OE.
word otherwise meaning
' success '.

speke v. 90, 183, 221 : **spak**
pt. 1 sg. 111, 3 sg. 507 ;
spoken pl. 531.

sporys n. pl. spurs 750.

sprynge v. inf. 87* ; **sprong,
sprange** pt. sg. 381, 746.

squyer n. 253, 410.

staff n. bishop's staff 459.

stande v. inf. 431 ; **stood** pt.
3 sg. 17, 634 ; pl. 609*.

state n. 102.

stede n.¹ place 55 ; **on þat
stede** 174* ; **in þat stede**
there 250 ; note to 652.

stede n.² steed 386, 396, 732,
741.

sterte v. pt. or pr. pl. 790.

stylle adv. 634.

stoken pp. stopped, shut or
stabbed, stuck 479*.

ston n. 546.

story n. 19.

stounde n. hour 662.

strete n. street 804 : highway
17.

strong a. severe 490 ; **stronge**
pl. 264 ; **stronge men of
honde** men formidable in
combat 487* ; **stronge** adv.
636.

strook v. pt. 3 sg. struck 750.

suffryd v. pt. 3 sg. 168.

sunne n. sun 456, 722.

sustyr n. 47, 108, 251.

swere v. ind. 1 sg. 681 ; **swoor**
pt. sg. 169, 437, 675 : pl. 23 :
sworn pp. 669.

swete a. dear 759 ; MS. **swete**
124*.

swych(e) a. 125, 812 ; note to
124 ; form in Prompt. Parv.

swylk(e) a. + a 562, 740 ; see
Gen. and Exod. ; Norf. Gilds.

swynke v. **gan me** (reflex.)
swynke toiled 323.

swyþe adv. also **swyþe** at
once 205.

swownyd v. pt. sg. swooned
284 ; pl. 604.

t

tayde pp. tied 802*.

take v. ; **takes** ind. pr. 3 sg.
179, 200*, 412 ; **take** imper.
sg. 207, 303 ; **took** pt. 3 sg.
gave 203 ; **token** pl. 582 ;
tooke 600 ; **took** 636 ; **tan**
(r. w. **gan**) pp. 495, 509, 768.

tale n. tale 153, 671.

teeres n. pl. tears 275, 368.

tel(le) v. inf. 10, 124 ; **telles**
3 sg. 19 ; **telle** imper. sg.
147 ; **tolde** pt. sg. 255 ; pl.
225 ; **tolde** pp. 193.

tydande n. news 124 ; from
OSw. tiþande.

tyde n. time ; **þat tyde** (conv.)
then 551.

tydyngys n. news 225, 255.

tyl(le) prep. (often northern
variant of **to**) 122*, 605,
647 ; 263, 445 ; **tyl(l)** conj.
222 ; with þat 171, 713.

to adv. too 799.

today adv. 685.

to-drawe pp. drawn asunder
706.

tofore prep. in front of 418.

tomorwen n. tomorrow 228 ;
tomorn 271, 445.

tonyȝt adv. 320.

toun n. 42, 347.

tour n. 42* ; **toures** pl. 526.

tourne *v. tr. inf.* 343 ; **turnys** 3 *sg.* 544; **turne** *imper.* change 441 ; *intr.* turn back 519.

trayne *n.* stratagem 165.

traytour *n.* 128, 139, 148, 181, 294, 700, 760.

trauayle *n.* toil 341*.

trewe *a.* faithful 63 ; **trewere** 580 ; **treweste** 694.

trewely *adv.* truly 311 ; *conv.* 24*.

trew(e)þe *n.* truth 776 ; troth 24 ; **trowþe** 151, 155.

trynyte *n.* the Trinity 420.

trowe *v. imper. sg.* (allit. with **trustly**) believe 679.

trustly *adv.* with confidence 679*.

twoo *a.* 66, 75.

þ

þey, þay *pron. pl.* 13, 370 ; for oblique cases see **here** *pron.*

þankyd *v. pt. sg. and pl.* 590, 595, 614, 644, 724.

þan(ne) *adv.* then 127, 143, 693 (r. w. **man**), 85, 738 ; **þenne** 33.

þan(ne) *adv.* than 307, 455, 566.

thar *v. pr.* 3 *sg. impers.* **hem thar** they need 575.

þare *adv.* r. w. **mare** there 22*.

þat *demons. pron.* 54, 55, 56, 100, 216, 586 ; **by þat** by that time 496.

þat *pron. rel. indeclin.* 1, 61, 101 ; as object 460, 685.

þat *conj.* 216, 248 ; 6 ; 702 ; 655, 122, 134 ; with princ. cl. 374*.

þe *def. artic.* 19 ; (*with n. in dat.*) 303 ; **þat** *before vowels esp.* **þat on, þat oþer** 43, 67, 68 ; merging into *demons.* 80.

þe *adv.* by so much 213, 785 ; OE. **þē** (**þӯ**).

þedyr *adv.* thither 547. Similar spellings in Sisam are from *Handlyng Synne, Gest Hystoriale, Towneley Play*.

the(e) *v.* (in asseverations) 145, 175, 666, 675 ; always *conv.*

þere *adv.* 111, 617 (r. w. **were**), 756 ; **þer** *indef.* 33, 125, 215, 473 ; *relat.* 98, 301 ; **þere þat** 359, 620 ; **þereat** 79 ; **þerfore** 30 ; **þerein** 9, *relat.* 349 ; **þeretoo** 207 ; in addition 324 ; **þerevpon** 679*.

þing *n.* 325 ; creature 192 ; **alle þyng** *sg. or pl.* 452.

þynk *v. imper. sg.* 397 ; **þouȝte** *pt. sg.* 82 ; from OE. *þencan* think.

þynke *v.* from OE. *þyncan* seem ; **me þynkiþ** 249 ; **me þynke** r. w. **swynke** (*inf.*) 326*.

þyrst *n.* 490 ; OE. *þurst*, the ME. vowel perhaps from OE. *þyrstan v.*

þis *a.* (*and pron.*) *sg.* 125, 136, 577*, 651, 673* ; **þese** *pl.* 273 ; **þis** *sg. or pl.* 126.

þo(o) *adv.* then 568, 597, 778.

þou *pron.* 2 *sg. nom.* 97, 102, 207 ; **þe(e)** *acc. and dat.* 112, 124, 134, 140, 683* ; **þi, þy, þyn** (before vowels and *h*) *poss.* 121, 139, 177, 209, 315 ; **þyselff** *nom.* 684.

þouȝ *conj.* 307, 686.

þorn *n.* 270, 444 ; 479*.

þorwȝ *prep.* 58, 64, 477.

þorwȝout *adv.* 611.

þre(e) *a.* 38, 697*.

þrydde *a. as n.* 633*, 786.

þrytty *a.* 321.

þryue, þryff *v.* 138 (note to 135) ; 692 (in asseveration ; cf. **thee**), *conv.*

þus *adv.* 41, 58, 86, 294.

v

vacant *a.* 52.

verrayment *adv.* assuredly 242, 279.

vnblemeschyd *pp.* unblemished, free from injury or mark (of ordeal) 588, 612, 642.

vnblyue *a.* not ready, unwilling, or, not glad, not eager 689*.

vncouþe *a.* strange, foreign (of lands) 486.

vndernbelle *n.* (*orig.*) midmorning (9 a.m.), (later) 9–12 a.m., but often applied vaguely (Tolkien's *Glossary*). At 351 probably between 9 and 10 a.m.

vndyr *prep.* 18, 394.

vndyrstande *v.* 269, 308 ; **vndyrstood** *pt.* 1 *sg.* 29* (*conv.*)

vnto *prep.* to 89 ; until 404.

voys *n.* 507.

vp *adv.* 154.

vpon *prep.* on 65, 298, 411 ; **þerevpon** (r. w. **ston**) 679*.

w

way *n.* 95, 110, 198, 321, 598, 684.

wane *n.* dwelling 104*: (worldly) **wan** resources 512.

war *a.* aware ; **were war** took the situation in 789.

warysoun *n.* reward (usually from superior) 402.

was *v. pt. sg.* 20 ; **wes** 15 ; **wase** (r. w. **spase**) 289; **were** (r. w. **bere**) *pl.* 285, 12, 13* ; **weren** 583 ; **were** *subj. pt.* 3 *sg.* 133.

watyr *n.* Holy water 552.

wax *v. pt.* 3 *sg.* grew 453.

we *pron. pl.* 247 ; **us** *acc. and dat.* 246 ; **oure** *poss.* 87*, 159.

weddyd *pp.* wedded 46; united in sworn-brotherhood 10*, 23, 132, 161, 691 ; cf. *wedbroþer* (Peterborough Chronicle) from ON. *veðbróþir.*

wede *n.* dress 602.

welcome *a.* 360 ; *as interjection* 93, 535*.

welle *adv.* r. w. **dwelle** 234 ; **weel** 31, 112, 118, 438, 468, 578, 726*.

wende(n) *v.* go. *inf.* 122*, 179, 223, 486 ; **wendes** 3 *sg.* 544 ; **wendes** *imper. pl.* 372 ; **went(e)** *pt. sg.* 333 ; *pl.* 237 ; **wente** 2. *sg.* came 105.

wene *n.* doubt ; **holde it for no wene** 680 ; cf. *wiþouten wene* (*conv.*) in *Sege of Melayne* 709.

wene *v. ind. pr.* 1 *sg.* think 184, 306 ; **wende** *pt. sg.* 694.

were *v.* wear ; **weres** *ind. pr.* 3 *sg.* 270; **were** *subj. pr.* 3 *sg.* 528; **weryd** *pt.* 3 *sg.* 553.

werk *n.* 50, 101, 113, 415; only in **goddys werk**; see note on 101.

wers *adv.* 785.

wete(n) *v.* know 265, 447, 667 ; **wot** 1 *sg.* 468, 796 ; **wate** (r. w. **state**) 2 *sg.* 108 ; **wetyng** *ger.* 505.

what *pron. interrog.* 247, 573 ; *a.* 95.

when(ne), whanne *conj.* 78, 330, 567 ; with **þat** 91, 130, 624.

wher *adv. rel.* 463 ; see **þere** *adv.*

why *adv. interrog.* 246, 794.

whyl *conj.* with **þat** 535.

whylys *conj.* **þe whylys þat** 398; cf. *þe quilis þat,* Cursor Mundi (*Gött.*) 1729.

whyt *a.* 70, 291*.

who *pron. interrog.* 449*.

wyde *a.* 542, 554, 770.

wyff (always spelt with **ff**) *n.* 46, 73, 214, 218.

wyȝt *a.* vigorous 314.

wyȝtly *adv.* 746, 790.

wyke *n.*[1] town 348 (OE. *wīc*).

wyke *n.*[2] office 54* (OE. *wīce*).

wil *v.* 1 *sg.* 8; **wole** 10, 140, 142; **wylt** 2 *sg.* 535; **wil** 151; **wole** ȝe *pl.* 246; **wolde** *pt.* 3 *sg.* 89; **woldest** 2 *sg.* 122*; **wolde** 3 *pl.* 35; **wolden** 11*, 14*.

wille *n.* desire 121.

wyn *n.* wine 329.

wynde *n.* wind 453.

wynke *n.* 332*.

wyn(ne) *v.* gain; *inf.* 6; get 220; **wan** *pt. sg.* 340; rescue 136; get away 200.

wyntyr *n. pl.* winters (for years) 67.

wyrke *v. inf.* 4; **wrouȝte** *pt.* 3 *sg.* 665; **wrouȝt** *pp.* 149.

wysse *v. inf.* guide 661.

wyte *n.* blameworthiness 798.

wyttyrlye clearly, truly (*conv.*) 80; here almost the equivalent of *videlicet*; see also *N.E.D.*

wiþ, with *prep.* with, against 17*; (**mette**) with 92, 239; along with 128, 214, 711*; together with 659; by means of 458; **ateynt wiþ** 696;

with wrong (ON. *meðˌ rǫngu*) wrongfully 518.

withinne *prep.* within, in 130 (postponed); of time 288.

withouten *prep.* 32; **wiþouten les** (*conv.*) truly 109; **wiþouten dwellyng** (*conv.*) quickly 96, 189.

wombe *n.* 283, 637.

wonde *v. inf.* flinch, hesitate (*conv.*) 282*; note to 716.

wone *v. inf.* delay 716.

wone *n.* dwelling; **kyngys wone** (r. w. **Athelstone**) 238; **Westemynstyr wone** (r. w. **Athelstone**) 755; note to 104.

woo *n.* woe; only in phrases as **woo were me** 133 : he was . . . **woo** 81; **my lord** . . **would be woo** 739.

wood *a.* mad, furious 250; **wodere** 454.

world *n.* 57; **worl** 136*.

worldly *a.* 512; **worldly wede** probably secular dress 602.

woundys *n. pl.* 144, 626.

wrong *n.* in phrase **with wrong** wrongfully 518.

wroþ *a.* angry 453.

wurd *n.* word = speech 87*; **wurdes** *pl.* 273.

wurþ *a.* worth 391, 493.

wurþy *a.* worthy (of honour) 104; + *inf.* 449; merited 443*.

INDEX OF NAMES

PRINTED IN
GREAT BRITAIN
AT THE
UNIVERSITY PRESS
OXFORD
BY
CHARLES BATEY
PRINTER
TO THE
UNIVERSITY

𝔈𝔞𝔯𝔩𝔶 𝔈𝔫𝔤𝔩𝔦𝔰𝔥 𝔗𝔢𝔵𝔱 𝔖𝔬𝔠𝔦𝔢𝔱𝔶

OFFICERS AND COUNCIL

Honorary Director
C. T. ONIONS, C.B.E., F.B.A.
Magdalen College, Oxford

Honorary Executive Secretary
Miss ELIZABETH MACKENZIE, M.A.
18 Walton Well Road, Oxford
Telephone: Oxford 47774

Honorary Editorial Secretary
Miss P. M. KEAN, M.A.
Lady Margaret Hall, Oxford

Council

Sir W. A. CRAIGIE, F.B.A., D.Litt.
Miss MABEL DAY, D.Lit.
Professor BRUCE DICKINS, M.A.
Miss DOROTHY EVERETT, M.A.

Sir WALTER W. GREG, F.B.A., Litt.D.
Professor J. R. R. TOLKIEN, M.A.
Professor A. H. SMITH, M.A.
Professor C. L. WRENN, M.A.

Bankers
THE NATIONAL PROVINCIAL BANK LTD.
Cornmarket Street, Oxford

THE Subscription to the Society, which constitutes full membership, is £2. 2s. a year for the annual publications, from 1921 onwards, due in advance on the 1st of JANUARY, and should be paid by Cheque, Postal Order, or Money Order crossed 'National Provincial Bank Limited', to the Hon. Executive Secretary, Miss Elizabeth Mackenzie, 18 Walton Well Road, Oxford. Individual members of the Society are allowed, after consultation with the Secretary, to select other volumes of the Society's publications instead of those for the current year. The Society's Texts can also be purchased separately from the Publisher, Oxford University Press, through a bookseller, at the prices put after them in the List, or through the Secretary, by members only, for their own use, at a discount of 2d. in the shilling.

THE EARLY ENGLISH TEXT SOCIETY was founded in 1864 by Frederick James Furnivall, with the help of Richard Morris, Walter Skeat, and others, to bring the mass of unprinted Early English literature within the reach of students and provide sound texts from which the New English Dictionary could quote. In 1867 an Extra Series was started of texts already printed but not in satisfactory or readily obtainable editions. At a cost of nearly £35,000, 160 volumes were issued in the Original Series and 126 in the Extra Series before 1921. In that year the title *Extra Series* was dropped, and all the publications of 1921 and subsequent years have since been listed and numbered as part of the Original Series. Since 1921 some sixty more volumes have been issued. In this prospectus the Original Series and Extra Series for the years 1867-1920 are amalgamated, so as to show all the publications of the Society in a single list.

LIST OF PUBLICATIONS

Original Series, 1864-1944. Extra Series, 1867-1920.

(One guinea per annum for each series separately up to 1920, two guineas from 1921)

2

O.S. 62. **The Cursor Mundi**, in four Texts, ed. R. Morris. Part III. 15*s.*   1876
    63. **The Blickling Homilies**, ed. R. Morris. Part II. 7*s.*   „
    64. **Francis Thynne's Embleames and Epigrams**, ed. F. J. Furnivall. 7*s.*   „
    65. **Be Domes Dæge** (Bede's *De Die Judicii*), &c., ed. J. R. Lumby. 2*s.*   „
E.S. 26. **Guy of Warwick**, 15th-century Version, ed. J. Zupitza. Part II. (*Out of print.*)   „
    27. **Bp. Fisher's English Works**, ed. J. E. B. Mayor. Part I, the Text. 16*s.*   „
O.S. 66. **The Cursor Mundi**, in four Texts, ed. R. Morris. Part IV, with 2 autotypes. 10*s.*   1877
    67. **Notes on Piers Plowman**, by W. W. Skeat. Part I. 21*s.*   „
E.S. 28. **Lovelich's Holy Grail**, ed. F. J. Furnivall. Part III. (*Out of print.*)   „
    29. **Barbour's Bruce**, ed. W. W. Skeat. Part III. 21*s.*   „
O.S. 68. **The Cursor Mundi**, in 4 Texts, ed. R. Morris. Part V. 25*s.*   1878
    69. **Adam Davie's 5 Dreams about Edward II, &c.**, ed. F. J. Furnivall. 5*s.*   „
    70. **Generydes**, a Romance, ed. W. Aldis Wright. Part II. 4*s.*   „
E.S. 30. **Lovelich's Holy Grail**, ed. F. J. Furnivall. Part IV. (*Out of print.*)   „
    31. **The Alliterative Romance of Alexander and Dindimus**, ed. W. W. Skeat. 6*s.*   „
    32. **Starkey's England in Henry VIII's Time.** Part I. **Starkey's Life and Letters**, ed. S. J. Herrtage. (*Out of print.*)
O.S. 71. **The Lay Folks Mass-Book**, four texts, ed. T. F. Simmons. 25*s.*   1879
    72. **Palladius on Husbondrie**, englisht, ed. S. J. Herrtage. Part II. 5*s.*   „
E.S. 33. **Gesta Romanorum**, ed. S. J. Herrtage. 15*s.*   „
    34. **The Charlemagne Romances: 1. Sir Ferumbras**, from Ashm. MS. 33, S. J. Herrtage. (*Out of print.*)
O.S. 73. **The Blickling Homilies**, ed. R. Morris. Part III. 10*s.*   1880
    74. **English Works of Wyclif**, hitherto unprinted, ed. F. D. Matthew. 20*s.*   „
E.S. 35. **Charlemagne Romances: 2. The Sege off Melayne, Sir Otuell, &c.**, ed. S. J. Herrtage. (*Out of print.*) „
    36. **Charlemagne Romances: 3. Lyf of Charles the Grete**, ed. S. J. Herrtage. Part I. 16*s.*   „
O.S. 75. **Catholicon Anglicum**, an early English Dictionary, from Lord Monson's MS., A.D. 1483, ed., with Introduction and Notes, by S. J. Herrtage and Preface by H. B. Wheatley. 20*s.*   1881
    76. **Ælfric's Metrical Lives of Saints**, in MS. Cott. Jul. E VII, ed. W. W. Skeat. Part I. 10*s.*   „
E.S. 37. **Charlemagne Romances: 4. Lyf of Charles the Grete**, ed. S. J. Herrtage. Part II. (*Out of print.*)   „
    38. **Charlemagne Romances: 5. The Sowdone of Babylone**, ed. J. Hausknecht. (*Out of print.*)   „
O.S. 77. **Beowulf**, the unique MS. autotyped and transliterated, ed. J. Zupitza. 15*s.*   1882
    78. **The Fifty Earliest English Wills**, in the Court of Probate, 1387–1439, ed. F. J. Furnivall. 7*s.*   „
E.S. 39. **Charlemagne Romances: 6. Rauf Colyear, Roland Otuel, &c.**, ed. S. J. Herrtage. 15*s.*   „
    40. **Charlemagne Romances: 7. Huon of Burdeux**, by Lord Berners, ed. S. L. Lee. Part I. (*Out of print.*)   „
O.S. 79. **King Alfred's Orosius**, from Lord Tollemache's 9th-century MS., ed. H. Sweet. Part I. 13*s.*   1883
    79 *b.* *Extra Volume.* **Facsimile of the Epinal Glossary**, ed. H. Sweet. 15*s.*   „
E.S. 41. **Charlemagne Romances: 8. Huon of Burdeux**, by Lord Berners, ed. S. L. Lee. Part II. (*Out of print.*) „
    42. **Guy of Warwick**: 2 texts (Auchinleck MS. and Caius MS.), ed. J. Zupitza. Part I. (*Out of print.*)   „
O.S. 80. **The Early-English Life of St. Katherine** and its Latin Original, ed. F. Einenkel. 12*s.*   1884
    81. **Piers Plowman**: Glossary, &c., ed. W. W. Skeat. Part IV, completing the work. 18*s.*   „
E.S. 43. **Charlemagne Romances: 9. Huon of Burdeux**, by Lord Berners, ed. S. L. Lee. Part III. (*Out of print.*) „
    44. **Charlemagne Romances: 10. The Four Sons of Aymon**, ed. Octavia Richardson. Part I. 15*s.*   „
O.S. 82. **Ælfric's Metrical Lives of Saints**, MS. Cott. Jul. E VII, ed. W. W. Skeat. Part II. 12*s.*   1885
    83. **The Oldest English Texts, Charters, &c.**, ed. H. Sweet. 20*s.*   „
E.S. 45. **Charlemagne Romances: 11. The Four Sons of Aymon**, ed. O. Richardson. Part II. (*Out of print.*)   „
    46. **Sir Bevis of Hamton**, ed. E. Kölbing. Part I. (*Out of print.*)   „
O.S. 84. **Additional Analogs to 'The Wright's Chaste Wife'**, O.S. 12, by W. A. Clouston. 1*s.*   1886
    85. **The Three Kings of Cologne**, ed. C. Horstmann. 17*s.*   „
    86. **Prose Lives of Women Saints**, ed. C. Horstmann. 12*s.*   „
E.S. 47. **The Wars of Alexander**, ed. W. W. Skeat. (*Out of print.*)   „
    48. **Sir Bevis of Hamton**, ed. E. Kölbing. Part II. (*Out of print.*)   „
O.S. 87. **The Early South-English Legendary** (earliest version), Laud MS. 108, ed. C. Horstmann. 20*s.*   1887
    88. **Hy. Bradshaw's Life of St. Werburghe** (Pynson, 1521), ed. C. Hortsmann. 10*s.*   „
E.S. 49. **Guy of Warwick**, 2 texts (Auchinleck and Caius MSS.), ed. J. Zupitza. Part II. (*Out of print.*)   „
    50. **Charlemagne Romances: 12. Huon of Burdeux**, by Lord Berners, ed. S. L. Lee. Part IV. 5*s.*   „
    51. **Torrent of Portyngale**, ed. E. Adam. (*Out of print.*)   „
O.S. 89. **Vices and Virtues**, ed. F. Holthausen. Part I. 8*s.*   1888
    90. **Anglo-Saxon and Latin Rule of St. Benet**, interlinear Glosses, ed. H. Logeman. 12*s.*   „
    91. **Two Fifteenth-Century Cookery-Books**, ed. T. Austin. 10*s.*   „
E.S. 52. **Bullein's Dialogue against the Feuer Pestilence, 1578**, ed. M. and A. H. Bullen. 10*s.*   „
    53. **Vicary's Anatomie of the Body of Man, 1548**, ed. 1577, ed. F. J. and Percy Furnivall. Part I. 15*s.*   „
    54. **Caxton's Englishing of Alain Chartier's Curial**, ed. F. J. Furnivall and P. Meyer. 5*s.*   „
O.S. 92. **Eadwine's Canterbury Psalter**, from the Trin. Cambr. MS., ed. F. Harsley, Part I. 12*s.*   1889
    93. **Defensor's Liber Scintillarum**, ed. E. Rhodes. 12*s.*   „
E.S. 55. **Barbour's Bruce**, ed. W. W. Skeat. Part IV. (*Out of print.*)   „
    56. **Early English Pronunciation**, by A. J. Ellis. Part V, the present English Dialects. 25*s.*   „
O.S. 94. **Ælfric's Metrical Lives of Saints**, MS. Cott. Jul. E VII, ed. W. W. Skeat. Part III. 15*s.*   1890
    95. **The Old-English version of Bede's Ecclesiastical History**, re-ed. T. Miller. Part I, 1. 18*s.*   „

4

E.S. 92. Lydgate's DeGuileville's Pilgrimage of the Life of Man, ed. Katherine B. Locock. Part III. 10s. — 1904
  93. Lovelich's Romance of Merlin, from the unique MS., ed. E. A. Kock. Part I. 10s.   „
O.S. 127. An Alphabet of Tales, in Northern English, from the Latin, ed. M. M. Banks. Part II. 10s. — 1905
  128. Medieval Records of a London City Church, ed. H. Littlehales. Part II. 10s.   „
  129. The English Register of Godstow Nunnery, ed. A. Clark. Part I. 10s.   „
E.S. 94. Respublica, a Play on a Social England, ed. L. A. Magnus. (*Out of print.*)   „
  95. Lovelich's History of the Holy Grail. Part V. The Legend of the Holy Grail, ed. Dorothy Kempe. 6s.   „
  96. Mirk's Festial, ed. T. Erbe. Part I. 12s.   „
O.S. 130. The English Register of Godstow Nunnery, ed. A. Clark. Part II. 15s. — 1906
  131. The Brut, or The Chronicle of England, ed. F. Brie. Part I. (*Out of print.*)   „
  132. John Metham's Works, ed. H. Craig. 15s.   „
E.S. 97. Lydgate's Troy Book, ed. H. Bergen. Part I, Books I and II. (*Out of print.*)   „
  98. Skelton's Magnyfycence, ed. R. L. Ramsay, with an Introduction. 7s. 6d.   „
  99. The Romance of Emaré, re-ed. Edith Rickert. 7s. 6d.   „
O.S. 133. The English Register of Oseney Abbey, by Oxford, ed. A. Clark. Part I. 15s. — 1907
  134. The Coventry Leet Book, ed. M. Dormer Harris. Part I. 15s.   „
E.S. 100. The Harrowing of Hell, and The Gospel of Nicodemus, re-ed. W. H. Hulme. 15s.   „
  101. Songs, Carols, &c., from Richard Hill's Balliol MS., ed. R. Dyboski. 15s.   „
O.S. 135. The Coventry Leet Book, ed. M. Dormer Harris. Part II. 15s. — 1908
  135 b. *Extra Issue.* Prof. Manly's Piers Plowman and its Sequence, urging the fivefold authorship of the *Vision.* 5s.   „
  136. The Brut, or The Chronicle of England, ed. F. Brie. Part II. 15s.   „
E.S. 102. Promptorium Parvulorum, the 1st English-Latin Dictionary, ed. A. L. Mayhew. 21s.   „
  103. Lydgate's Troy Book, ed. H. Bergen. Part II, Book III. (*Out of print.*)   „
O.S. 137. Twelfth-Century Homilies in MS. Bodley 343, ed. A. O. Belfour. Part I, the Text. 15s. — 1909
  138. The Coventry Leet Book, ed. M. Dormer Harris. Part III. 15s.   „
E.S. 104. The Non-Cycle Mystery Plays, re-ed. O. Waterhouse. (*Out of print.*)   „
  105. The Tale of Beryn, with the Pardoner and Tapster, ed. F. J. Furnivall and W. G. Stone. 15s.   „
O.S. 139. John Arderne's Treatises on Fistula in Ano, &c., ed. D'Arcy Power. 15s. — 1910
  139 b, c, d, e, f, *Extra Issue.* The Piers Plowman Controversy: b. Dr. Jusserand's 1st Reply to Prof. Manly; c. Prof. Manly's Answer to Dr. Jusserand; d. Dr. Jusserand's 2nd Reply to Prof. Manly; e. Mr. R. W. Chambers's Article; f. Dr. Henry Bradley's Rejoinder to Mr. R. W. Chambers (issued separately). 10s.   „
  140. Capgrave's Lives of St. Augustine and St. Gilbert of Sempringham, ed. J. Munro. 10s.   „
E.S. 106. Lydgate's Troy Book, ed. H. Bergen. Part III. 15s.   „
  107. Lydgate's Minor Poems, ed. H. N. MacCracken. Part I. Religious Poems. (*Out of print.*)   „
O.S. 141. Earth upon Earth, all the known texts, ed., with an Introduction, by Hilda Murray. (*Out of print.*) — 1911
  142. The English Register of Godstow Nunnery, ed. A. Clark. Part III. 10s.   „
  143. The Wars of Alexander the Great, Thornton MS., ed. J. S. Westlake. 10s.   „
E.S. 108. Lydgate's Siege of Thebes, re-ed. A. Erdmann. Part I, the Text. (*Out of print.*)   „
  109. Partonope, re-ed. A. T. Bödtker. The Texts. 15s.   „
O.S. 144. The English Register of Oseney Abbey, by Oxford, ed. A. Clark. Part II. 10s. — 191
  145. The Northern Passion, ed. F. A. Foster. Part I, the four parallel texts. 15s.   „
E.S. 110. Caxton's Mirrour of the World, with all the woodcuts, ed. O. H. Prior. (*Out of print.*)   „
  111. Caxton's History of Jason, the Text, Part I, ed. J. Munro. 15s.   „
O.S. 146. The Coventry Leet Book, ed. M. Dormer Harris. Introduction, Indexes, &c. Part IV. 10s. — 191
  147. The Northern Passion, ed. F. A. Foster, Introduction, French Text, Variants and Fragments, Glossary. Part II. 15s.   „
  [An enlarged reprint of O.S. 26, Religious Pieces in Prose and Verse, from the Thornton MS., ed. G. G. Perry. 5s.]   „
E.S. 112. Lovelich's Romance of Merlin, ed. E. A. Kock. Part II. (*Out of print.*)   „
  113. Poems by Sir John Salusbury, Robert Chester, and others, from Christ Church MS. 184, &c., ed. Carleton Brown. 15s.   „
O.S. 148. A Fifteenth-Century Courtesy Book and Two Franciscan Rules, ed. R. W. Chambers and W. W. Seton. 7s. 6d. — 191
  149. Sixty-three Lincoln Diocese Documents, ed. Andrew Clark. 15s.   „
  150. The Old-English Rule of Bp. Chrodegang, and the Capitula of Bp. Theodulf, ed. A. S. Napier. 7s. 6d. „
E.S. 114. The Gild of St. Mary, Lichfield, ed. F. J. Furnivall. 15s.   „
  115. The Chester Plays, re-ed. J. Matthews. Part II. 15s.   „
O.S. 151. The Lanterne of Light, ed. Lilian M. Swinburn. 15s. — 191
  152. Early English Homilies, from Cott. Vesp. D. xiv, ed. Rubie Warner. Part I, Text. 15s.   „
E.S. 116. The Pauline Epistles, ed. M. J. Powell. 15s.   „
  117. Bp. Fisher's English Works, ed. R. Bayne. Part II. 15s.   „
O.S. 153. Mandeville's Travels, ed. P. Hamelius. Part I, Text. 15s. — 191
  154. Mandeville's Travels, ed. P. Hamelius. Part II, Notes and Introduction. 15s.   „
E.S. 118. The Craft of Nombrynge, ed. R. Steele. 15s.   „
  119. The Owl and Nightingale, 2 Texts parallel, ed. G. F. H. Sykes and J. H. G. Grattan. (*Out of print.*)   „

O.S. 155. The Wheatley MS., ed. Mabel Day. 30*s.*   1917
E.S. 120. Ludus Coventriae, ed. K. S. Block. 30*s.*   „
O.S. 156. Reginald Pecock's Donet, from Bodl. MS. 916, ed. Elsie V. Hitchcock. 35*s.*   1918
E.S. 121. Lydgate's Fall of Princes, ed. H. Bergen. Part I. (*Out of print.*)
     122. Lydgate's Fall of Princes, ed. H. Bergen. Part II. (*Out of print.*)   „
O.S. 157. Harmony of the Life of Christ, from MS. Pepys 2498, ed. Margery Goates. 15*s.*   1919
     158. Meditations on the Life and Passion of Christ, from MS. Add., 11307, ed. Charlotte D'Evelyn. 20*s.*   „
E.S. 123. Lydgate's Fall of Princes, ed. H. Bergen. Part III. (*Out of print.*)
     124. Lydgate's Fall of Princes, ed. H. Bergen. Part IV. (*Out of print.*)
O.S. 159. Vices and Virtues, ed. F. Holthausen. Part II. 12*s.*   1920
     [A reprint of O.S. 20, **English Prose Treatises of Richard Rolle of Hampole**, ed. G. G. Perry. 5*s.*]
     [A re-edition of O.S. 18, **Hali Meidenhad**, ed. O. Cockayne, with a variant MS., Bodl. 34, hitherto unprinted, ed. F. J. Furnivall. 12*s.*]
E.S. 125. Lydgate's Siege of Thebes, ed. A. Erdmann and E. Ekwall. Part II. 20*s.*   „
     126. Lydgate's Troy Book, ed. H. Bergen. Part IV. 15*s.*   „

O.S. 160. The Old English Heptateuch, MS. Cott. Claud. B. IV, ed. S. J. Crawford. 42*s.*   1921
     161. Three O.E. Prose Texts, MS. Cott. Vit. A. XV, ed. S. Rypins. 25*s.*   „
     162. Facsimile of MS. Cotton Nero A. X (Pearl, Cleanness, Patience and Sir Gawain), Introduction by I. Gollancz. 63*s.*   1922
     163. Book of the Foundation of St. Bartholomew's, Smithfield, ed. N. Moore. 10*s.*   1923
     164. Pecock's Folewer to the Donet, ed. Elsie V. Hitchcock. 30*s.*   „
     165. Middleton's Chinon of England, with Leland's Assertio Arturii and Robinson's translation, ed. W. E. Mead. 25*s.*   „
     166. Stanzaic Life of Christ, ed. Frances A. Foster. 35*s.*   1924
     167. Trevisa's Dialogus inter Militem et Clericum, Sermon by FitzRalph, and Bygynnyng of the World, ed. A. J. Perry. 25*s.*   „
     168. Caxton's Ordre of Chyualry, ed. A. T. P. Byles. (*Out of print.*)   1925
     169. The Southern Passion, ed. Beatrice Brown. 15*s.*   „
     170. Walton's Boethius, ed. M. Science. 30*s.*   „
     171. Pecock's Reule of Cristen Religioun, ed. W. C. Greet. 35*s.*   1926
     172. The Seege or Batayle of Troy, ed. M. E. Barnicle. 25*s.*   „
     173. Hawes' Pastime of Pleasure, ed. W. E. Mead. 15*s.*   1927
     174. The Life of St. Anne, ed. R. E. Parker. 10*s.*   „
     175. Barclay's Eclogues, ed. Beatrice White. 25*s.*   „
     176. Caxton's Prologues and Epilogues, ed. W. J. B. Crotch. (*Out of print.*)   „
     177. Byrhtferth's Manual, ed. S. J. Crawford. 42*s.*   1928
     178. The Revelations of St. Birgitta, ed. W. P. Cumming. 10*s.*   „
     179. The Castell of Pleasure, ed. R. Cornelius. 12*s.* 6*d.*   „
     180. The Apologye of Syr Thomas More, ed. A. I. Taft. 30*s.*   1929
     181. The Dance of Death, ed. F. Warren. 10*s.*   „
     182. Speculum Christiani, ed. G. Holmstedt. 25*s.*   „
     183. The Northern Passion (Supplement), ed. W. Heuser and Frances Foster. 7*s.* 6*d.*   1930
     184. The Poems of John Audelay, ed. Ella K. Whiting. 28*s.*   „
     185. Lovelich's Merlin, ed. E. A. Kock. Part III. 25*s.*   „
     186. Harpsfield's Life of More, ed. Elsie V. Hitchcock and R. W. Chambers. (*Out of print.*)   1931
     187. Whittinton and Stanbridge's Vulgaria, ed. B. White. 12*s.*   „
     188. The Siege of Jerusalem, ed. E. Kölbing and Mabel Day. 15*s.*   „
     189. Caxton's Fayttes of Armes and of Chyualrye, ed. A. T. Byles. 21*s.*   1932
     190. English Mediæval Lapidaries, ed. Joan Evans and Mary Serjeantson. 16*s.*   „
     191. The Seven Sages, ed. K. Brunner. 24*s.*   „
     Extra Issue. On the Continuity of English Prose, by R. W. Chambers. (*Reprinting.*)   „
     192. Lydgate's Minor Poems, ed. H. N. MacCracken. Part II, **Secular Poems**. 30*s.*   1933
     193. Seinte Marherete, re-ed. Frances Mack. 15*s.*   „
     194. The Exeter Book, Part II, ed. W. S. Mackie. 18*s.*   „
     195. The Quatrefoil of Love, ed. I. Gollancz and M. Weale. 5*s.*   1934
     196. A Short English Metrical Chronicle, ed. E. Zettl. 20*s.*   „
     197. Roper's Life of More, ed. Elsie V. Hitchcock. (*Out of print.*)   „
     198. Firumbras and Otuel and Roland, ed. Mary O'Sullivan. 18*s.*   „
     199. Mum and the Sothsegger, ed. Mabel Day and R. Steele. 12*s.*   „
     200. Speculum Sacerdotale, ed. E. H. Weatherly. 16*s.*   1935
     201. Knyghthode and Bataile, ed. R. Dyboski and M. Z. Arend. 16*s.*   „
     202. Palsgrave's Acolastus, ed. P. L. Carver. 20*s.*   „
     203. Amis and Amiloun, ed. E. Leach. 12*s.*   „
     204. Valentine and Orson, ed. Arthur Dickson. 20*s.*   1936
     205. Tales from the Decameron, ed. H. G. Wright. 16*s.*

The Original and Extra Series of the 'Early English Text Society'

The following is a select list of forthcoming volumes. Other texts are under consideration:

Ro. Ba.'s Life of Sir Thomas More, ed. Elsie V. Hitchcock and Msgr. Halett. (*At press.*)
Tretyse of Loue, ed. J. H. Fisher. (*At press.*)
King Alisaunder, ed. G. V. Smithers. (*Volume I, Text, at press.*)
Barclay's Life of St. George, ed. W. Nelson. (*At press.*)
The English Poems of MS. Harley 2253, ed. Hilda Murray.
The English Text of the Ancrene Riwle, edited from all the extant manuscripts:
  B.M. Cotton MS. Nero A. XIV, ed. Mabel Day on the basis of a transcript made by J. A. Herbert. (*At press.*)
  Gonville and Caius College, Cambridge, MS. 234/120, ed. R. M. Wilson on the basis of a transcript made by J. A. Herbert. (*At press.*)
  B.M. Royal MS. 8.C.1, ed. A. C. Baugh. (*At press.*)
  Bodleian MS. Vernon, ed. F. P. Magoun.
  Corpus Christi College, Cambridge, MS. 402, ed. J. R. R. Tolkien.
  B.M. Cotton MS. Titus D. XVIII, ed. Francis Mack.
  B.M. Cotton MS. Cleopatra C. VI, ed. A. H. Smith.
  (*It is also hoped to issue a revised edition of Magdalene College, Cambridge, MS. Pepys 2498.*)
The French Text of the Ancrene Riwle:
  Trinity College, Cambridge, MS. 883, ed. W. H. Trethewey.
Athelston, ed. A. McI. Trounce. (*Revised edition, at press.*)
The Homilies of Ælfric, ed. J. Pope and Edna R. Williams.
Non-Ælfrician Homilies, ed. R. Willard.
Jacob's Well, Part II, ed. Elsie Smith.
Whitford's Version of the Imitation of Christ, ed. E. J. K. Klein.
Thomas Castleford's Chronicle, ed. A. McIntosh.

September 1950.

Publisher

LONDON: GEOFFREY CUMBERLEGE, OXFORD UNIVERSITY PRESS
AMEN HOUSE, E.C. 4

QUEEN MARY
COLLEGE
LIBRARY